# JEWS
## IN THE
# GARDEN

A Holocaust Survivor, the Fate
of His Family, and the Secret History
of Poland in World War II

**JUDY RAKOWSKY**

**Cover: In the Rakowski lumberyard, Kazimierza Wielka Poland, 1926.**
Back row: Frymet (sister of Sam's father), Rita (cousin), Jozef Rakowski (Sam's father), Jozef Banach, (brother of Sam's mother married to a Rakowski sibling).
Front row: Pearl Chilewicz Rakowski (Sam's grandmother, Judy's great grandmother), young Sam, Moshe David Rakowski (Sam's grandfather, Judy's great grandfather). Moshe David died in 1929. Everyone else, except for Jozef and Sam, was killed in the Holocaust.
*Courtesy of Sam Ron to the U.S. Holocaust Memorial Museum*

Published by Sourcebooks
P.O. Box 4410, Naperville, Illinois 60567–4410
(630) 961-3900
sourcebooks.com

Cataloging-in-Publication Data is on file with the Library of Congress

Printed and bound in the United States of America.
VP 10 9 8 7 6 5 4 3 2 1

*To the truth tellers who reveal the tales*
*of lives discarded, rescuing them and*
*us from denial of a dark history.*

"We all need peace. Memory,
meanwhile, breeds unrest."

—Dr. Piotr M. A. Cywinski, director,
Auschwitz-Birkenau State Museum

# Prologue

# Hena in Hiding

ZAGÓRZYCE, POLAND 1944

Heavy footfalls thudded on the road that rainy May night. Passing miles of freshly plowed fields, men moved in menacing formation.

Eighteen months in hiding had honed Hena Rożeńka's hearing, alert to sounds of danger from Germans or anyone who would betray her and her family. Perched on a hilltop in central Poland, it was easier to notice approaching intruders. The farm hideout lay a few kilometers and a world away from the house and shop where she had spent her life nestled among so many relatives. But who were these men out here shouldering long guns? Why were they heading directly toward the farmhouse as if it was their target?

Hena's apprehension grew with every footstep the gunmen took toward the house. Her parents, her sisters, and her brother were inside. This late in the war, with liberation expected any day, they had dared to seek comfort and refuge from this raw spring soaker.

The dark forms encroached on the house. Fear and help-lessness gripped her gut. She could not warn her family without revealing herself. She could only steal peeks from her hiding place. That night, she may have had a thousand reasons for not joining them inside. After all, at age sixteen, she had been with her family every moment since September 1942. She longed to be on her own. The last time she saw peers in school, she was eleven.

Her parents kept telling her how lucky they were. Pan (Mr.) Radziszewski, a kind man and customer from their hard-ware store, had rescued them before the roundup. Otherwise, they would have been forced onto wagons and trains with the rest of the Jews of Kazimierza Wielka.

Out here on this farm so far away from everything, that brutality did not seem real, but their brave protector told them what had happened. The Germans shipped nearly two hun-dred Jews off to Bełżec, the nearest death camp. No one heard from any of them again. A second roundup happened not long afterward. Throughout the fall and winter of 1942, Pan Radziszewski brought back news from town of Nazis scouring the countryside, murdering any Jews they found and terror-izing townspeople with threats of punishing whole villages if they dared harbor Jews. The Rożeńeks took in these reports from their hideout, willing themselves invisible.

Since their arrival here, they had weathered two winters.

Along the way, the farmer's teenage daughter went away, one of the many Poles involuntarily deported for forced labor in Germany.[1] But recently her parents as well as Hena's siblings were elated by word Pan Radziszewski brought back from town: Red Army troops were approaching. Their suffering wouldn't last much longer.

Hope made her parents so much lighter. Some moonless nights, they stole out of the cramped outbuildings and took in fresh air, heavenly respite after interminable stillness crouching in the dirt. They had even dared to dream of ordinary life back running their shop, and that Hena might see her schoolmates again.

She strained for a furtive peek. Nothing about the approaching gunmen indicated they were Russian troops, or Germans for that matter. And why would they be taking up positions around this farmhouse?

Dark forms now massed at the door. Muffled voices carried on the cold, wet air.

Then came the sounds she would long remember. Metal on metal, guns poised for action. Thunderous banging on the front door ricocheted off nearby houses.

Men shouted in Polish. "Give up your Jews! We know you have Jews. Hand them over!"

Hena could not believe this was happening. How many times had she imagined an attack by storm troopers pulling up in big black cars in front of the house, soldiers fanning out across the farmyard before anyone could run? Now those shuddering fantasies had turned real.

A bleary Pan Radziszewski appeared. Light from within silhouetted him cradling a small child. Gunmen stormed into his house, shouting and beating the farmer with the butts of their rifles. Pan Radziszewski clung to the child, protecting the baby instead of shielding himself.

"We know you have Jews. Hand over your Jews. Where are they?"

"What are you talking about?" Radziszewski protested. The child screamed. "What are you doing here?" he demanded. "Who are you?"

The gunmen stormed the house, breaking dishes, ransacking everything. Their noisy assault and accusations reverberated across the fields to surrounding farms. Hena heard no German, no Russian. Only Polish.

The stately cherry tree outside the house, now freighted with wet blossoms, had just shaken off winter doldrums. Knotty buds had emerged, opening with clusters of pale petals that cheered the wartime landscape. Hena may have huddled under it. Maybe the attackers would not find her family, she consoled herself. Maybe they would not look in the space behind the stove or in the attic, where some Rożeńeks had hidden during other scares, like when a neighbor's daughter came by to play.

The house erupted with sounds of furniture tumbling and more assaults on the farmer. After moments of quiet came exultant shrieks. Her heart sank. The gunmen must have found their quarry. Her beloved family.

"We got them!" someone shouted in triumph. The muffled

shouts from inside the house turned sharp and clear. She saw why. Windows at the top of the house had been thrust open. Gunmen inside yelled to others swarming below.

Next she saw the form of her sister Frania. Her teacher and protector, Frania was five years older than Hena. She appeared in the opening, her face twisted in terror. Her body lurched into view. The gunmen laughed while shoving her out the window. Her slight form floated for a moment. Bullets sprayed upward. She landed with a sickening thump.

Acrid gun smoke drifted to Hena's hiding place. The vicious attackers laughed and shouted, egging each other on for the next, her sister Frymet. How could she watch this again? The sounds and images repeated. Her stomach knotted in horror at the sight of her mother's haggard face in the window. She must have been looking down on her daughters lying crumpled below. Ita was in her fifties and had calmed them over so many days and nights while they had to sit still on damp earth. She moved awkwardly. The sadistic attackers prodded and poked. Then came the push. Her screams rang out amid the barrage of shots.

Hena could glimpse the ends of the barrels of the guns aimed upwards murdering her family one by one. She struggled to believe her mother and sisters—who only moments before huddled together in fear—were already dead.

Her brother and father watched helplessly, restrained by other assailants. Again came the sickening sounds. The forms of her brother then father were pushed into a hail of bullets, their bodies falling onto the others.

The gunmen whooped and hollered, triumphant in their murderous cruelty, congratulating each other for killing the "Yids."

The attackers made no attempt at secrecy. They staged the executions brazenly, their shouts and gunfire reverberating through the hamlet. No one in the village responded. No Germans. No Polish police.

For hours after the massacre, Hena did not move. The gunmen seemed to have gone. But she had heard them warn the farmer not to take any belongings of the Jews. They would be back.

How soon?

Long after the shuffling boot steps had receded, she remained frozen in place. She was alone in the world.

Where could she be safe? She could not ask Pan Radziszewski for ideas. What if the gunmen found out she was alive and tortured him?

The cherry tree turned into the burial site of her family. But the location of the Rożeńeks' remains would not stay secret. The tree itself refused to conceal the crime.

Each spring, it blossomed as usual. The flowers gave way to promising little stone fruits colored lime green. They cast a hopeful look. But never would they turn the blushing orange-red of Poland's famed sour cherries. They withheld their promise as Poland's pride and never ripened. Instead they turned black and rotted, refusing to allow villagers to forget what lay beneath.

Over time, the tree drew notice in the village and beyond. For miles around, people heard of the cherry tree. Murdered Jews, the Rożeńeks from Kazimierza, were buried under it. Was it cursed?

Word trickled out in whispers that someone escaped the fate of her family. It was Hena, the youngest daughter. Only she could walk away.

# PART I

The eightieth birthday party of Benjamin Rakowsky, who immigrated to the U.S. in 1913. Ben celebrates with his younger brother, Joe, father of Sam (Rakowski) Ron, who stayed behind and survived the Holocaust. Judy attends this celebration as a seven-year-old.

# 1

# Lost and Found

LIMA, OHIO 1966

P oppy sat at the head of a long table at Lost Creek Country Club, beaming at his family, who were all turned out in shimmery dresses and sharp suits for his eightieth birthday celebration. Ben Rakowsky, my beloved grandfather, had married Jennie Stokfish in Warsaw before anyone knew even one world war. From his family of eight children hailing from a village near Kraków, only three had survived and made it to this country. On this night, Poppy's pale blue eyes shone between his wide cheekbones and heavy brow, indelible family features repeated on the squarish faces of his siblings and progeny around the table, including his only son, my father, Rudy.

Poppy's path to that birthday celebration started on another continent when his country did not even exist. Ben left home in his twenties, encouraged by his mother to avoid the draft. Poland had been carved up by Russia, Austria, and Germany.

Jewish parents willed sons to emigrate rather than forfeit their lives to the Russian army. Family lore has it that he was involved in a plot against Czar Nicholas II, an added incentive to leave the country in times of pogroms against Jews and prewar turbulence. Ben evaded the czar's clutches by leaving the country with a group of Polish Jews sponsored for immigration to the United States. Landing in Galveston, Texas, on September 11, 1913, the ship *Breslau*'s manifest recorded his arrival. At twenty-seven years old, he left behind his wife, Jennie, and baby daughter, Helen, in Warsaw. Filling swamps in Texas, malaria befell Ben's group of immigrants. Their sponsor put them on a train to the Mayo Clinic. Ben, we were always told, was the only one healthy enough to walk off that train. After treatment, Benjamin Rakowsky, whose surname now ended in a *y* thanks to the stroke of an immigration official's pen, headed east from Minnesota, stopping in a small town in northwest Ohio that once enjoyed an oil boom before Texas struck a much larger vein. Ben was earning money by measuring college students for tailored suits, and living in Lima, Ohio. Here he would settle. Why Lima, Ohio? He was so impressed by the warm reception: a bank president held the door open for him, a poor Polish immigrant.

Six years and a world war later, Jennie and Helen joined him in Lima. They left a place that once again had reclaimed its identity as Poland. No one else in their extended families followed.

After Germany and the Soviet Union invaded Poland in 1939, Poppy sent letters that drew no response from his family in Europe. Finally, in 1946, a telegram arrived. It was from his "unknown nephew," Samuel Rakowski, a son of his younger brother, Józef. Sam had helped the Red Cross locate Poppy using a clue he remembered from old letters to his grandmother: the return address included the word *buckeye*, part of the name of the company Ben started in Ohio, known as the Buckeye State.

"From our family survived your sister Lily with her son, nineteen years old, and your brother Józef, who is my father, and my mother survived. The rest of the family, I am sorry to say that they are all destroyed by *y'mak shmo*—his name should be blotted out—Hitler."

Ben sponsored the survivors for visas to America. Only then did he learn that American liberators of Mauthausen had found his once-brawny brother lying on a pile of corpses, barely alive at eighty-eight pounds. Joe's son Yisrael, Sam's brother, had perished in the same camp two months shy of liberation. Joe's wife, Sophie, had survived three concentration camps and a death march from Gross-Rosen with her sister Minna.

Joe and Sophie came to stay with Poppy and Grandma in Lima, but my grandmother struggled with welcoming these immigrants, despite all they had endured. A prickly, thin-skinned woman, Grandma cringed at the reception Joe got around their adopted hometown, where after decades of trying to fit in, they finally felt accepted. But people kept mistaking her brother-in-law for her husband. All over again, she felt the sting of being a greenhorn and a Jew in a small white Christian town. Grandma hardly concealed her feelings, offering the newcomers instructions in table manners and begrudging them a second slice of toast.

By the time of the birthday celebration, those tensions had long since disappeared. Joe and Sophie had moved away from Lima soon after immigrating. Joe created a successful home-building business in Canton, Ohio. The two couples had grown close. In fact, at the party, Ben was still tan from their annual vacation in Miami.

For seven-year-old me, none of this background would mean anything for decades. The party loomed in my memory in flashed impressions—the itchiness of my dress and the pinch of my black patent leather shoes.

That night, I almost didn't recognize Grandma with her flaming apricot hair sprayed into an elegant cloud. She clutched a mink stole over a champagne-colored dress. She chatted with visiting relatives in Yiddish, their cone of secrecy. They sounded just like her even when they spoke English: *th* sounded like *t* (*ting* for *thing*) and *w*'s were *v*'s (*vat* for *what*). And every sentence rose an octave at the end, always sounding like a question. But my eyes were on Poppy, whose smile flashed like sunshine. I tried to catch his eye, those blazing ocean blues he had passed down only to me, not to any of his three children or the other six grandchildren. He smiled in my direction, which I took as an invitation to wriggle off my seat and sneak under the tray of a waitress who was shouting at the old-country relatives as if their accents made them deaf.

At Poppy's side, I waited. I expected him to pull me onto his ample lap as he usually did on our weekly visits, when anything I did or said made him laugh in belly-jiggling delight. But that night he left me standing there under his protective arm, riveted by his brother, Joe.

They seemed caught up in memories a world away.

_____

Until I was in fifth grade, I didn't think much about where Poppy and Grandma came from. The teacher said that people in America came from all over the world. We made up a wonderful melting pot with everyone casting off those former identities to pursue the American dream as one. She asked that we volunteer our families' countries of origin. The class shrugged. Few of the white multigeneration American kids had a clue. A boy named Smith might be English, the teacher suggested. He did not know.

I piped up, "I am of Polish-Jewish descent." The teacher found that interesting, and I shared the little I knew about my immigrant grandparents. I repeated the reference in the carpool after school. The mom at the wheel spun. She accused me of fibbing: "Everyone knows all Polish people are Catholic." I was dumbstruck. Why would I lie about that?

I had a vague sense of why we had few relatives on Dad's side. We knew Hitler killed many Jews, including our relatives. The ending had an American spin. Poppy was smart to leave Europe before the war and found freedom in the United

States. No one mentioned the life our family left behind, who was lost, or how.

———————

Twenty years later in Canton, Ohio, I slipped a tin of macaroons onto the table among the home-baked Passover treats, frowning at my store-bought offering. I was a guest at the home of that unknown nephew, who was born Shmul Rakowski in Poland; after the war, he and his wife changed their surnames to Ron, Hebrew for *joy*. He cast off the dark memories of destruction in Europe, renewing life in a new country.

I greeted the hostess, Sam's wife, Bilha, who was stirring a pot of matzo ball soup like a pro. Bilha, a lively Israeli with sapphire eyes, asked, "Did your mother teach you to make matzo balls?"

I murmured, "Just from the box." I recalled the high-anxiety seders my mother made in the years after Grandma Rakowsky could no longer manage the effort. Grandma's scrutiny persisted long after her stamina flagged. Mom worked hard to follow her recipes and example. But when Grandma walked in, tension gripped our house. She toddled straight to the kitchen and our avocado-green range. Steam fogged her thick glasses over the soup pot. Arthritic hands spooned out a matzo ball. Pursing her lips, she took a bite. We held our breath. Then she issued her judgment with a snap of her tongue. My mother turned away, her hopes sinking like the third batch of matzo balls she'd made that day. It was hopeless. She could have made a zillion perfect matzo balls. But to Grandma, Mom's heartfelt conversion and efforts to raise us in her adopted faith would never cut it. She could never compensate for not being born Jewish.

Here in the house of Sam and Bilha, the holiday was delightfully devoid of such undercurrents. These were second cousins I did not know well. Still I was on edge, wondering if they were noticing I'd lost weight since my recent divorce. No one mentioned it or that at twenty-three I was already divorced. Maybe they were judging me like my grandma would have if she were still alive, thinking, *You're better off, because he wasn't Jewish.* It turned out, their focus was not on me.

Bilha, a deeply knowledgeable Jewish educator, took center stage for the long seder, telling stories and singing songs while also serving a home-cooked feast. Sam sat at the head of the table, reminding me of my late poppy with the same accent and attempts to move us along and maybe skip a few pages of the service. I listened politely but was painfully aware of what I did not know, having grown up as the fourth kid, who got to trade Hebrew school for swim practice. By the last song of the night, I was looking at my watch, thinking about my long drive home and the news story I was in the middle of reporting.

Then Sam shot out of his chair like somebody had flipped a switch.

"I want to show you guys something," he said, pulling out a slide projector. "I'm going to show you where you come from."

He pulled down Bilha's Israeli art collection, turning a

living room wall into a screen. He loaded a wheel of slides that looked like they could keep us there until dawn. The projector hummed, beaming images in the dark living room of relatives I'd never seen in a place I'd never heard of.

"This," he said, "is Kazimierza Wielka." He pronounced it in whooshing syllables that made it sound as grand as Paris and as down-to-earth as Cleveland.

The buildup hardly matched the images of forlorn stucco buildings filling the screen. Sam clicked away, describing his first trip back to Poland since the war. He had gone there with his son David, who was watching the slideshow along with his wife, sister, brother-in-law and my brother Mike. Slide after slide displayed monochrome gray streetscapes familiar from news footage of life behind the Iron Curtain. But Sam saw something else.

He was still smiling over memories of his first homecoming since the war to the town northeast of Kraków where generations of our family had thrived. He could not believe the warmth of his reception. He and David had left a tour for Sam's last-minute decision to visit his hometown. Sam said he was nervous in the taxi nosing through his old neighborhood.

Then a former neighbor shrieked with joy at the sight of him. She told the taxi driver, "In your cab, you have the prince of the city."

Until that night, my memories of Sam were of a wallflower at large family gatherings. He sat with the old-country relatives who were speaking Yiddish and smoking cigars. He looked like a leaner, subdued version of my father, who was holding court across the room in an electric peach sport coat, twanging away in an Ohio accent with a Lucky Strike pressed in his lips.

Cousins born one year and worlds apart, Dad and Sam, with their serious brown eyes and thick brows, looked like brothers. For cousins who met only after they were fathers themselves, their telltale mannerisms were uncanny. The arching brow of skepticism, the quick wink after telling a joke. But until that night I saw them as opposites.

Sam was full of pizzazz, holding forth about his hometown. He kept hopping up and darting to the screen, admiring the images, particularly one of him standing in a blue blazer and photo-gray glasses beaming by a road sign for his town. He brimmed with pride. Was he running for office or selling time-shares? My upbringing in Lima, Ohio, known for producing the country's school buses, hearses, and army tanks, did not turn me into a booster. And no one there ever forced us to wear yellow stars or targeted us for slaughter.

Sam showed us a 1929 photo that introduced my imposing great-grandfather Moshe David Rakowski and his stern-looking wife, Pearl Chilewicz Rakowski, posing in front of the family lumberyard, the business that Moshe David established when he moved to Pearl's hometown of Kazimierza Wielka. Two-year-old Sam sat cross-legged in a sailor suit at his grandfather's feet.

At the sight of his grandmother's image on the screen, Sam's voice dropped. He took us back to the night his family went into hiding. His ninety-three-year-old grandmother was a formidable woman and quite healthy, but she could not keep up with a group dashing in the dark to a distant hideaway. The decision was excruciating. They had to leave her behind, even knowing what that meant.

Early Monday morning, locals later described, Nazis swarmed the city, thundering through the streets, blaring demands from loudspeakers for all Jews to report immediately to the market square. Heavily armed Germans scoured the houses for Jews who failed to obey.

Sam's voice caught and he cleared his throat.

Pearl ignored the orders. A group of German soldiers who had been swigging vodka on a nearby stoop barged into her house, finding her alone. The two families—eight Rakowskis and Banachs—who lived there had vanished. Several Nazis dragged Pearl out. In front of neighbors, they cocked their weapons and opened fire. The townspeople remembered: It took many bullets to kill her. Pearl went down shaking her fist.

I shivered. The lights flicked back on and I froze, sitting like a bad guest, not even offering my help with the dishes. I stared at my scrawl on cocktail napkins, words I could no more pronounce than spell. As Sam talked, I'd tried to record the names, dates, and places as if they were shooting stars that would disappear if I did not capture them. The tragic end of my great-grandmother's life filled me with pride and horror. The electricity around Sam was stunning, as if a sleepwalker had awakened.

Two newspaper reporting jobs later, after covering all manner of misdeeds from organized crime to priest sex abuse to a corrupt judge who exchanged leniency for a Mercedes-Benz from a drug dealer, I pulled out those napkins. I turned my sights on Sam and the remarkable untold story in my own family.

In the mid-1980s, the world had started paying more attention to Holocaust survivors. Elie Wiesel said something in a talk I attended that I could not ignore: "Listen to the survivors." I lobbied Sam until he agreed to describe his long-bottled Holocaust experiences for a Sunday magazine story. In his first-ever interviews, we sat at his white-clothed dining room table for marathon sessions. I coaxed him back over painful terrain. He unpacked memories he had carefully boxed away. I found every detail of Sam's stories compelling and his attention to accuracy reassuring. He embellished nothing.

My crime reporter veneer fell away. I asked him questions in a childlike voice that surprised me when I transcribed my interview tapes. He responded in kind, starting answers, "You see, honey..." Over time, I tried harder to push him to fill in more blanks and flesh out my understanding of scenes. He resisted. He started each response with "No, no." Eventually, I learned that his noes were a throwaway, a beat of space, a chance to think. I sought constantly to tease out the way things looked, smelled, or felt. But Sam, whether by nature or experience, remembered action, not color.

In those interviews, he brought me along with the family into hiding in a barn for two months in the fall of 1942. Germans were flushing Jews out of hiding places and executing them all. Sam's father decided they'd be safer in the ghetto in Kraków, thirty miles away. A nobleman friend of Sam's father dating back to their service in the Polish army arranged their transport to the ghetto. The eight Rakowskis and Banachs dressed like farmers and rode a horse-drawn wagon into Kraków and jumped down just before they reached the ghetto. But before they could gather any belongings, the driver sped away. "So," Sam said, "we went naked into the ghetto."

For nearly five months, he lived in the part of the Kraków ghetto designated for Jews healthy enough to leave the barbed wire confines for slave-labor jobs in area factories. Sam worked a night shift in the Wachs metal works. A Polish woman who was his supervisor snuck food and milk to him and helped him meet his work quota.

In March 1943, the Germans stormed the ghetto, killing two thousand Jews in the liquidation. Sam was forced to bury the remains of people he recognized.

He joined survivors in the nearby concentration camp Plaszów, built atop Jewish cemeteries. Plaszów's sadistic commandant Amon Göth was known for impulsively shooting Jews from his office window if he thought they were moving too slowly. He killed a Jewish cook because the soup was too hot.[1] Sam remembered hauling stones back and forth across the grounds in an exercise solely intended to induce exhaustion, hastening death. Fear haunted every crew, knowing that at any moment, Göth might shoot them just for "fun."

Plaszów was terrifying, but it was full of family. One day, Sam was ordered into a line leading to a cattle car crammed with other Jewish prisoners. None of them were his parents, brother, aunts, uncles, or cousins. The train stopped in a forest northeast of Warsaw by a camp called Pionki. He had no idea what was in store. "I didn't know when they turned on the showers whether they would be water or gas."

He later learned that his mother was in a nearby subcamp for women, serving the same munitions factory. She managed to keep in her shoe a photo of Sam and his little brother, Yisrael. Despite harrowing risks, she and Sam passed messages to each other in missile shells.

Later, the Red Army advanced from the east, endangering the munitions factory. The Germans decided to disassemble the factory and move it to Germany. The owner persuaded the Reich to allow designated Jews to go along so they could reopen the factory outside Berlin. Chosen as one of those precious workers, Sam was once again trapped in a cattle car on another precarious trip across Poland. Allied shelling stopped the train near Częstochowa. The German officers rousted Sam and other prisoners off the train and handed them shovels. They had to dig anti-tank ditches. The Germans hoped to slow the Russians' advance across the rolling carpet of south-central Poland.

Sam was relieved to get back on the train, especially when it kept going past Auschwitz. Finally, the journey ended in Oranienburg, outside Berlin, at the concentration camp

Sachsenhausen. But the camp denied admittance to the Jewish prisoners.

For weeks, Sam's group of Jewish prisoners was stuck in quarantine outside the camp. By then, Sachsenhausen housed mainly political prisoners and POWs from across Europe. The camp authorities presumed Jews carried typhus. The only other Jewish prisoners in Sachsenhausen at that point in the war were working on a secret operation producing counterfeit British pounds for a German scheme to destabilize the currency system of the United Kingdom.[2] The factory that Sam and his workmates were spared for was never reassembled. Sam was interned at two different subcamps until the spring of 1945.

One day, the guards assembled all the prisoners, who by then numbered more than eleven thousand.[3] Fearing greater danger in line with the Jews, Sam ripped the yellow star off his uniform and jumped in with the Christian Poles. Some Poles pushed him out of the line, calling him a dirty Jew. With one small loaf of bread allotted to each prisoner, he left Sachsenhausen on a death march. For more than two weeks, they got no more food or water. Guards shot anyone who stepped out of line. At night, they stopped in fields or forests. The starving prisoners ate bark off trees and drank from puddles. Sam and a friend took turns dozing and guarding one another's precious shoes. One morning they awoke. The guards were gone.

On roads teeming with refugees, Sam met American GIs who gave him a sip of cognac, "my first taste of freedom." He and his friend barged into a house near Schwerin, Germany, and found a woman huddled in fright with her children. Sam said, "When I saw her fear, any desire for revenge evaporated." They showered but could not get clean. For a few weeks, they helped American GIs pick out German guards from the camp who were trying to melt into the civilian population. A month after liberation, in June 1945, Sam hopped on a free train heading back to Poland in search of surviving family.

Sam unspooled his story to a cousin half his age whose youth was devoted to swim meets and cheerleading. I gobbled up every detail he shared. He kept pivoting from his war experiences to how wonderful his life was growing up. But I kept pushing him back to the part that started in September 1939 when he peered out a neighbor's cellar window at Panzer tanks steamrolling into town.

Why, I asked Sam, had he not spoken in detail of this before? His answer was surprising: "I didn't think anyone would care."

His survival was as miraculous as it was riveting. My big question was how. How could he keep up his spirits and his resolve amid constant fear and so much suffering?

At first, his response to my asking how he survived the Holocaust was, "I'm a Rakowski. We're strong."

I inhaled that answer like a child worshiping a superhero. I ran with it, telling myself I too could have weathered freezing winters in paper clothing. I could have gotten by on watery soup and an occasional potato. I could have endured Nazis forcing me at gunpoint into crammed cattle cars for endless journeys in squalor, not knowing the destination. I could have kept my sanity on arrival, forced to strip and be shaved. I could have abided the ill-fitting shoes and sleeping many to a bunk. I could have done it, I told myself, glomming onto our shared DNA. By some transitive formula, I hoped that Sam's extraordinary resilience was braided into my genes as well.

But I wondered how he kept it together over such a long haul. He said he coped by avoiding the doomsayers spreading grim gossip that the next day, they would all be killed. He walked away from them. "If I'm going to die tomorrow," Sam reasoned, "why start today?"

But I pressed him for philosophy or a prayer, some mantra he kept in mind.

"What was I thinking about, young lady?" he finally said, losing patience. "I was thinking about a piece of bread. Maybe a potato."

He shared dazzling tales of intuition and luck. Like the time he spent months digging an escape tunnel from a concentration camp, only to decide at the very last minute not to use it. Those who did succeeded in leaving the camp, but in the vast forest outside, most perished from hunger and exposure. That decision reinforced Sam's belief in trusting his gut. Late in the war, he followed another impulse and hid in the barracks rather than joining the work crew heading out of Pionki. That selective malingering saved his life. The rest of his work crew that day was forced onto trains bound for Auschwitz.

These stories left me in awe. No pedestal was high enough for this man, my cousin.

But he would not let stand this notion that luck or cunning was sufficient for surviving the Holocaust. One night after another marathon interview session at his dinner table, I tossed my perennial question his way again. How did he survive? Glib from fatigue, I answered my own question: "It's because you're a Rakowski, right?"

But this time, he took off his glasses. His dark brown eyes bored into me, freezing my Cheshire cat grin.

"You know," he said, "a lot of Rakowskis burned up in Treblinka."

That knocked me down from my cloud. I also came to see it as a turning point from him indulging a younger family member to engaging me as a collaborator. I would learn Sam often did not answer a direct question, then later piped up with it at the time of his choosing. In a phone conversation one day, he acted like I'd never asked.

"When we were standing around in the camps and they were counting us endlessly like we were a precious commodity, you know what we'd say to each other?"

"Sam!" I exclaimed. "Do tell."

"We'd say to each other *durkh leben*. You know what that means?" he asked, his accent as thick as ever. "That's Yiddish for 'live through it.'"

I repeated it to myself, stumbling over the consonant clusters that make Yiddish and Polish so challenging. It stayed with me. I wrote it on a scrap of paper and taped it near my computer. In my own moments of frustration and exhaustion, I repeated the phrase that had helped him endure greater trials.

Sam's personality emerged like a relief sculpture over the course of working together on the story. Recovering and reconnecting his memories, however grim, seemed to spark satisfaction from talking about them. Learning from him, a living survivor, was exciting. It fired my imagination and curiosity far beyond the dramatic experiences of anyone else I'd written about. I got caught up in telling Sam's story as the origin story of my family and the tragedy of a people. He was a miraculous survivor and reliable witness with an infectious deadpan humor who also brought me closer to my forebears, revealing traits that resonated in my branch of the family. Sam had Poppy's unflagging optimism and my father's stubbornness and ego. But they were never tested like he was. It surprised me that despite all he had endured, being with Sam was uplifting. He may be a survivor, but he was no victim.

In the spring of 1987, the *Providence Journal* Sunday magazine published my story with historical and present-day pictures of Sam and his family. The cover showed a stylized painting of me wearing a Jewish star bearing Sam's face as a teenager through barbed wire. The headline starting with "Survivors," depicting me as a survivor too, added to my self-consciousness. I hardly qualified, but it captured the life-changing experience of getting to know Sam and the family history. With the story's publication, I struggled with my unusual emotional investment in it and my clear loss of journalistic distance. But Sam had no ambivalence. He embraced the public attention to his story.

On the Sunday that it ran, I met Sam in New York, where he was visiting his uncle Isaac Levenstein, a survivor from Kraków. Sam took me out to a fancy restaurant for brunch with a great view of Manhattan. I asked him what he would do next. Was this the end or the beginning of more talk about his experiences? He bubbled with reports about what he called his "Holocaust business," posting testimonies with organizations and museums chronicling the fate of victims and survivors in the Holocaust. He was also getting more involved in sharing his experiences with schoolchildren.

Meanwhile, the story of how more than one thousand Jews, including Sam's uncle Isaac and aunt Sally, were rescued by a German industrialist named Oskar Schindler had been published in a prize-winning nonfiction book. And, Steven Spielberg had optioned it for a movie that would become the first Holocaust film to rate as a box office success, *Schindler's List*.[4] Somehow, the Holocaust was a topic people wanted to hear about.

I asked Sam if this attention made him want to return to Poland. He had still only been back once, seven years before with his son David.

"I told you I promised my mother not to go back," he said. Of course he had. That was after his mother and her sister Minna survived a death march from the concentration camp Gross-Rosen in 1945 and made their way back to Kazimierza

Wielka after liberation. While they were visiting a Jewish man who had survived in hiding, locals barged in and attacked. They fled, with Minna jumping out a second-story window, breaking her leg. Sam reunited with his mother in Kraków while Minna was in a hospital. "She told me, 'Sam, you can never go home again.'"

"Sure," I said. "But you already did, and that went well."

In fact, the balm of that reception had profoundly affected him, releasing a flood of memories from before the war when he was a good student and popular guy who felt woven into the fabric of his community.

"What's next?" I asked. "Will you return again to Poland?"

"I don't know. Maybe," he said. "I want to look up some people when the government situation improves."

"If you ever need a sidekick," I said, "I'd love to tag along and lend my skills to the cause."

He chuckled and gave me his double wink. "I'll let you know."

On the first trip to Poland together in 1991, Sam and Judy find a monument to slain Jews of Kazimierza Wielka desecrated, and Sam scratches his name on the back with a rock in an act of defiance.

# 2

# The Old Country

My connecting flight to Warsaw was delayed. I surveyed my waiting plane mates, rows of men who looked like toughs in a James Bond movie. With faces as wide as jack-o'-lanterns and pants hiked up to their armpits, they looked like old pictures of my grandfather. But he would never have worn such awful suits, garish plaids with all the tailoring of a burlap sack. In lieu of luggage, they leaned on plastic grocery bags held together by bungee cords. So much for the romantic allure of the old country.

Cousin Sam and I were traveling separately, which gave me time to switch gears from the intense story I'd been covering about a Rhode Island lawyer, his wife, and their daughter murdered with a crossbow by their financial advisor.

Other travelers, wearing smart suits and fancy watches, clearly were Western businessmen, swooping into Warsaw to help jump-start capitalism after five decades of communist rule. Poland was suddenly a global rock star after the trade union Solidarity and allies toppled the communist government, spurring a domino effect all the way to the Berlin Wall and spreading democracy throughout eastern Europe.

On the flight we passed from Germany into Poland, and I half expected the view out my window to show a shadow on the ground below, like the newspaper maps that had depicted the Soviet bloc in a menacing shade.

I was eager to see Sam in action on his home turf. I'd been reading about Warsaw, the city where my grandparents met in the time of the last czar. It was hard to believe my family had lived here for hundreds of years. I turned back to cribbing on the history of this place where kings welcomed Jews, and one in the 1200s, had granted Jews civil rights unequaled anywhere. Another king—Kazimierz, the namesake of our ancestral hometown—codified those rights, spurring further Jewish population growth, which the court saw as a means of increasing literacy and entrepreneurship. By World War II, Jews comprised the largest minority in Poland and lived in higher concentrations than anywhere in the world,[1] despite Poland's proud reputation as the most Catholic country in Europe.

Poles historically called themselves the "chosen people" and their country the "Christ of nations," designated to suffer for Europe's sins. Poland's historic narrative of victimhood is one of those generalizations that goes beyond stereotypes like the French are romantic and Italians are volatile.

The martyr identity aligns with Poland's history of extended domination by foreign occupiers and homegrown strongmen. Its military history is also imbued with a messianic narrative. For instance, the decisive victory in 1683 by the Polish king and military leader Jan Sobieski and forces of the Holy Roman Empire over the Ottoman army not only saved Vienna but enshrined Sobieski as Europe's "Savior of Christendom."[2]

In the Romantic era during the 1800s, the notion of Poles as the "chosen people" gathered strength. And in 1920, with full support from the Catholic Church, Polish general and prime minister Józef Piłsudski launched a war on the Soviet Union to save all Slavs. In what became known to Poles as the Miracle on the Vistula in the Battle of Warsaw, Piłsudski's forces delivered a humiliating and costly defeat to the encroaching Bolsheviks. The victory preserved the newly independent republic, and Poland saved Europe from the communist threat.

Sobieski and Piłsudski endure as great military heroes for those epic triumphs, in part because the list of major Polish battlefield victories is relatively short.

Surrounding empires—Austria (later the Austro-Hungarian Empire), Prussia (later Germany), and Russia—cannibalized Poland out of existence for two centuries until 1918, embedding deep and lasting insecurities in the Polish psyche. That sense of resignation to conquest resonates in the lyrics of its anthem of independence, written after Poland's dismemberment in the 1700s: "Poland is not yet lost, so long as we still live."

Some have linked Poland's military shortcomings to the topography itself. Its broad swath of arable land makes a great breadbasket, but conquerors have taken it for a welcome mat. Without rugged mountains slowing tanks or troops, conquerors from Napoleon and Hitler from the south and west, to the czars and Stalin from the east have steamrolled Poland's defenses and carved up its lands.

Germany and Russia have savaged Poland repeatedly over time, leaving a deep imprint of victimhood and grievance. Long stretches without autonomy have limited Poland's experience with independence and holding itself accountable for its own behavior. After all, blaming a big bad neighbor is easier than taking responsibility for a nation's own actions.

But what nation could have withstood an invasion like Hitler's blitzkrieg of 1.5 million troops, two thousand tanks, and over one thousand bombers and fighter planes? And two weeks after Hitler launched World War II on September 1, 1939, from the west, the Soviet Union invaded from the east. Germany quickly claimed victory and occupied the country. It proceeded to turn Poland into its prime theater for history's most systematic extermination of humans, which the Germans rationalized by designating Jews in particular as subhuman. The Reich built all six death camps—Chełmno, Bełżec, Sobibor, Treblinka, Auschwitz-Birkenau, and Majdanek—on occupied Polish territory. In total, the Germans established forty-four thousand concentration camps across the footprint of the occupation but confined the killing factories to Polish turf.[3]

Why pick Poland? Hitler found the world's largest Jewish population right next door. In mid-1930s Poland, anti-Semitism was already making life hard for Jews, a minority comprising less than 10 percent of the population. After Piłsudski died in 1935, the Polish government shifted right, and anti-Semitism surged as it had in other European countries with large Jewish populations. Poland's legislature closed a vise on Jews, implementing laws and regulations that shut Jews out of jobs and positions in universities and the legal and medical professions, and also denied them credit.[4] Polish nationalists, like the National Democratic Party, called for Jews to be evicted from the country, insisting that the Polish nation was traditionally Catholic, and led widespread boycotts of Jewish businesses, as Germany had modeled three years earlier.[5] The boycotts often escalated to violence.

None of these facts diminish the egregious losses and suffering of Poland, which endured the longest German occupation of any nation and yet its government never turned collaborator. Throughout the war, Poles suffered incomparable destruction and deprivation, and the country lost six million of its citizens, half of them Jewish Poles.

The decades of communist rule that followed gave no respite to already downtrodden Poles. Besides quashing personal expression, the Soviets suppressed religion, hoping to deny the influence of the Catholic Church and push the society toward atheism. The communist government also whitewashed Jews out of the war's narrative. No Polish monument

or textbook mentioned what later became known as the
Holocaust. Victims of Hitler's fascism were all the same, leaving generations to grow up with no awareness of the systematic
extermination of Jews, eliminating the Holocaust from historic
consciousness.[6]

Into that opening after communism, Poland elevated
the profile of Catholic victims of Auschwitz-Birkenau to the
principal martyrs, despite the fact that 1.1 million of the 1.3
million murdered there were Jews. Dating back to the 1950s,
management of Auschwitz focuses on the side "that is associated with Catholic Martyrdom or Polish Nationalism, but not
Jewish Martyrdom," in the words of a leading authority, Dr.
Robert Jan van Pelt.[7]

The Poland that Sam and I visited in 1991 was flush with
confidence and pride. It was a heady time. The nation was still
absorbing the amazing triumph of the trade union Solidarity
and its ally the Catholic Church. Unshackled from aggressors
at last, Poland had every reason to take a bow. Like a dewy-eyed
ingenue strutting on the world's economic stage, it was drawing widespread admiration for outstripping its Warsaw Pact
siblings in transforming from communism to a market econ-
omy. Global news outlets had descended, making Warsaw the
regional launchpad for covering the unraveling Iron Curtain.

I was focused on a more distant past in this city where my
grandparents had married. I doubted I'd find a trace of them
or their nuptials with only one surviving synagogue, but it was
exciting to see the city shake off a dreary past of bread lines and

anonymity. On my cab ride from the airport, I saw streets full of matchbox-sized cars, with drivers careening around corners and racing to beat trams like newly licensed teens. Free expression abounded in varied forms. Solidarity bumper stickers still shouted from light poles, alongside peep show trailers sprouting on downtown street corners and generating long lines of men. Spray-painted swastikas climbed walls and tagged street signs.

I paced in my room in the Grand Hotel in Warsaw. With my bags lost in transit, I couldn't freshen up much. Although I was too jet-lagged to remember my three words of Polish at check-in, I learned that Sam was already here but not in his room. Settling in to wait, I pulled back heavy old red drapes that reeked of stale cigarettes. My room seemed like a time capsule from when the Red Army kicked out the Nazi brass.

I cracked a window on dishwater skies and idly noticed a gray-haired guy in a black leather jacket down front. I looked away from that Western businessman and gazed at the skyline. But then I did a double take. That leather jacket guy was Cousin Sam.

Ever since my dad died three years before, the sight of Sam gave me a jolt. With his bristly brow and thought-stopping stare, I thought I was seeing a ghost. The resemblance was so strong that when Sam showed up at Dad's funeral, Mom nearly fainted. Now I was traveling with this man who was at once family and stranger.

I waved and called out his name. No response. Maybe he wasn't wearing his hearing aids.

Sam was fussing with something in a rental car. He got out and sidled up to a sneering cab driver slouched against a Mercedes. Warsaw cabbies had a reputation as rip-offs, but I watched Sam persuade the guy to lend him a hand. The cabbie got in Sam's car and fiddled with something and apparently fixed it. Sam was smiling and nodding, and the driver walked away with no tip. That's some charm.

Sam disappeared. Almost immediately, I heard a sharp knock. I opened the door and a breathless Sam nearly fell into my room.

Before I could speak, he fired off questions: "Which airline did you take? Did you exchange any money yet? How did you get from the airport? How much was your cab?"

I hugged him. "I yelled to you out front."

"Oh, you saw me out with the car?" He peered out my window like he didn't believe me. "I couldn't figure out how the car goes into reverse."

This was not the subdued old Sam. He was as hyper as a teen on prom night.

Sam had flown straight from a family bar mitzvah in Jerusalem. He wasn't much of a phone talker, so we'd just stitched together flights and hotel reservations, but no detailed schedule. I figured he had an itinerary roughed out in his mind. The formal tours would retrace his steps through the ghetto and camps, but I was keen on the unscripted visits in his hometown where relatives died far from barbed wire and gas chambers.

I asked about Israel and the bar mitzvah.

"Very nice. Very fancy, very meaningful." He nodded. Then he shoved his hands in his pants pockets and looked away. "But everybody wants to know why I'm coming here."

"Oh?" I giggled as if I knew the answer.

"I tell them it's a Polish vacation," he said. "You must be a Polack to go on a Polish vacation." His chuckle deepened to a belly laugh.

"Well," I said, smiling, "it's a great place for a crime reporter. It's one big crime scene."

———

The next morning, Sam steered the rental car through Warsaw, which was rebuilt after suffering more destruction than any other major European city in World War II. The worst came when the Nazis were in retreat but still retaliating for the sixty-three-day Warsaw Uprising. The Polish Home Army (Armia Krajowa) valiantly tried to liberate the country, but it did not happen before 85 percent of Warsaw was razed. Hitler's carpet-bombing played out while the Red Army sat and watched from across the Vistula River.

The postwar building boom replaced neoclassical structures with giant LEGOs of concrete. Coal dust left the endless rows of high-rise apartments looking like sooty prison blocks with windows the size of peepholes. The combined effect offered the city all the aesthetic charm of a dungeon.

We lurched and braked through morning rush-hour traffic

with Sam relearning the finesse of driving a stick. I had a five-speed car in the States but would not dream of offering to take the wheel here. It was Sam's country. The road signs alone, with their unpronounceable combos of consonants, froze my brain.

After a few hours of driving, we approached Kazimierza Wielka. Sam whistled when he wasn't reminiscing. He squinted at a road sign and said, "I drive through here and I get electric shocks. I see the barns and buildings that our lumber went in. And I remember coming this way delivering Christmas trees as gifts to good customers."

He delighted in seeing the rolling landscape of farms where beets and cabbage were being harvested by old methods.

"You see that rich soil?" Sam said, pointing out the window. "People lived better here than other places in Poland during the war and even under communism, because they could grow cash crops, tobacco and sugar beets."

Agriculture was still old-fashioned; horsepower came on four legs. The bucolic scenes stirred something timeless and beautiful. Maybe I was taken in by what he saw here now that I had a 3-D view of what this unexpected pitchman displayed in that living room slideshow.

Why was he so excited to be back in a place where he suffered so much?

I changed the subject to something Sam had just shared the previous night. He had revealed that he had a tip about a surviving relative whom he'd been told about on his last trip here two years earlier. "Sam, tell me more about that lead you got on that cousin that you had never heard about. What are the chances that she's still alive?"

"It's interesting," he said. She was from the Rożeńek family. "We never knew where the Rożeńeks went to hide. But we thought they did," he said. And his mother's sister Ita and her family had never turned up on any of the meticulous records the Germans kept from concentration camps and death camps, so there was no proof of what happened to that family.

On Sam's previous trip, Stefan, the husband of a former schoolmate, revealed that the family was killed in hiding, but one member, a daughter, had survived. Sam had asked where this daughter had gone. Stefan said, "She went west."

In Poland, "heading west" referred to the western side of the country that had formerly been part of Germany. At the end of World War II, Stalin punished Breslau, the last strong-hold of the Third Reich against the Red Army, by grabbing it away from Germany.[8] It became the Polish city of Wrocław.[9]

In those early days, Wrocław was chaotic, between the dis-placement of Germans and arriving Poles from lands to the east given to Ukraine and Lithuania. That left Wrocław with no entrenched population. It became a safer harbor for Jews who had tried to return to prewar homes and businesses only to be rebuffed—often violently—by the current occupants.

The tip came during Sam's 1989 visit, a fortieth anniversary trek with Bilha, which included a stop by the house of Wojciech Guca, the brother-in-law of Sam's father's business partner. Guca was the Christian Pole to whom Sam's father entrusted the family lumberyard when the Germans barred Jews from owning businesses or earning money. When Stefan spilled the news about the surviving cousin, he told Sam, "Go ask Guca." Guca lived a few doors from where the family was killed during the war so he would know about the daughter who survived.

The possibility that a cousin had survived all these years and no one in the family had ever known about it was riveting. I was fine with visiting monuments and camps with Sam, but tracking someone still alive, as a reporter, *that* was my bread and butter. But here, I had no idea if such a pursuit was even practical. I had never done any reporting in a foreign country and had no knowledge of how they kept records, not to mention that I didn't speak the language. Oh, and there was another big hitch: the trail was cold—on ice for half a century.

Still, the prospect of tracking down the last of the twenty-eight first cousins Sam had grown up with in a village of three thousand was compelling. So few extended family members even saw the end of the war. In the decades that followed, like many survivors, he had put his head down and focused on rebuilding his life. His parents tracked people they knew in Israel, South America, Canada, Europe, and the United States while Sam was raising a family and moving back and forth between Ohio and Israel. He and Bilha struggled with obligations to their respective parents, but ultimately, they landed permanently in Ohio where Sam worked in his father's thriving home-building business. Also services were better there for their younger daughter, Daphne, who was born with cerebral palsy.

A horse-drawn cart piled high with beige beets filled our windshield. The beast looked like a Clydesdale right out of an American beer commercial, stepping high with the white tufts near his hooves. Sam strained at the horse's pace, the wagon swaying into both lanes.

"C'mon, mister, make up your mind."

The hunched driver turned his leathery face and shrugged. Why should he risk his harvest by pulling over?

Sam squinted at the farmer. "I look at every face, like maybe I recognize him from before and he knows something about my people."

Sam pulled into the lane of oncoming traffic, zigging around the cart, shouting something in Polish. The driver did not flinch. We gathered speed. Then Sam slapped his forehead.

"Sam, you dumb Polack," he said, swinging a U-turn.

"Where are we going?" I asked.

"You'll see."

The little white car scudded down a side road Sam had missed in the jolt from horse pace. It galumphed across railroad tracks, kicking up dust in the sunshine. The road faded to dirt. Tall weeds formed a tunnel ahead. Brush clawed the undercarriage, slowing our pace. Sam leaned forward, squinting at the fork in the path. He chose the right one. A stand of goldenrod swayed with ambivalence. Sam nodded, confirming his choice.

The perfume of autumn decay transported me back to my childhood pine tree, which offered a bird's-eye view of the flat farmland in Ohio where my grandfather had chosen to settle. It must have reminded my Poppy of this beautiful land.

I did not know our destination, but Sam knew this place. He had crossed continents and scaled inner walls of grief. Something was bringing him here, whether for some kind of "closure" or "unfinished business," something pulling him back and also keeping him from letting go.

The spindly treetops rustled. Sam peered at the shedding trees.

"We used to play here in these woods."

At a clearing, he stopped and jumped out of the car. By the time I had circled around to his side, he emerged from the back seat brandishing a new camcorder, unshackling batteries. His glasses were pushed up onto a crown of thinning white hair. He peered through the viewfinder.

"You know how to work that gizmo?" I teased.

He handed it over. "You can figure it out."

"How would I know how to use this thing?" I sounded whiny, like a sullen teenager snapping at my father. "Is it on? Where's the microphone?"

He ignored my snark. "Just look through and you'll see R-E-C in the window there if it's recording." He looked around. "This used to be a good place for romance." Lowering his glasses, he drifted to something that made him smile.

"Did you bring a lot of girls here?"

He grinned. Just then, we heard a muffled giggle nearby. We froze. Apparently, it was still a dating destination.

Sam's head tilted at the trees, searching. I panned the camera across a line of skinny trees framing a plowed field.

"We're in these woods, beautiful woods," he narrated to the camera. "It smells alive. And we're trying to figure out where they buried two or three hundred people." Sam stood very close to the lens, ignoring my fluster. Staring into the camera, he pronounced, "In this place, a group of scouts dug a big pit ahead of time."

"You guys were in hiding then, right?"

"We'll get to that later, young lady," he said. "We are near to the place where my friend Ari Mellor, who resettled in Winnipeg, Canada, put up something to remind people what happened here to the Jews of Kazimierza Wielka." Sam turned on his heel. "We're walking toward this monument."

I tried to keep Sam in the frame. I stumbled. The lens turned to the treetops. He kept talking and walking.

"After the Nazi roundup in October 1942, the Germans were kind of disappointed. They didn't get anywhere near all the Jews of Kazimierza Wielka."

"How many were there?" I tried not to sound breathless.

"Well, there were more than usual because some Jews had run away from other towns," Sam narrated. "A lot of people thought that the Nazis might forget about the little villages and small towns, so they came here thinking they'd be safe. You know your great-aunt Frymet; she did that. She ran away from Warsaw and left her husband there."

The population of 350 Jews before the war had swelled to 550. The trains to Bełżec carried less than half that number.[10]

A week after the roundup, Jews with less durable hiding places filtered back to town. Nazi propaganda lured many with the promise that they would only be sent away for forced labor. But the Germans locked them in the school. Days later, on a Monday morning in November, many townspeople remembered the sight of German soldiers pointing guns at a line of Jews walking out of town. Witnesses saw the panic when the Germans turned the line left, heading away from the train station, instead turning on the road we took. They came here to Słonowice. To these woods.

The camcorder followed Sam approaching the clearing of the monument.

"They marched them out here, sturdy guys, tin benders and craftsmen, mothers and small children." His voice faded.

They forced the women to strip in front of men who were their neighbors, keepers of stores they visited, parents of schoolmates, he said. Mothers held their babies, standing by the pit, waiting for the crack of the bullets meant for each, I would read in accounts of the slaughter at the Jewish Historical Institute in Warsaw.

"What kind of shape are we going to find the monument in?" he asked aloud.

"I wrote to the city manager. I asked him if he could have somebody check on this place. Maybe he got somebody to fix it up."

Wind fluttered. Sam gasped.

I turned the camera to a bald upright stone. Swastikas painted in black covered what had been a monument. Holes pocked the face, where letters that once told the story in English and Hebrew had been yanked out and left in a pile of twisted metal in the dirt. I panned to Sam's hunched form.

"Why do they have to destroy this one thing we have left here?" he asked, his voice cracking.

We both turned to the woods. Narrow white trees stood impassively. A breeze chafed upper branches, swishing dry leaves like cymbals. The warm autumn air twirled, wafting the earthy perfume of decay.

Sam picked up a sharp stone from the dirt and walked around to the back of the monument. I followed the camera's tunnel vision. An impish smile creased his cheeks. Ignoring the defaced front, he found a blank canvas on the flip side. Like a wily tagger, he scratched with the prehistoric implement. I expected a Hebrew slogan like *am yisrael chai* (the people of Israel live), harking back to his newlywed days in Israel when he left his family name behind, shaking off the past.

R-A-K- He scratched slowly in giant letters that showed white on the dark rock. O-W-

"Not Ron?" I asked. No answer.

S-K-I.

He beamed at the camera. "I'm back." He laughed dryly. "They missed one."

---

Walking back to the car, I stared at the fields and trees, reflexively looking for a hiding place, feeling the panic of the doomed

Jews, so long a part of the town, marched here at gunpoint. I shuddered. All these lives taken and forgotten.

Sam knew who they were in detail. During the occupation, he was put in charge of keeping track of everyone in the Jewish community. His father decided it was a good use of Sam's year of high school, which made him one of the most educated in town. His job was to make sure they could even out the burden of the Germans' onerous demands for physical labor on the Jewish families. Sam kept lists of every able-bodied Jew in town, who was ill, who was widowed, and who had already shoveled snow or swept streets. It meant that he knew every Jew in town by name, age, and address.

That was why he was certain that no one in his family had ever heard about a surviving daughter from that family. Other related Rożeńeks had appeared in displaced persons camps after the war, but none were the sister of Sam's mother Ita or her husband or three children. Not in the Germans' detailed records from concentration or death camps, and no survivor in the Rożeńek family had ever reached out to anyone from their hometown after the war.

Driving away from the monument, Sam shrugged off his disappointment in the vandalism. The sight of familiar streets seemed to buoy his spirits.

It wasn't until after he started attending survivors' events in the early 1980s that Sam allowed himself to think about his home turf, spurred by seeing familiar faces and playing hopscotch with names and places. His wheels started turning, and pretty soon he had filled envelopes with pages of names and phone numbers. Every city he visited in the United States, Europe, or Israel, he called, visited, and debriefed anyone who could fill in blanks. The list builder kept updating the ones on paper and in his head, leading him back home again.

"Everywhere else I have lived, I have been a stranger," he said. "When I come and stand on the streets of my town, I feel at home, even though there are no Jews here anymore." He laughed from someplace deep. "It's crazy."

Turning back into a tour guide, Sam spun the car around a small traffic circle. The island held a sign with an oversized metal cutout of a big beige vegetable, a sugar beet.

"You see that? That's the sugar factory," Sam gushed. "This was one of the largest in the country. When the factory got electricity in the 1930s, we got lights in our house."

He wheeled along the main artery, Sienkiewicz Street, where people referred to their location by whether it was closer to the church or the cemetery.

"This was a Jewish street," he said. "There was a bakery across the street, making fresh bread every day." Flanking the bakery on both sides were shops owned by two families in which the wife was a sister of Sam's mother, the Dulas and the Rożeńeks.

"Over there was a shochet. You know what a shochet is? That's a kosher butcher. He was right there. Down the street was the hardware store. Now that was the Rożeńeks.'"

I tried to see through his eyes the lively streetscape of his childhood in a stretch of desolate buildings with crumbling facades and peeling paint. Who could tell from this scene that it was a street of Jewish shops that drew customers from several towns around on Mondays, market day?

This was Sam's domain. He used to stop by the Rożeńeks' hardware store even when he didn't need anything. They were always there: Frania, who was a few years older than him, minding the store and her little sister, Hena, playing or just hanging around.

Sam walked this street daily from his first days of school to his teenage years, when he ran invoices from the lumberyard up to the sugar factory. He was such a familiar sight that they waved him through the gate up there. Later, during the occupation, he had a slave-labor job on the grounds of the sugar factory in the garage, servicing the vehicles that ferried Nazi officers around.

Sam rounded a block and pulled up to a mustard-colored stucco house with a tiny balcony outside a second-floor window. Growing up, he knew it as the mayor's house and also the home of his classmate Sofia Prokop. Sam and Sofia were academic rivals, vying for best student. She always won, which he chalked up to her being the mayor's daughter and him being the only Jewish boy in his class. Sofia had married a clerk from the sugar factory, Stefan Pierchała. Sofia still lived in the house where she was born, and she was able to raise her family there. It was Sofia's husband who had revealed on Sam's last visit that the Rożeńek family had been killed during the war, but one daughter escaped and survived.

Ever since that visit, Sam had been following up by phone and letter for two years, seeking details or some elaboration from Stefan. No response. No answer to his letters and no calls back. So Sam figured he'd show up in person again and it would be harder to ignore his inquiry, which matched my journalistic playbook. It was harder to turn someone away on your doorstep than to ignore calls and notes.

Sam swung the car into the driveway, saying to me, "We're going to the horse's mouth. Let's see if he'll tell us more about this cousin."

Just after Sam turned off the ignition and was climbing out of the car, Stefan, a bear of a man with a helmet of gray hair, barreled down the driveway. He waved his arms, nostrils flaring. This man twice Sam's size shouted in rapid-fire Polish, commanding him to pull the car up the driveway and into the courtyard.

Sam got back in and obliged, moving the car out of sight.

Stefan darted out to the street, scanning side to side like he was harboring a bank robber.

Were we welcome here?

Once we were out of view, Stefan gripped Sam's hand warmly. He turned to me, clicking his heels and lifting my hand to his lips in the manner of a Polish gentleman.

Sofia emerged from the house, looking grandmotherly in bright white dentures and dyed brown curls. She hugged Sam like a long-lost friend. She ushered us past ambling chickens and tall purple hollyhocks into the house, eyeing the big suitcase Sam carried with the excitement of a child at Christmas. Sam hoisted it on a table and opened it with a flourish. Out came the gifts: entire skirt suits for Sofia, along with nylons, lipsticks, chocolate bars, and toys for the grand-children. Communism had fallen, but such goods remained scarce and pricey in Poland.

Sam turned on his video camera, offering an upbeat nar-rative in English, panning from Sofia to Stefan. "These are my friends, the best ones for helping me find my people here."

Stefan and Sofia spoke little or no English, but they had to know from all Sam's correspondence that he was on a mission to find the cousin who Stefan had first mentioned and who we would later confirm was Hena Rożeńka, the feminine case of Rożeńek.

That line Sam had spoken for the video camera was the last English I would hear for quite a while. We sat down at their dining table, and they started talking. Sam had promised to translate, but in the moment, it was the last thing on his mind. But I could tell that Sam wasted little time on small talk. He brought up the Rożeńeks right away.

Stefan looked away.

Not a promising sign. Also not a good interviewing tech-nique. No warm-up at all. But it was Sam's show. He needed to know why Stefan had not answered him the past two years.

Sofia emerged from the bedroom beaming. She modeled her new tweed jacket and skirt from America.

Marooned behind the language barrier, I paid attention to the furnishings and noticed pictures of Jesus and Pope John

Paul II watching us from every wall of the dining room and living room. Had the communist government allowed such religious displays from the beginning in Poland or only after the Vatican named a Polish pope in 1978, I wondered. Or were these the free expressions that only came after the fall of communism? I had no chance to ask. Sofia did not sit with the men, instead donning an apron and disappearing into the kitchen. Was she avoiding the conversation about the Rożeńek cousin?

Stefan put on his thick glasses, looked at Sam, then took them off again, seeming agitated. He spoke for a long time, winding through stories about his memories of the war. I was encouraged by the length of Stefan's speeches, thinking it might mean he was revealing something new. But Sam occasionally turned to me with a roll of his eye and said in English, "I've heard all this before."

Sam tried to bring Stefan back to the topic: What happened to the Rożeńek daughter? What happened to her family?

Stefan's close-set dark eyes scanned the room. I was writing down everything I noticed on a reporter's pad. Stefan tossed his glasses on the table and stared at me accusingly. What was I writing, he asked Sam. Sam told him not to worry about it.

"She's my secretary," he said in Polish, then again to me in English.

I looked Stefan in the eye. He looked away.

Stefan pivoted from Sam's question. He turned to the day the Germans rounded up all the Jews in town in the autumn of 1942, weeks before the killings by the monument. Stefan described what he personally saw, and Sam gave me snippets in English. Stefan got animated when he told Sam that he saw the grown daughter of the kosher butcher darting back and forth in the street. He used exaggerated hand motions to show that she had a big bosom. His eyes were shining with the memory, reminiscing about a big-busted woman getting gunned down by Germans before his eyes. I got the sense from his practiced telling that he had repeated this story ad nauseam at coffee klatches around town.

Sam looked at me, unsmiling, and shrugged. He asked Stefan again about Hena.

Sofia was rolling out homemade noodles, calling out something from the kitchen. Had she cautioned Stefan before our arrival to hold back on spilling any more about the Rożeńek cousin while maintaining the facade of helpful friendship?

Sam pressed Stefan again. I did not need a translator for the phrase Stefan pronounced and repeated: "*Nie wiem.*" It means, "I don't know."

Stefan's eyes darted back and forth, and then he looked away. If I had to guess, it seemed he was regretting ever telling Sam about Hena. He did not add the slightest detail to his first utterance about her. He sure acted like he knew more but had reason to button up.

Stefan retreated. As Sam later told me, he said, "Go ask Guca."

"I will," Sam said. "But you were the one who told me about her."

Why wouldn't he say more?

Sofia interrupted by ferrying in bowls of chicken soup heaped with her fresh noodles. I hopped up to help serve, stepping into her kitchen suffused in the smells of bleach and boiled chicken, noticing her sofa-sized coal stove. The fragrances took me back to my own grandmother's kitchen. Sam had told me that growing up, Jews and Poles would never have eaten at each other's houses because of kosher restrictions. He had not always abided by such restrictions, and sometimes joined his father when he broke bread with non-Jews to seal business deals. Now all four of us stared into our bowls of soup. Then we slurped in silence. Sam's jaw was set. He waited for Stefan to say more, but nothing changed.

After the plates were cleared, we offered wan smiles to our hosts.

Sam stood up. "C'mon, young lady. We're not gettin' anywhere."

The entire drive to our hotel in Kraków, Sam fumed about his so-called friends. Why did they stonewall him? Why wouldn't they help him with this search for Hena? What did they think he was going to do? Try to prosecute? No way. That was not on his mind. He just wanted to see her. He just wanted to thank whoever had hidden her.

All through dinner in the hotel, Sam brooded. Late in the evening, he phoned Stefan and Sofia. "Why do you welcome me with kisses and cakes, but you won't tell me the truth? If my cousin is alive, why won't you let me know how to find her?"

He raised his voice. It cracked with disappointment. I could not hear the response on the other end, but from Sam's end, it did not sound promising. He told them he was canceling his plans to return the next day. "I am done with you people," he said in Polish.

I found Sam in a better mood the next morning at breakfast. He said that Stefan called, begging Sam to come back again. He said he had a surprise. I wondered why Sam readily accepted this missive given how upset he was the night before. But Sam wanted to believe him. We hopped in the car and headed back to Kazimierza Wielka.

"Maybe it was a good thing I got angry," Sam suggested.

The closer we got to the Pierchałas' house, the higher Sam's hopes soared. Maybe this would be the day, he said. Maybe Stefan had found her, and Sam could finally have a reunion with the Rożeńka cousin.

---

Waves of blue-green rye shimmered in the October sunshine. The rental car rolled through the countryside. I was sitting in the back next to Sofia, dressed in her new American tweed suit, lips pressed in a tight smile. Stefan rode shotgun with Sam at the wheel.

We passed a sign for the hamlet of Chruszczyna Wielka. From the front seat, Sam said to me in English, "We are very near Zagórzyce." He was signaling to me our proximity to the Rożeńeks' wartime hiding place.

The vibe with Stefan and Sofia was confusing. The epiph-any Sam hoped for when we arrived at their house that morn-ing had given way to another round of Stefan's bobbing and weaving over coffee and home-baked apple strudel. Sam got impatient again and asked Stefan why he'd asked us back. Stefan raised his hands and said, "Wait, I have something for you. We know who has your dinner table. Want to see it?"

I wondered how the table fit into the search for the cousin.

We pulled over by the side of the road in front of a large property with a brick farmhouse surrounded by fields. The house was set far back from the road.

Off to the side sat a windowless gray building. "That's a flour mill," Sam said in English to me. "We used to walk out here to visit relatives on Saturdays. My mother's family owned a lot of land around here."

A squat man in dusty coveralls emerged from the gray build-ing, peering at our car through thick glasses. Stefan jumped out and lumbered down the drive. He threw his arm around the guy and turned him away from us in what looked like a furtive effort to keep us from overhearing them or seeing the man's expressions. They huddled for several minutes. Finally, Sofia got out and tot-tered down to them, calling out in a friendly voice. The caucus-ing continued. Sofia turned to eye us warily, as if we were some kind of threat. The man in overalls kept squinting at the car.

"What's going on, Sam?" I asked.

"I don't know, honey. Apparently some big negotiations," Sam said. "We have to be very diplomatic about it."

Sofia marched back toward the hot car, her pale blue eyes gleaming with triumph. Stefan, meanwhile, was waving his arm, motioning for us to join them.

Sam turned to me in the back seat. "OK, young lady. We're going inside."

We walked gingerly down the long drive. Sam introduced himself and me in Polish to the man of the property, Maxwell Majdecki. He nodded and smiled formally, as if he was doing us a big favor.

Sofia and Stefan watched him warily, like they expected a last-minute change of mind. But Majdecki gestured for us to enter the house. A small brown puppy whimpered and barked, scampering underfoot. We climbed concrete steps. Sofia led us down a dark corridor that opened into a large room walled with windows and five old television sets in dark veneer cabinets. It faced a vast expanse of woods and tilled fields.

Suddenly at home, Sofia began clearing dishes off a large table and peeled back layers of plastic tablecloths.

She announced something that sounded admonishing. I turned quizzically to Sam.

"She says, 'To look, not to take,'" he translated.

"Why would we...?" I asked aloud in English, not expecting an answer.

Once she had removed the last skin of polyester lace, she smiled grandly and said, "*Proszę bardzo*." (Please and welcome.)

Sam stood frowning before the heirloom. He videotaped the scene and our hosts showing us the oak table that may have been built in the 1920s, the interwar period and a time of great optimism in Poland. This rectangle of wood had more detail than a basic farmer's table but little decoration or style. It had been stained walnut and looked worn and grooved. Sam knew those scratches and nicks.

Stefan, Sofia, and Majdecki stared at him. Did they think he might suddenly hoist the table on his shoulder and bolt out the door?

That was the last thing Sam was likely to do even if he wanted to. He had a well-developed habit of leaving houses full of furnishings behind ever since he left Poland. He had moved again and again in Israel and the United States—twelve times in all—without a backward glance. He left behind or gave away whole houses of furnishings without giving his wife a chance to pick a dish or a painting she might want to keep.

But now he did not hurry. His hands navigated the weathered wood, fingering the surface as if reading braille. For a lumberman's son, every grain in the wood table told a story from another lifetime.

*His* other lifetime.

This table had been at the heart of so much of that life, of big holiday meals with family and small weeknight dinners with only his mother, brother, and grandmother while his father was away on business, exploring forests for timber harvesting or visiting the sawmill they leased in another town. The table was at the center of Shabbat dinners on Friday nights with roast chicken and springtime seders that lasted long into the night.

In his mind's eye, he saw faces around this table. His brother, Yisrael, who always picked at his food, and his father, who led discussions of local Jewish leaders around it after curfew during the three years of German occupation. The Nazis never locked the local Jews into a ghetto, but they still issued edicts and demands. At this table, the leaders had decided to pool money for food for hungry families in their community and cash for bribing the Germans, hoping to buy time and, maybe, lives.

Majdecki strode over to the table with the exaggerated gestures of a game show host. He offered Sam a seat at his table. Sam hesitated, then sat down.

Majdecki sat opposite him in a straw-yellow shirt buttoned tightly to the neck. He started telling stories with a flourish, sounding like he had regaled other audiences with them many times. Sam left the camera on, recording the conversation.

"After the Jews were gone, the Nazis put all their furniture in the Rakowski lumberyard," Majdecki said. (His exact words came later from transcribing Sam's video.) "I was newly married, and I needed a table. I got such a good price for this," he crowed. His pale blue eyes lit up at the memory.

Sofia beamed at Sam.

"The price was so good," Majdecki said. "Only two hundred złoty [under fifty dollars today]."

At the time, Sam sat stone-faced. He turned to me. "He's telling about his good deal," he said, giving me a look with an arched eyebrow.

I watched Majdecki fold his arms across his chest in a

self-satisfied way and wondered if it occurred to him that while he was scoring his bargain, the man sitting before him was stranded in the countryside struggling to stay alive in hiding after the roundup.

Majdecki seemed oblivious. He went on, regaling us with the story of how he scored this sprawling property, complete with a stately house and flour mill. The Jew who owned it survived, but was unable to return amid the dangerous postwar atmosphere. Majdecki said he found the owner, a man named Brenner, huddling with other survivors in a cellar in a nearby city. Assaults on Jews were rampant, and they were hiding out. Majdecki said he persuaded Brenner to sign over the property to him before he left the country.

He turned to another topic, leaning forward in his chair to share the drama of the day of the roundup, reminiscent of Stefan's eagerness to offer his account of that day.

Majdecki was passing through town that day and remembered seeing Germans herding Jews onto wagons and lorries. He recognized a horse and wagon belonging to a Jew, a customer named Spokojny. He had just agreed to sell some grain to Spokojny, who had not yet paid for the order.

I didn't know what Majdecki was saying, but his voice rose, simulating how he called out to Spokojny. He said he told him not to worry about paying for the grain yet to be delivered. He smiled and nodded, like this was generous.

Sitting in the wagon, Spokojny had thanked him. That was when Majdecki noticed Spokojny's bloody hands. The men sitting with him in the same uniforms were also stained with blood. The Nazis had made the Jewish police go around and pick up the bodies of Jews killed during the roundup and forced deportations.

Spokojny pleaded with Majdecki, "Please, go to my wife. She is in Glogów, and please tell her I went to Miechów."

In Miechów, the Germans forced the Jews onto trains headed for the death camp Bełżec. When Spokojny's wagon arrived, the trains were already crammed with doomed Jews. "The trains were locked there," Majdecki said. "So they just shot them all."

Sam asked him if he had ever fulfilled his promise. "Did you go tell Spokojny's wife?"

Majdecki shook his head. "No," he said with a shrug.

He started humming a klezmer song he recalled Jewish musicians playing at Christian weddings. He turned, as if noticing me for the first time. He asked if I knew the tune.

I shook my head. He looked surprised.

"I miss the Jews," Majdecki said. He looked to me for a reaction. I forced a polite smile. Talk about mixed messages.

Sam asked him about the Rożeńeks, the cousins Sam's father had always believed found a hiding place in Zagórzyce. Did he hear that a daughter escaped their massacre? Majdecki shook his head.

Sam looked pointedly at Sofia and then at Stefan. They looked away. So we really were just visiting furniture.

Sam asked Majdecki about some other cousins, the Dula

family. "Abraham Dula was my uncle," Sam said. "He and his wife, Esther, used to run a fabric store in town. My father believed that the Dulas had found a hiding place nearby, some place in this very village."

"Oh yes," Majdecki said, nodding. "Next door," he said matter-of-factly. "They are buried in the root cellar."

A curtain of drying tobacco leaves cordons off the mass graves for the Dula family. We discover this after the man with Sam's dining room table says the Dulas are buried next door.

# 3

# Barnyards

We trudged through tall grass separating farmyards and houses that nudged up close to each other. I caught up with Sam and asked him who the Dulas were. Sam said he had aunts in both families. One of his mother's sisters married a Dula and another married a Rożeńek, and the two families ran shops one door apart from each other, separated by the bakery on the main street in town.

Crowing roosters and barking dogs announced our arrival at the neighboring property. A man appeared and Majdecki, the table man, gave him a familiar nod, signaling that the strangers were with him.

The aging farmer in soiled coveralls nodded back at Majdecki and surveyed us. He did not seem surprised by the sight of five people entering the farmyard. Oddly, it seemed as though he had been expecting us.

Sam ambled over, extending his hand formally. "I am Szmul Rakowski from Kazimierza Wielka," he said slowly in Polish.

The farmer tilted his moon-shaped face in puzzlement but said nothing.

Everyone seemed to be holding their breath, wondering how this guy would take our intrusion and inquiry about the remains of our relatives on the property. What had happened to them here, and what role might this farmer or his family have played in the events?

"I understand that my uncle and the Dula family were hiding here during the war," Sam said. "I came really to thank you for hiding them." Sam moved in very close, looking the farmer straight in the eyes. "Thank you," he said in Polish. "For your generosity."

The farmer nodded. He held Sam's handshake for what seemed like a long time. His sad eyes turned and stared at the ground. "Sam," he said, "it is a tragedy for your family and for mine."

The farmer, who identified himself as Władysław Sodo, shook his head. With a big sigh, he then told the story. On a May night in 1944, gunmen surrounded the house and banged on their door. They barged into the house, shouting at his father and demanding that he turn over the Jews he was hiding. Sodo said his father, Kazimierz Sodo, had insisted, "There are no Jews here."

The gunmen roughed up his father and ransacked the house. But his father kept denying he was hiding anyone. The attackers left. A few hours later, they returned and went straight to the barn. After a lot of shouting and scuffling, someone yelled that they had found the Jews.

Five adults emerged from the hiding place, prodded from behind by gunmen aiming at their backs. It was the Dula parents and three grown children. The assailants forced them to walk single file up to the top of the hill overlooking the barnyard. Almost immediately, shots rang out.

The attackers beat Sodo's father brutally, punishing him for putting the entire neighborhood in jeopardy; if Germans discovered the hidden Jews, they told him, the entire village would pay with their lives. The men made his father strip every personal item off the bodies of the people he had been feeding and protecting for eighteen months. Then the killers forced the father to dig a mass grave around the farm's root cellar. After he tossed the bodies there, they made him climb down in the grave and threatened to shoot him too.

Sam was shaking his head slowly, absorbing what Sodo was revealing. The people killed were cousins he saw almost every day growing up. He turned back to Sodo, who had more to share. For weeks, one particular killer kept returning to threaten Sodo's father, accusing him of keeping for himself gold and jewels the gunmen presumed the Jews had left behind. Sodo said that no matter how many times his father protested that there was no booty, nothing beyond what the murderers had already taken, he could not convince them. In fact, suspicions that the Sodo family somehow profited from harboring Jews would persist in the area for decades to come.

After Sam told me more details of what Sodo said, we stood in silence. Sodo bowed his head and sighed. He turned and led us past a brood of chickens up an incline to an area where a curtain of drying tobacco leaves obscured what was behind it. I saw that a mound of earth rose behind the tobacco drape.

I swallowed hard, imagining that night. Gunmen crawling all over the property hunting for the Dulas. The terror of imminent discovery. Knowing they were about to be executed.

Sam asked, "How do you live with this for fifty years? You never wanted to move these bodies from there?"

Sodo lowered his eyes. The murderous raid had traumatized his father. The family blamed his early death on the experience of the local harassment and horror of the executions. "This is a tragedy for my family," he said.

Both men looked away.

Sam asked, "Maybe there's something left over here, a picture, a Jewish object left for memory?"

The farmer shook his head and said, "There's nothing left here. They took everything."

Sam asked, "These were Germans, hunting Jews so late in the war when the Red Army was so close?"

"No," Sodo said. "The gunmen were Poles."

"Stealers! Bandits!" Sofia chimed in.

Sodo nodded. "Yes, they were stealers, all right." But someone had tipped them off to the presence of Jews. Twice Sodo called the gunmen *partyzanci*, or Polish partisans, and I watched Sofia wince at their mention.

It was shocking enough to happen upon a family of five buried in a working farmyard, not to mention discovering they were Sam's aunt and uncle and three grown cousins. And here we were talking with a gentile Pole whose father had rescued this family, harboring them for eighteen months, only to have fellow countrymen wipe them out in a brutal attack. Who were these partisans, and how was killing Jews part of their mission?

It turned out that we had just waded into one of the most controversial topics of wartime Polish-Jewish relations, which has only gotten hotter over time. Later I would learn that in Poland, almost everyone claimed to have been a partisan during the war. Dating from 1942, the largest clandestine organization operating across the country was known as the Armia Krajowa (AK), or Home Army.[1] It was the military arm of the Polish underground state and an umbrella of resistance groups.[2] Formed in the wake of the German and Russian invasions, it was the largest and most dominant resistance group, with ranks swelling to four hundred thousand by 1944. Its membership fell into three types of members: full-time operatives, many of whom had been members of the Polish army and had formal training; uniformed fighters in the forests openly fighting Germans; and a third, part-time contingent that was unpaid and called on less often for operations.[3] The AK's leaders in the Polish armed forces in London sent financial support, and the Allies clandestinely dropped arms to aid in sabotage and other efforts to undermine the Germans.[4] The AK was best known for its role in the heroic sixty-three-day

Warsaw Uprising in 1944, and it provided significant intelligence to the Allies throughout the war. But despite support and connections with the government in exile, it was known to operate independently and without seeking permission or sharing knowledge of its activities.[5]

The partisans label also applied to a network of groups, some with sizable ranks whose units did not always submit to direction from the Polish government in exile and in fact sometimes clashed with other underground units. One of the largest, the Narodowe Siły Zbrojne (NSZ, National Armed Forces), formed in 1942, was openly supportive of the German campaign of genocide against Jews.[6] "The liquidation of the Jews in the Polish territories is of great importance for future development because it frees us from a multimillion-dollar parasite," said the NSZ newspaper in March 1943.[7]

The other major resistance guerrilla group operating around Kazimierza Wielka, I would learn, was the Bataliony Chłopskie (BCh, Polish Peasants' Battalions). It originated as a defense organization for farmers exploited by the Germans and grew to 160,000 members at its height in the summer of 1944. Its tactical units joined the AK late in the war. While Jewish partisans operated in commando units that had some affiliation with AK, including getting some financial support from the Polish government in exile, they were not active in the rural areas around Kazimierza.[8] But the operations of the AK and some other resistance groups, I would learn, were not always so different from the attitude, policies, and practices of genocidal Nazis.[9]

Standing in the Sodo farmyard that day, I had no knowledge of wartime partisan activities in the area. I just noticed that the farmer seemed to react to Sofia switching his reference to bandits. After we'd piled back in the car and headed back to town, Sofia again lamented the actions of the "bandits," as if repetition might blot out Sodo's reference to partisans. Sam did not challenge her.

Bandits or partisans. Surely Sofia, the top student in Sam's class, was smart enough to expect we would have a strong reaction to finding a whole family of Sam's cousins murdered by Poles. But if she did, she was in denial. Driving away from the Sodo farm, she asked Sam if he liked seeing his table. Sure, he told her, like Abraham Lincoln's wife complimenting the play. I mentally rolled my eyes. How was he supposed to dwell on furniture now? However, when we dropped them off—Sam pulled in well out of sight this time—he said we'd see them tomorrow. The day had started with a tall order of making progress on finding Hena. Even though none of that happened, Sam acted as though Stefan had redeemed himself.

Driving from the hinterland in the dark toward the lights of Kraków, I could not help but compare the discovery of the graves of the Dulas with the fresh crime scene to which I'd devoted my days and nights leading up to this trip. The slayings of a lawyer and his librarian wife and their young daughter by their financial advisor in Rhode Island had garnered national headlines. The summer before, I'd spent months covering a major Mafia trial in Connecticut, involving a series of mob hits

aimed at toppling the leadership of the crime family that con-
trolled the rackets in New England.

Those crimes drew vast law enforcement efforts for investigation and prosecution. The public did not expect the killers
in either case to get away with what they'd done. But here I was
in Poland, leaving a fifty-year-old mass grave that seemed like a
ho-hum part of the landscape. I thought of stories I'd covered
in the United States involving remains discovered by dog walk-
ers or dug up in a construction project. Not the same here. Had
these murders ever been investigated?

I told Sam that Sodo struck me as credible, a good guy.

Sam was also impressed. "We met a good man today, young
lady. I'm just thinking about how they took good care of five
people, grown-ups, for eighteen months. What a sacrifice.
Such good people."

But it was not enough to save the Dulas.

Someone had betrayed them. The houses near the Sodo
farm were clustered together, and some neighbors had a clear
view of the farmyard and the house. Sodo said people were
always watching them, checking his father's store purchases or
making unusual movements.

The gunmen's confidence in their quest and the beeline
they made for the hiding place when they returned implied a
tip from someone nearby. After all, the attackers had not gone
house to house. They went directly to the Sodo farm at a time
when most people were expecting the war to end soon.

I was still stuck on Sodo's revelation that the killers were Poles.

"Can you believe that Poles killed them?" I asked.

"Who else was around in the spring of 1944?" Sam wondered. "The Germans were being chased away by the Red Army."

"Sam, do you think the Rożeńeks' killers were Poles too?" I asked.

"Maybe so," he said. "Everyone in the countryside here was either in the partisans or helping them," Sam said. "But they cannot stand to have that legacy of the underground tarnished. A lot of them were fighting Nazis and killing Jews too."

He pulled up to the hotel. The weight of the day's discoveries hit him.

What a day.

Sam said, "We went looking for one live cousin, and instead we wound up with five dead ones."

———————————

When we drove up the next morning, Stefan was waiting. Sam had made the point that neither the table nor the Dula graves brought us any closer to finding Cousin Hena. Stefan said he had another idea. He climbed in and directed Sam to a farm in Zagórzyce, the hamlet where the Rożeńeks had hidden. Stefan said the people we were visiting should know something about what happened to Hena.

Sam parked on the road by the farm's entrance. It was a sultry October day. We tromped up the drive, stirring dust and trepidations. At the top of the hill, we found a scene that turned on the soundtrack from *Deliverance* in my head. Run-down buildings surrounded a farmyard littered with empty vodka bottles of varying sizes. The barn slouched as if it too had been on a bender. Even the wooden well house in the middle of the barnyard leaned off-kilter.

"Nobody home," Sam pronounced.

Stefan scanned the barnyard as if scoping out an escape route.

Sam said, "They'll probably come back soon from the fields for lunch."

I had a bad feeling about this. "Maybe we should wait for them off the property," I suggested, thinking of many door knocks I'd made as a reporter that had not gone well. I half expected to see shotguns emerge.

Eyeing the well house, I wondered if a young Hena had sought refuge here. Maybe after the shock of what she'd witnessed, she hid under the barn or even in the well house. That could have easily become a trap. Maybe the farmers were kind to her and took pity after her trauma. Maybe she fell in love with a son. Or maybe people in this house had tipped off whoever killed her family.

Roosters started making a racket, alerting us to the horse-drawn wagon just cresting the hill. The guy holding the reins had bloodshot eyes under a cap askew. I pegged him as a day drinker. Another guy sat in the wagon with a tiny woman in a babushka. Sam called out a greeting in Polish, apologizing for the unannounced visit and asking for a moment of his time. He said that he came from Kazimierza Wielka and was trying to piece together some history. He did not wait for responses, hurrying to put them at ease, particularly the driver, who was squinting at us with smoldering eyes.

Without hearing a word of English, I read their body language. No signs of anything hospitable.

Sam courteously addressed the old woman frowning at him beneath her sun-bleached babushka. She dismounted, showing torn white stockings under a skirt caked in mud. The other man hopped down from the wagon without a word, deferring to the woman.

Sam continued, asking for answers about the Rożeńeks, saying he understood they had hidden in a house nearby and had a surviving daughter.

Before Sam finished the question, the old woman answered with that reflexive mantra, "*Nie wiem.*" (I don't know.) She waved us away like she was swatting flies.

Here we were, right near where the Rożeńeks hid, and yet amnesia abounded. I watched her frown and turn away. She kept repeating "*Nie wiem, nie.*" Fat chance she was going to become chatty and cooperative.

It was so frustrating. In this place where roosters outnumbered people, surely back fence chatter abounded. Both Majdecki and Stefan had told us how much people chewed on old gossip and war stories.

But the old woman's shaking head delivered another gut punch to our expectations. Another brick wall.

I pulled out my camera and started snapping frames. This

scene was worth remembering, particularly the old woman with the Baba Yaga look. My little Instamatic seemed unobtrusive, especially while Sam was talking to the farmers. I was framing shots of the vodka bottles, the well house, the roosters, and the old woman leaning heavily on the horse-drawn cart.

Then the wagon driver appeared in the viewfinder. His face darkened like a storm. His cheeks puffed, and his mouth puckered. He flamed red. He lunged at me with a pitchfork. I tucked the camera in my pocket and backpedaled. Everyone reacted. The three guys and the old woman all threw their arms trying to restrain the guy. He ranted and reached for me. The old woman, who came up to his waist, held little sway. She was shouting and poking at him, but she could not even reach his swinging arms. He writhed and jabbed the air, yelling at me.

Sam shot me a look.

"He wants your camera. He wants you to erase the picture of him," Sam said.

"I know. I am not giving him the camera," I said.

"He's upset about the picture," Sam said.

"Yeah, uh, that's pretty clear," I said. "But did you find out what happened? Was Hena here?"

"They don't know anything. Like all the rest."

Between the wagon driver's flashing eyes and that pitchfork, I decided to cut our losses.

My Nikes did a one-eighty and I hightailed it down the driveway. The camera would be safer in the car. And so would I.

I closed the car door but did not lock it. Good thing. A few minutes later, Sam jogged down the driveway. He hopped in and fired up the engine. Somehow Stefan, moving awfully fast for a big man, managed to get to the car, plopping in the back seat. We sped off, kicking up a cloud of dust.

Now I second-guessed myself. Had I ruined our chances of getting information? I had been a benign presence on this trip until now. I might be slowing Sam's progress by always asking him to translate. Maybe they saw Sam as a Pole, and he could have charmed these folks. Maybe I put them off—a young American in a jewel-toned Gore-Tex shell, staring suspiciously.

We drove in silence. "I'm sorry, Sam. I couldn't give my camera to that guy. I hope I didn't ruin everything."

Sam didn't say anything until after we dropped off Stefan.

When we reached the hotel, I started to get out.

He said, "Well, young lady."

I froze.

"Today it is very clear," he continued.

"What's that?" I asked.

"I saw the stubborn look on your face when I asked you for the camera. There was no way you were going to give it. And I thought, *Today, I know you are a Rakowski.*"

Sam interacts with a woman living in an apartment in the former Kraków ghetto. He is remembering where he lived.

# 4

# Origins

S am was already digging into his breakfast the next morning when I found him in the hotel dining room. He did
not even look up. He was so intent on spooning out the sunny
center of a boiled egg perched on a ceramic cup. "You know,
this was my favorite when I was a boy," he grinned.

"You didn't knock on my door this morning," I said, sti-
fling a yawn.

"I didn't want to wake you, honey. Let you sleep in."

I headed to the buffet, scowling at platters of eggs and
squares of sweating lunch meat. Memories from recent days
reverberated: the tobacco-leaf curtain guarding the Dulas'
graves and the laughter in the woods at the trysting place by
the monument in Słonowice. So far, nothing I had seen diminished the widespread Jewish perception that Poland was a giant
graveyard. Also, nothing had prepared me for the big shrug,

the indifference an entire generation of grandparents paid to these victims who were not strangers, but former neighbors and schoolmates. They were the people who made their shoes or sold them the fabric for a favorite dress. It was one thing to witness the Germans deporting people to be gassed and burned or starved and worked to death somewhere else. It was quite another to know the family that is buried in your neighbor's yard.

Perhaps those who lived on here after witnessing so much wartime carnage had turned numb. But if they really didn't care that five hundred people from a town of three thousand were wiped off the planet, what explained their warm welcome of Sam? Maybe the taboo communism imposed on so many topics, particularly regarding Jews, ingrained habits of denial. In fairness, Stefan had looked emotional remembering the five-year-old boy he used to pass on his way to work who was killed at Słonowice, where we visited the monument by the mass grave. Call me a cynical reporter, but I wondered did he select that memory to share for our benefit? He seemed to prefer talking about the Jewish butcher's voluptuous daughter.

Over the past few days, the language barrier had sharpened my study of body language and facial expressions. I had some experience evaluating credibility, having sat through hundreds of hours of court testimony and having interviewed plenty of suspects and witnesses for investigative stories. Even so, Stefan was a puzzle. He kept his arms folded tightly across his chest when talking with Sam, looking around suspiciously without

making eye contact. What was he avoiding? Why did he introduce us to people in the countryside but make us hide the car
by his house so no one would see us visiting him?

In contrast, Sodo was as open as the Polish landscape, his
furrowed brow and sad eyes a balm for the soul. I wish I could
have asked him some questions at the scene, where Sam did
very little translating. Sam was juggling a lot, using the Polish
of his childhood and absorbing Sodo's shocking revelations.
Translating was the last thing on his mind. But by the time he
filled me in with the details, it was too late for my follow-up
questions. I still did not know if anyone ever investigated these
five murders on Sodo's farm. Was anyone ever held responsible?

Majdecki and the Pierchałas showed no reaction to what
Sodo revealed to us about the massacre of the Dula family.
Did they know about the fate of the Dulas? Majdecki had
spoken in a mechanical monotone about his grain customer,
covered in blood, being carted off to his death. If Majdecki
had felt anything about that experience, how could he listen
to the man's pleas for him to go tell his wife where he had gone
and done nothing? In fact, Majdecki seemed to think nothing of it. But his tone changed, and his wire-rimmed glasses
steamed up with excitement when he crowed about the nice
price he got for Sam's dinner table at the Nazi auction. And
he had gushed about his own cleverness in getting his stately
house and sprawling property signed over after the war by the
survivor who was fleeing for his life. Talk about not reading the
room. Did he expect Sam and me to congratulate him? And

yet Majdecki was the only one we had met who volunteered that he "missed the Jews," referring to klezmer musicians who used to play at weddings.

Majdecki seemed to share a mindset with Stefan and Sofia, a blithe acceptance of the annihilation of the Jewish population. To be sure, many like Majdecki who had no complicity in the genocide nevertheless benefited materially—from furniture to real property. They somehow rationalized the destruction of the Jews. Sofia, whose father had taken great risks while mayor in hiding Jews for brief periods in their house, shared with me a shocking victim-blaming analysis: "A lot more Jews would have survived if they just didn't look so Jewish."

In fact, the Germans used Polish police to identify Jews because many looked just like "Aryan" Poles and unlike the anti-Semitic caricatures. All the more reason to make Jews wear yellow stars on their clothes and lock them in ghettos.

Perhaps Sofia meant the remark to reassure me, but "passing" was always confusing.

I grew up wanting to blend in like everyone, yearning to resemble the lithe blonds in *Seventeen* magazine. With Poppy's sky-blue eyes, some of my mother's features, and an ambiguous surname, I was pretty incognito.

For my first year of college, I attended Tulane University in New Orleans and decided to try sorority rush, which gave me whiplash. At known WASP sororities, ladies at the door welcomed me, gushing that I looked like the "all-American girl." I remember their words making the smile freeze on my face,

engraving imposter syndrome in my psyche. The greeters at the
Jewish sororities looked right through me, reminding me of
the refrain I'd heard from older Jewish ladies eyeing me skep-
tically and sniffing, "She doesn't look Jewish." I didn't know
how to feel about this chameleon quality that enabled me to
code-switch my Jewish identity.

I benefited from changing times. In contrast, my grandfather in the American South in the 1930s and 1940s struggled
to find lodgings that would accept a Jewish businessman. My
father faced no such challenges, but he dreamed of joining the
club with the better golf course in my hometown, which until
the mid-1970s barred Jews and Blacks. I was fourteen when
my family was invited to break the barrier. I felt the X-ray eyes
of the entire dining room when we walked in and took seats at
their tables.

In Poland with Sam, there was no wiggle room. I could not
avoid the stark realization that had I lived here in the 1940s,
my chances of survival were almost nil.

I told Sam what Sofia said about more Jews surviving if
they did not look so Jewish. Sam said, "This does not matter."

Neither did Sam allow himself to react to seeing his old
dinner table or the insult of being warned not to run off with
it. I was astonished by Sofia's admonishment "to look, not to
take." Sam was full-on pragmatic. "Majdecki's all right," he said.
"If it wasn't for him, we would not have found the Dulas."

Part of me wished I too could silo emotion and reaction on
the ground in Poland, as I did routinely as a reporter. But the

dismissiveness of these locals to what happened during their lifetimes to our relatives was not easy to accept.

I marveled at how Sam did it. He kept his own traumatic experiences under wraps to reconnect with his old neighbors.

Sam may have stayed clinical in his town, but over breakfast his memories of the Dulas flooded back. It had started the previous night at dinner. Details had emerged in short spurts, like water releasing from an unkinked hose. The whole family was tall and slim in stature, he said, and always bustling around the fabric store, just down the block from Sam's house and the family lumberyard. His aunt Esther was his mother's sister; he would drop by the store to hang out with his cousin Kalman, a few years Sam's senior, and his older brother Wulf, who was in the Polish army and died in 1939 during the German invasion. Kalman and Sam had both attended a business-focused private Jewish high school in Kraków. Kalman graduated from the school in Kraków that Sam attended for one year. That made them more educated than anyone else in town. In Poland then, education was only compulsory through seventh grade. But Sam and Kalman remembered not only the girls in their coed school but also the ones they wanted to meet at the neighboring Jewish girls' high school.

Sam recalled that Abraham and Esther Dula's oldest daughter had moved to another Polish town after she married, and he did not know what happened to her. Abraham was more religious than Sam's family and other relatives. When Sam stepped into the Dulas' shop, he had to be ready for the elder Dula to pepper him with questions on the weekly Torah portion. But even though Abraham was steeped in Jewish texts, he and his family wore modern clothing and displayed no outward signs that they were Jewish until the Nazi occupiers forced them to wear the yellow Star of David on their clothes.

"The way that the Dulas got to that farm was that Sodo was a customer at the fabric store, and Kalman probably asked him to hide the family," Sam suggested. "The Dulas were secretive," he said. "We thought they went to hide somewhere, but they didn't tell anyone where they were going." In fact, sharing such arrangements, even with close relatives, was too dangerous.

I could see Sam's wheels turning, consulting his mental map of the town in prewar times, one he would actually draw for me later. He could identify every shop on the main thoroughfare and the relatives who ran each one.

Sam had walked that street for the last time in September 1942. His own supervisor at the German motor pool where Sam had a slave-labor job had forewarned him of the impending roundup of Jews. His Polish boss even broached the idea of hiding him. But Sam carefully demurred. He believed his father had a plan for his family and his upstairs cousins, the Banachs, who had two children and who were siblings of Sam's parents.

The following midnight, they took what they could carry and walked from their comfortable house to the farm where they would hide. Józef Rakowski had arranged this through a friend who was a township official. The official could not hide them on his own property because he had a jail cell that regularly drew visits from Polish police and German officers. But he had relatives who lived in a remote location that hedged the obvious. The two families—minus Sam's young female cousin Masha Dina, who they placed with a different family—reached that tucked-away farm before dawn. Once secure in that out-of-the-way barn, Sam felt the full weight of their predicament. They had turned from people into prey.

At the breakfast table, I nibbled on crusty bread and cheese, finding this whole swirl of memories hard to digest. I knew traveling here would be distressing, but I stared at my coffee—which came unfiltered here, and required patience until the grounds settled in the cup. I wondered if any amount of coffee would be enough to help me understand all this.

"Sam, how could anyone live in that house all these years knowing there were people buried in the courtyard?"

He shook his head. "God knows."

"And who were these Poles killing Jews in these parts that late in the war?" I asked.

"Some call them bandits, and some people say it was partisans, but," Sam reminded me, "that's a controversial thing to say here." He defended Poland's underground as the largest under occupation, even though the French resistance got a lot more attention and credit.[1] "And you know Poles saved more Jews than any other country in Europe." In Poland, he said, "The partisans are the heroes. You saw those gleaming eagle monuments along the roads? Those are for the AK."

"And meanwhile, our people are lying at the edges of fields and in root cellars," I grumbled.

"Whatever it is," he said. "Honey, a rose garden I never promised you."

"No, the gardens here seem to have Jews planted in them," I said darkly, feeling the weight of history he had lived.

Sam's reliance on his old contacts had sent us on side trips that proved revealing, but they did not advance the hunt for Hena. How many more unmarked graves would we stumble upon, and how much furniture would we visit? They seemed like a distraction from the search for a living relative. But why all the feints and distractions from his old friends? There must be someone we could visit in the place where the Rożeńeks lived who would not greet us with pitchforks. Someone who would be willing to level with us.

I realized that I had not considered what it would be like to find her. I was intent on helping Sam have a reunion with this mysterious cousin. I assumed, of course, that she would be delighted to see him.

I twirled my fork in the bland cheese and scanned the room for a waitress with coffee. Did Sam's village mates not want us to find Hena for some nefarious reason, or did it just not matter to them whether we found her? It was almost impossible to know based on what we had witnessed. And I had not had enough caffeine.

Sam pushed away his plate. He pronounced, "No Holocaust today, honey."

I felt my face brighten.

"Today we're just tourists on a Polish vacation." He let out a loud belly laugh that startled groggy diners at nearby tables. "Are you ready to go?" he asked.

"Almost," I stalled. Was it even possible to get away from the Holocaust here? In my mind, I'd just spent my breakfast in impromptu graveyards, rewinding recent scenes. My expectations for a Sunday off were low. I'd settle for not being stared at like a zoo animal. In Poland, no one doubted I was a Jew, unlike in the United States, where I often heard, "But you don't look Jewish." The definition of a Jew Hitler set was quite inclusive: anyone with one Jewish grandparent qualified for extermination. I wondered if that definition endured in postwar Poland when surviving Jews intermarried.

Maybe in postwar Poland, Hena had found a way to "pass" too.

Sam seemed to have a thick skin, but the anti-Semitic threads running through so many conversations made my jaw drop. Sam had context for the extreme: slave labor, the Kraków ghetto, cattle cars, and the brutality of the camps. He acted as though he could see past it. Ever since he'd been coming back to Poland, he drew strength from reconnecting to experiences in his early life. He was surprisingly upbeat. When Sam was growing up, he had told me, "people were anti-Semitic, but here they weren't anti-me."

On the way down from Warsaw, Sam had deliberated aloud about the historic sources of anti-Semitism. Farmers

thought Jewish shopkeepers had it easier because they weren't
in the fields, even though Jews had been legally barred from
agricultural enclaves and had to find other means of earning
income. Throughout history, the nobles had made Jews col-
lect the tenants' rent, which built up resentment against the
middlemen rent collectors. Jews were literate because they
were obligated to read the Torah, requiring parents to educate their children to fulfill the obligation. That literacy qualified the Jewish population for higher-paying occupations in
commerce and banking. While Jews were heavily involved in
running taverns and breweries, socially they kept separate lives
from their Christian neighbors, with Jewish dietary laws lim-
iting shared meals.

Before the war in 1939, Jews accounted for a sizable minority—10 percent in a nation of thirty-five million. Warsaw was 30
percent Jewish, with 375,000 Jews.[2] But after the population was
wiped out, anti-Semitism in Poland persisted. In 1968, the communist government blamed the remaining Jewish population
for a widespread student uprising and an internal government
power struggle. The purges spurred Jewish flight, leaving about
eight thousand Jews by 1972. At the time of our visit in 1991,
thirty-seven hundred self-identified Jews lived in Poland, comprising .01 percent of the population.[3]

But even that number loomed larger in perception than in
reality. Sam was crossing a street in Warsaw early in our trip
and saw graffiti in German echoing Nazi-era signs. It said,
"Jews Out." Sam turned to the guy next to him reading the

same slogan and asked him in Polish, "What Jews?" The man responded, "Oh, there are a lot of Jews. I know one."

These anecdotal experiences were striking. On a stop at a house where Stefan took us in search of Jewish relics, Sam faced a tough negotiator in an old woman whose apartment was crammed with furniture left by Jews. He purchased a small painting of a Hasidic rabbi from her, offering less than her asking price, which matched my round-trip airfare. On our way out, a younger woman popped out of her apartment and sneered at us. She lobbed a verbal bomb, her face contorting as she spat out the words, that Sam only translated once we were outside: "I don't know why you Jews complain. So many of you survived." It knocked the wind out of me. Apparently for her, for 250,000 Jews to survive out of 3.3 million was still too many.

How could Hena stick around here with attitudes like that?

I put down my coffee cup and raced off after Sam, who was melding into the tourist crowd of white-haired guys in jeans and sneakers in the hotel lobby. I caught up with him chatting away in Polish with the concierge, who might never have guessed that Sam had been out of the country for five decades. Sam got directions for a tour of Kraków, an ancient riverfront city full of magnificent churches, monasteries, and convents, and anchored by the fourteenth century Wawel Castle. Kings had built it, but the Nazis choice of the Wawel for their national occupation headquarters spared it from attack during the 1939 blitzkrieg.

We parked near the edge of the old Jewish quarter and

strolled along downcast blocks of hollowed-out buildings oozing despair. Beneath sagging cornices and coal-stained facades, locals had turned a weedy lot into a makeshift market. Zombielike sellers hawked sad wares. They had not seen the promise of postcommunism. An unshaven guy who looked like a junkie from 1980s Bedford-Stuyvesant stood over some beat-up boots. Nearby, a toothless babushka hawked mud-caked vegetables and browning apples.

The sun burned through coal-dusted clouds. Along our walk, the merchandise improved. Tidy boxes of fresh cucumbers and heads of cabbage flanked racks of gently worn wool blazers.

Sam sped ahead in search of more sites on his tour of what used to be where. I tried to imagine him arriving in this city at age fourteen for high school. Leaving his small village, he had to learn the ways of trams and trains. He treasured that year and rode the train home on weekends in his spiffy blue school uniform, drawing adoring looks from female passengers.

The next time he saw Kraków was when his family snuck into the ghetto in November 1942. Even though more than a dozen relatives were packed into a single apartment, he looked back on those times wistfully because they were together.

"We also were not hungry then, because we could buy extra food on the black market on the outside when we went to work," he recalled.

I was looking around, wondering if we were close to the factory where he worked. I realized that Sam had peeled off. Up ahead, I noticed a young man hoisting merchandise above his head on a long stick. He displayed a parka that looked brand new, with an orange lining and a furry collar, something worth a second look, even here.

My eyes followed the coat back down to its salesman, a handsome guy about my age, with curly brown hair and luminous green eyes. Tracking the coat or the guy, I wasn't sure which, I threaded through pedestrians who had filled the streets this Sunday morning. I lost him but followed the raised coat. The crowd parted and there was the coat seller. He was turned away, chatting with someone. I jostled for a better look. Maybe he spoke English. Maybe I could have a conversation with someone my age in this unlikely place. He turned and I saw who he was talking to: Sam.

I walked up, smiling, but they kept talking in Polish. Sam was smiling mischievously. He said something to the fellow, nodded, then let out a hearty laugh. It was a release, like he was budging a heavy door. The man with the parka grinned at Sam, green eyes twinkling like they shared a secret. Then he shrugged. He said something else I could not understand.

"What are you talking about?" I finally interrupted.

"I told him he looks like he has some Jewish blood in him."

My eyes widened. I looked back at the parka seller, expecting to see anger or annoyance. But he just kept smiling. Maybe he did not want to show offense so he could make the sale.

Out of nowhere, I felt anger boiling up in me.

"Sam, how could you say that to him? That's a terrible thing to say to someone here!"

In the noisy market, I was nearly shouting. But Sam just kept smiling like he had been catching up with a long-lost nephew.

"That poor guy," I said. "Why did you say that?"

Sam shot me a sideways glance.

Then I was mortified. Where did I get off telling Sam what it meant in 1991 Poland to say someone looked Jewish? On these same city streets during high school, Sam had to make himself scarce around Easter. Fueled by the lie that Jews took blood from Christian children to make matzo for Passover, young men left church looking for Jews to beat up.

What was I doing defending a stranger who like many Poles may carry some Jewish DNA? Now I was really mixed up. Since my magazine story on Sam, I had taken flak from religious Jews questioning my Jewish bona fides because my mother had converted to Judaism. It was the opposite in Poland, where the mere implication of having Jewish roots had recently scotched the political aspirations of a candidate for prime minister. Sam gave me that look that said I could not possibly understand this country. He declared, "There used to be over three million Jews in this country. They didn't all just disappear."

I walked on. "What did he say?"

Sam shrugged, raising those hairbrush eyebrows. "He said maybe it's possible. He doesn't know too much about his grandparents."

"Of course," I said. "Maybe that's what happened to Hena. She could have melted into the population and now she could have kids that guy's age."

Sam bristled at this idea. "No," he said. "That doesn't make sense. Why wouldn't she contact family after the war?" Sam's parents had stayed in touch with a man named Singer, the one Jew in Kazimierza Wielka who survived in hiding and stayed there after the war. "She could have gotten word to people in our family."

"Maybe she had suffered enough for being Jewish already," I countered.

He didn't seem to be listening. After all he had been through, he had told me he did not know how he felt about his actual faith. "But I didn't want to be the one to break the chain either." The possibility that Hena married a non-Jew did not seem to be the sticking point with Sam. But no outreach to family, that was something else. Family was paramount to him, the rarest of survivors who came through the Holocaust with both parents.

I followed him distractedly. My mind was fixed on Hena. With Poland's new openness, there had to be a way to track her through government records. Under communism, everyone had to hold a job, even menial ones taking patrons' coats at restaurants or selling sheets of toilet paper at public restrooms. The government kept records of everyone's address and employment. Somewhere, documentation of Hena's movements *had* to exist. My reporter's brain was shifting into gear. The challenge— and a bit of the thrill—of the chase was kicking in.

"I have filed requests with the International Committee of the Red Cross, and I'm working with the tracing folks at the

Jewish Historical Institute in Warsaw," I said. "Someone must have an address or a listed job that will help us track her down."

Sam said, "Good luck." He tossed his head in dismissal. "I'm counting on my people here, my so-called friends, to lead us to her while she is alive."

I followed him off a curb and into traffic. Sam had picked up his pace, heading toward the next landmark, an apartment where he lived in the Kraków ghetto during the war.

Maybe his villagers would come through. But I was looking both ways.

Crystal bell Judy receives as a gift from Guca's granddaughter.

# 5

# Some Friends

The next day, Sam was back behind the wheel in his hometown, maneuvering along familiar streets and slowing for pallid children playing in the street. The kids sized us up like gatekeepers, weighing whether to let the strangers pass onto their turf. In fact, they were treading on Sam's old stomping grounds, where he had traipsed long before they were born. Sam squinted at the old houses we passed. He remembered them from before they had electricity and indoor bathrooms.

"We're going to visit my money today, young lady," Sam chuckled. "And maybe we'll get some answers."

In five days on the ground in Poland, I had seen Sam charm a lot of people, embracing widows and widowers with real intimacy, even kinship. But now we were headed to see a man Sam shouldn't have to cajole or sweet-talk, someone who should jump at the chance to help a Rakowski, particularly Sam.

Sam was convinced Wojciech Guca had knowledge of the fate of the Rożeńeks' younger daughter because he lived a few houses away from the Rożeńeks' hiding place during the war. And who better to be helpful but the brother-in-law of Sam's father's business partner in a timber brokerage and other ventures.

As a young teen, Sam traveled together with Guca, a guy twice his age, on summer trips checking on remote logging operations. By night, they bunked together in tiny huts. During the day, they checked on the transfer of fresh-cut logs that workers lashed together as rafts and sent downriver to sawmills, where they were cut into boards for sale in the lumberyard. Sam had waxed nostalgic for the rides he took on those log rafts. Even during the occupation when the Nazis barred Jews from riding the trains, Guca walked for hours with Sam, even though he could have taken the train.

On this sunny October day, Sam had reason to believe he would get help from his old friend. Back when the Nazis prohibited Jews from owning businesses or making money, Sam's father had handed over the Rakowski lumberyard to Guca before the Nazis could pick someone else. The Rakowskis never got a dime for the business. Guca got the largest and most prosperous lumberyard in the area. He should be the best candidate to help with the quest for Hena.

All these years later, villagers remembered Sam's family for the lumberyard. Locals knew who took it over. The lumberyard joined the Rakowskis and Gucas in the minds of everyone in town.

We pulled up to a modern brick split level, a dandy in a dowdy row.

An aging platinum blond who had squeezed herself into a tight red dress was waiting on the porch. She grinned at Sam through a slash of red lipstick, waving like she was flagging down a cab. Sam had told me one of Guca's daughters was divorced. This might be her.

"*Dzien dobry, Pani się.*" (Good day, madam.) Sam hugged his former schoolmate. "*Jak się masz?*" (How are you?) He turned back and gave me the double wink. "You see, I have lots of girlfriends here."

The front door opened on a tweedy couple who looked like they belonged in a Pendleton catalog. Guca's other daughter, a nurse, and her husband, a pediatrician, kissed Sam on both cheeks and offered me courtly handshakes. They ushered us inside, past a room lined with glass display cases lit to show off many rows of cut crystal.

In a wood-paneled den, a slight old man rose from a leather chair that matched his earth-toned slacks and brown cashmere pullover. He and Sam shared an unsmiling, back-slapping hug. Guca sank back into the chair and faced Sam, favoring his good eye over the second, drooping lid.

On the way over here, Sam had said, "I want to know about my cousin. I'm going to eat his *kaczka* (dinner) and spend a lot of time here and probably get nowhere."

Once again, despite downplaying his hopes to me, Sam had built up expectations for a big reveal. After Stefan had tipped

Sam about Hena surviving the war, he kept urging Sam to "ask Guca. He knows." Now here we were.

Sam complimented Guca's beautiful home. His old work-mate cut him off in mid-sentence. A relative in Canada had paid for it, Guca said. Sam just nodded.

On Sam's first trip back, he went by the train station, fig-uring he'd find old-timers hanging around. Sam walked in and one pensioner greeted him as if he'd never left. Then he said, "Guca lives in town now." He gave him directions to Guca's house, where the entire family greeted Sam as if he were a celebrity. Clearly villagers saw Guca as having benefited from the Rakowskis' misfortune.

But Guca downplayed it all. "Sam," he said, "they took everything. The Germans, then the Russians."

Sam nodded. Sitting together in the living room, the two men seemed to be starting off on a good note, as far as I could tell.

But my opportunity for observation was quickly cut short. Guca's daughter came to me with her teenage granddaughter, Monika, in tow. Our hosts decided that even though she was much younger than me, we girls should go off together like kids on a playdate. "You two can talk to each other," Sam said. "She knows some English."

Monika led me upstairs, asking "Do you like the Beatles? I have all the Beatles records. All compact discs."

In her tidy pink bedroom, she opened a thick album of CDs sleeved in pages and pages of discs. I marveled. CD sales may have eclipsed cassettes back in the States, but I was still hauling boxes of tapes around in my car and only had a few CDs. She started singing along with John and Paul to "Penny Lane."

The moment was lovely, but my mind was downstairs. I was out of earshot of Sam and Guca and unable to witness the whole point of our visit. It was bad enough that Sam was spotty on translating. At least when I was present, I could glean something by observation and could ask later what had been said.

But this smiling teenager was being the perfect hostess to her American guest. Next, Monika pulled out a neatly kept photo scrapbook full of pictures of herself in groups of peers grinning from ski lodges and beaches. Maybe all the kids in Poland got to travel like this, but it did seem remarkable. My leisure travel seemed odd by comparison. I had traded scuba vacations for visiting unmarked graves with people twice my age unspooling tales of mass murder.

Monika and I had clearly hit our limit of small talk and mime. I was relieved when Sam called me back downstairs. He and Guca were talking animatedly in Polish.

"Anything?" I asked Sam.

Sam shrugged, looking disappointed. "I've heard all these stories before."

Our hostess appeared and announced that dinner was ready. She directed us to the table in an oak-paneled room with crystal goblets winking under lights.

The table was beautifully adorned with fine linens, china, and crystal. Guca's daughters and granddaughters ferried in heaping platters of cold cuts, cheeses, and rye bread. A special treat was clustered at the center of the table: cold bottles of Pepsi, still a coveted commodity.

Guca's son-in-law spoke at length about something I could not understand, plunging me back into a foreign film without subtitles.

Sam clued me in. "They're talking about how the prices are too low for the crops, and it hasn't gotten better since the Russians left."

I sipped Pepsi and smiled.

The red-dress lady grinned across the table at Sam.

I forked seconds onto my plate, having already wolfed down a few Dagwoods. It wasn't like I could contribute much to the conversation.

The Pepsi soon took its toll and I excused myself and visited one of the beautifully appointed bathrooms. I stuck my head into the kitchen on the way back and admired the custom wood cabinets, dishwasher, and the latest model cooktop. The only other local kitchens I had seen so far were vintage like Sofia's, with its coal stove and reliance on manual labor.

Monika's mother was loading her up with platters of food to follow the soup course, which was already on the table.

Uh-oh. I had mistaken the cold cuts for the meal. I returned to find the table groaning from steaming heaps of roast beef, pierogies, green beans, roast potatoes, and tureens of gravy. The Guca family had pulled out all the stops for us.

The mood seemed warm and festive. Sam laughed and put his arm around Guca, like old pals on a summer jaunt in the forest.

Then Guca launched into a monologue.

"What's he saying, Sam?" I asked.

Sam waved me off. "Nothing I haven't heard before."

Sam cleared his throat, and I could tell he was trying to find an opening to bring up Hena. When Guca took a breath, Sam jumped in. I heard the word Zagórzyce, the hamlet where Guca and his family had lived during the war with his sister and brother-in-law. Sam also mentioned the Rożeńek name in the feminine case, a clue that he was mentioning the daughter we were trying to find.

But Sam's topic got short shrift from the patriarch. Guca waved off Sam's questions like a bad smell.

"*Nie wiem,*" Guca said and frowned.

I needed no translation. I was starting to think this was what people said around here instead of hello.

Sam was not dissuaded. He continued to talk and ask questions.

Guca repeated his mantra in response again and again.

Monika turned to me, smiling and helpful. "He said it was a long time ago."

How relevant was it that time had passed? If Hena was alive, how much longer would that be the case? Her family may be long gone, but Guca could at least offer some help before she was.

This brick wall of resistance, the reflexive "*nie wiem,*" reminded me of the many witnesses suffering from selective amnesia I had met while covering gangland and racially motivated slayings and corruption. But what kept Guca, with his historic affections for Sam, not to mention how directly he benefited from the Rakowskis' departure, from trying to help Sam now? If he knew something, anything, about where Hena went after the war, why not tell Sam?

Sam chided. He cajoled. He had the floor to himself. The others had fallen silent, not even making eye contact.

Guca stared blankly.

Sam turned to one daughter and then the other, asking in Polish, "How could you not know about this cousin? You lived right in Zagórzyce."

The gravy congealing on their plates seemed to rivet all our hosts' attention.

"What is the reason now not to let me find my cousin if she could be alive?"

Sam raised his voice briefly, then turned and was almost beseeching Guca. He *had* to know a lot more. With so many connections with people all over the area, how could he not? Why wouldn't he share a single detail that could help Sam have a reunion with his only relative left alive in Poland?

Sam shook his head. He turned to me. "We're gettin' no place here, honey."

The heavy food sat like a boulder in my belly. I looked at each person at the table, but no one met my gaze.

Sam stood up. He was on the move again.

I rose too.

Then everyone was on their feet.

I followed Sam down the corridor toward the door. The granddaughter intercepted me, all smiles and warmth. She must

have thought we were just impolite. She did not seem to understand the tension, or perhaps she accepted her relatives' explana-
tions at face value. She reached into one of the display cases and
withdrew a cut crystal bell, its etched edges gleaming in the light.

"Please accept a small gift," she said haltingly in English.

"*Dziękuję bardzo*," (Thank you very much) I said, using up
my Polish vocabulary.

The Gucas were all smiling as they saw us out, as if the gift
had set everything right.

I clutched the bell with ambivalence, a trinket, my inheritance, from the Guca family to ours.

Sam was shaking his head.

The entire forty-five-minute drive back to Kraków, he
vented his annoyance, alternating between saying, "To hell
with my friends," and asking aloud, "How could he not know?"
and "Why won't he tell me?"

Sam had relied on his relationships with the people he had
known from a young age in pursuing our mystery cousin. He
figured the bonds could withstand his asking for their help.
I shared his frustration but could not match the emotional
investment in these locals or his expectation that they would
eventually deliver what we needed to find her. Even if Guca did
not know exactly what became of Hena, he could have at least
shown an interest, based on their history, in trying to help.
Given Guca's age, Sam might never see him again.

"Well," Sam said, rebounding. "I'm going to have to push
Stefan harder. He knows something!"

After Augustyn starts talking to Sam, Stefan takes him aside and speaks privately, apparently trying to discourage him from talking.

# 6

# Breakthrough

After six days on the ground, Sam had satisfied his own curiosity about what life had been like for some relatives who stayed in hiding after his family snuck into the ghetto in Kraków and how some had met their fate. His investigative method was a bit scattershot: he chatted up anybody he found on his home turf with crow's-feet, reminding me of a roving reporter parachuting in and working a story. Along the Sam tour, I'd gathered impressions of the place where generations of my relatives had built lives and livelihoods. We had stopped by the former estate that my great-grandfather's brother once ran—Sam found a relative of a former employee who described the big harvest feast that my great-great-uncle put on each autumn for all the workers. In another town, Sam chatted up a guy who remembered the flour mill that another ancestor ran until his bloodline was also snuffed out.

But we seemed no closer to finding Hena.

The old-timers we encountered who offered these accounts were strangers who had no relationship or history with Sam. The puzzle was the resistance he got from those who gave him the warmest welcome. It was not as though the fate of various Jews in town, their businesses and possessions were forgotten. Clearly, they were a persistent topic of discussion among locals.

Stefan seemed eager to trade gossip he'd picked up but sent mixed signals about shedding further light on his original tip about Hena.

Sofia, who had grown up as the mayor's daughter and had the juice and contacts to be helpful, deflected Sam's entreaties to help find Hena. After one of our visits to her house, we had gone to the local (Catholic) cemetery, where Great-Grandma Pearl was buried in a mass grave with a dozen other Jews whom the Germans murdered during the deportations in 1942. I saw an older woman tidying a grave and leaving fresh flowers. She turned and we recognized Sofia. Startled, she looked like she'd been caught out. Again she had offered that same tight smile, pressing her lips together as if her fidelity to Poland depended on it. What secrets could she spill?

Sam held out faith—more than I could muster—that his warm relationships with local contacts who had known him as a top student and son of the owner of the largest local lumberyard would win out. That these people, some of whom had directly profited from the extermination of the Jews and who were protective of local reputations, would produce real clues to Hena's whereabouts. He hoped they would still see him as one of them. He had locked on these people as providing the best avenue to the answers we needed.

Despite the language barrier, I felt sure they knew a lot more than they were sharing.

My mind tumbled back and forth over these well-worn subjects on yet another morning drive from Kraków to Kazimierza Wielka, where we picked up Stefan and headed to another farm in another hamlet outside town.

What little Sam and Stefan said to each other was in monotone Polish, offering no clues to our destination. I hoped for a better reception than we had gotten at what I privately called the vodka farm. Stefan was selling Sam on how much he had done for him over the past three days, using his inside knowledge to make connections on Sam's behalf. He wanted credit for the visit to the table and for taking Sam to the lady who sold him a small painting of an old rabbi, albeit for an extortionate sum.

Stefan also seemed to sense my wariness—or perhaps he merely disregarded the thirtysomething American scrutinizing him. He had yet to look me in the eye. I did not understand what was behind the resistance about helping us find Hena. Sam made it clear again and again he had no designs on taking back property or bringing legal action against anyone for anything. He just wanted a reunion with this one surviving cousin. Stefan could be a hero to Sam, his wife's childhood friend, if he delivered Hena or even helped us find who had hidden her after her family's massacre so we could thank them.

These contradictions were looping in my mind when I saw the sign for Gabułtów, another hamlet near Kazimierza.

Sam parked under a tree by what looked like a gentleman's farm. Brilliant autumn sunshine bathed the cavernous barn in a harvest halo beneath a cobalt sky, framing blushed leaves reminiscent of a postcard from Vermont. In the middle of harvest season, it was quiet.

Stefan hoisted his ample girth from the back seat, his retiree's legs loping up the hill with surprising speed. I cocked my head, wondering why he would try to outpace Sam. I had not even budged from the car yet. Chastened by our recent experience, Sam said maybe I should stay put as a precaution, until it was clear that we were welcome.

An elderly man wearing a wool blazer and a beret appeared on the rise by the barn. His high cheekbones and tweedy look distinguished him from the rough-hewn farmers we'd seen.

Through the open car windows, I watched Sam introduce himself. He moved in very close, in his intimate way with countrymen. His host, whom I would learn later was a man named Augustyn Wacław, smiled and nodded. They chatted and seemed to be getting on fine when Stefan moved to intervene. He took Wacław by the elbow and steered him into the open garage on the right side of the barn. In the shadows of the garage, the strapping Stefan seemed to be insisting on something quite intently to the slight, professorial Wacław, who I later learned had run a bookshop in town. Although they remained well out of earshot, Stefan kept turning the elder man away, maneuvering him like a reluctant dance partner, as if he thought Sam might read their lips.

This scene got me out of the car. Moving closer for a better look, I snapped photos, trying to capture the scene. But despite Stefan's finger wagging and whispering, Wacław shed him like a wet towel.

He rejoined Sam in the barnyard, where Sam finally got to state his purpose. I understood he was asking if the man knew about an attack that had happened in a nearby village, Zagórzyce. That was where a family named Rożeńek, Sam explained, had hidden during the war until they were murdered. Did he know anything about it or what happened to the daughter who escaped?

Wacław nodded and, without hesitation, laid out what he knew. He had been commander of a battalion of partisans during the war, Bataliony Chłopskie, the peasant farmers' group. Late in the war, some groups—including some men from his own— went around murdering Jews in hiding. Wacław didn't know who ordered these killings, but some of the squads didn't want the Jews to survive and take back their homes and businesses.

Wacław said he knew for a fact that members of his own group of partisans had murdered the Rożeńek family in Zagórzyce.

Watching Sam and his elegant host, I noticed that Stefan seemed very nervous.

Moments later, all three of them hopped in our rental car. Sam forgot to release the emergency brake. He stepped on the gas, and the tiny Fiat groaned. Sam turned to me and started talking in Polish and then asked Wacław for directions in English. He slapped his forehead. He was really excited.

Wacław had confirmed that Hena survived, Sam said. After the war, she appeared at some sort of court proceeding at which she was asked to identify two men, one whose last name was Marzec and another named Grudzień, suspects in the murders. I jotted down the names, eager to follow up on tangible leads. Also, a man Wacław knew had sat with Hena during the proceeding. He lived nearby. We were headed to his house now.

Sam was flying. This was the first solid lead we'd had this whole trip, and I could see his mind was jumping ahead to the reunion he might have with his cousin. He forgot to manage the seesaw of clutch and accelerator, sending us lurching and juddering along the country roads to our next destination, the tiny crossroads of Dalechowice, southwest of town.

Sam's elation would not last. We soon pulled up to a vast mud pit of a farm ringed with all sorts of fences and chicken wire enclosures. Outbuildings wobbled on rotting wood foundations. This place made the vodka farm look like the Ritz. In my mind, the soundtrack of *Deliverance* turned into *The Haunted and the Hunted*.

An old woman missing most of her teeth ambled over to the metal fence and waved her arms. Even with the validation of locals like Wacław and Stefan in the car, she shooed us away. Over the raucous barking of three scrawny dogs, I heard that old familiar "*nie,*" or no.

Wacław kept talking, appealing to the babushka naysayer

to let us in. Finally, the farmer of this fine property emerged—a wiry fellow with a peg leg and a birdlike face who was about as welcoming as a shotgun aimed at our heads.

Here was Adolf Poremski, whose first name must have endeared him to mates in the *milicja* of the Polish People's Republic. This Adolf even sported a little mustache. His beady eyes, set impossibly close on a pencil-thin face, darted wildly.

After a week of barnyards and graves and people who seemed inured to the dispatch of their Jewish neighbors, I was feeling punchy. Watching Wacław use his commanding persistence—and perhaps the authority of his old partisan stature—to persuade the Poremskis to open the gate, filled me with admiration. He was the only one who had volunteered the truth about what had happened to the Rożeńeks even though it implicated his own partisan group.

Next I watched Poremski play the opposite role, repeating "*nie*" again and again before anyone could ask him anything. A bizarre scene ensued of three elderly men holding up the tottering Poremski while poking his chest and firing questions. They held his arms like they were maneuvering a puppet. Wacław already knew about Poremski's old job in the *milicja*, and yet when he suggested that he share that with us, he kept pivoting backward, saying, "*nie, nie wiem*" (no, I don't know), over and over. Poremski said, "*nie,*" so many times, it seemed like it was the only word he knew.

The pleading and coaxing went on. Wacław reminded Poremski that he had already admitted to sitting with the surviving Rożeńek on the day she was asked to identify two suspects in the murders of her family. She had declined to finger anyone, saying it was too dark that night to be sure of the murderers' identities.

Sam tried a softer approach, saying we just wanted to know how Hena looked and where she had been staying when she came to court.

But Wacław was all business. He leaned into Poremski, offering a glimpse of his forceful younger self as a leader of the farmers' partisans. Finally Poremski, in grudging monosyllables, admitted he had been in the *milicja*. And after another endless stretch of obfuscation, the three of them holding fast to the tottering Poremski, he admitted that indeed he'd sat with Hena Rożeńka and witnessed the proceeding when she was asked to identify her family's killers. Even then, he tried to undercut his contact, saying it lasted only a few hours.

In that mud pit, I stared into Poremski's face, which was twisted with fear, his eyes darting back and forth while he pulled away from the other men like he wanted to jump out of his clothes. Was he afraid we would find out about something he did during the war or for the communist regime afterward? Or was he afraid of the same people Hena feared reprisals from, people who might still live nearby? In that post-communist stretch when archives were opening and evidence from the dark days of the war was bubbling to the surface, he might be one of many who was not a fan of the reckoning with history Poland was starting to embrace.

Poremski, who looked like a terrified version of Sad Sack, the goofy and inept soldier in American cartoons, could have answered so many basic questions about *when* he had sat with Hena. Was it right after the war or years later? Did she come alone? Were the suspects ever implicated in other cases? The Dulas' murders, perhaps? Was the proceeding part of an investigation that continued?

Ultimately, the sum total of Poremski's grudging admissions did not advance what we knew upon arrival. But to my mind as a reporter, they counted as confirmation from a second source of the existence of a court proceeding and official awareness of the Rożeńeks' execution by Poles.

We piled into the car, heading back to Wacław's farm. I'd been reading news that Poland was about to hold a monumental election in two weeks, the first free parliamentary elections in seventy years. It was a heady time for Jewish-Polish relations. Just months before, Polish president Lech Wałęsa, the global hero credited with bringing down Soviet communism, had become the first Polish leader to visit Israel after the two nations had renewed diplomatic relations. Wałęsa had made history by apologizing to the Israeli parliament on Poland's behalf for the behavior of Poles during World War II under German occupation.

"We helped you as we could," Wałęsa said, hailing the many Poles who were righteous gentiles. But he acknowledged that "there were also evil-doers among us."[1]

Wałęsa's candor, which played well in 1991 Warsaw, fell flat out here in the hinterland. The notion of Poland facing up to any complicity in the Germans' total annihilation of the Jewish population stood little chance of scaling a mountain of "*nie wiems.*"

Wacław had not hesitated to tell us the truth even though it implicated Polish partisans. He had no problem leveling with people looking for a surviving cousin. But the humanity of our search was lost on Poremski. Maybe he feared the way political winds had shifted in Warsaw, and now he might suffer for his actions in aiding the communist government as part of its *milicja*, or maybe he himself had a role in partisan activities that he was intent on concealing. No matter his motivation, this guy was not about to say any more about his contact with Hena, even though he was the last person we knew of who'd seen her alive.

We took Wacław home then Sam dropped off Stefan, thanking him for a good day of discoveries. Sam had not asked him what he had been whispering about to Wacław in the garage. For all his puzzling behavior, Stefan was smiling and emphasizing to Sam how much he had delivered for his Hena search.

Sam pressed on, asking him where we should go and who we might speak with the following day, our last in town. Stefan raised his hands in retreat. He was too busy, he said, to do more.

Sam drove off, saying, "Now we know there was a court proceeding and she was alive. This is our biggest day yet!"

"And, Sam, that means there have to be records of what happened. What were those suspect names? Marzec and Grudzień?" I was thinking of all the ways to track files of a court proceeding, with investigative files and docket information.

"Don't get your hopes up, young lady," Sam said. Proceedings under communism were not public and transparent. It probably took place in a quasi-military court set up by the Russians, who kept everything under wraps. It wasn't like an American courthouse where you walked right in as a member of the public and monitored criminal justice.

Was it really that bad, or was Sam just less comfortable with chasing records, doubting my abilities, or realistically handicapping chances of success? My optimism might have been overblown given the opaqueness of record keeping here. But an investigation would generate paperwork, a report that might list an old address for Hena, offering a trail. I had to believe a trove of information existed, waiting to be found. The postcommunist openness breezing through the highest levels of the government might ease the way. I compiled a mental checklist of ways to track records and witnesses from an actual court proceeding. And I had two suspects' names.

On the other hand, three guys had spent an entire afternoon trying to get one guy just to admit to information he'd previously revealed. But it was now confirmed, credibly, that Hena had survived and had been called as a witness to her family's murders. Authorities had tracked her down, believing she could identify the killers. She was out there somewhere.

# PART II

Danuta Sodo Ogórek, her son, Dominik Ogórek, and her uncle, Władysław Sodo. Sodo has just been interviewed by a crew from the Spielberg Shoah Foundation, during which he describes the episode in 1944 when Polish partisans beat his father and killed the Dula family. Danuta and her son, who live on the property, have come upon the scene and learned about these events for the first time. She says she was teased at school about the "Jews in the Garden" but did not know it was true.

# 7

# Jews in the Garden

The next time we returned to the Sodo farm where the Dulas were buried, we knew that the two families—the Dulas and Rożeńeks, who had lived and worked just doors apart—had both been executed by Polish gunmen in 1944 after eighteen months of surviving under the protection of courageous Polish farmers.

Unlike before, this visit was well-planned. And it created a spectacle that the neighborhood would remember for decades.

A cavalcade of vehicles roared up the narrow lane that raw April day. It included a film crew, an American newspaper reporter, and "some Jews," in neighbors' parlance (Sam, me, and his older daughter, Tamar Heller). Sam shot out of the first car like a fireball. He found Władysław Sodo camera-ready in a light-blue V-neck and dress slacks. Sam introduced Sodo to Tamar and nodded at me, reminding Sodo that we'd met. The subsequent three cars carried professionals there to capture the event: a Kraków-based film crew as well as a reporter and a photographer from the *Akron Beacon Journal*, a northeast Ohio newspaper covering their local survivor's journey home with his daughter. Sam's interviews for my magazine story, his media debut, had been his warm-up for a long line of interactions with other chroniclers.

Perhaps channeling the neighbors' reception to prying outsiders, several farm dogs decried our arrival. The newspaper photographer tripped over a dog while the burly Polish videographers wielding a fuzzy boom mic and a suitcase-sized camera debated where to set up and how to frame their shots. Their equipment had already drawn attention earlier in town where they shot Sam and Tamar outside Sam's family home, next to his old school, and in Słonowice at the monument by the mass grave. Accompanying them was a bilingual interviewer from Kraków.

As a speaker and a participant in Holocaust commemoration events, Sam had become a busy guy. At some events, he even represented the survivors in the family who worked in the factory of Oskar Schindler and made it on that infamous list. He even attended the screening at the U.S. Holocaust Memorial Museum of the 1993 film *Schindler's List* that President Bill Clinton attended. There he met famed Hollywood director Steven Spielberg, who had spent months filming in Kraków.

So moving was the experience that Spielberg afterward formed a foundation for recording and preserving firsthand accounts of every Holocaust survivor in the United States, which later became the USC Shoah Foundation. As part of that effort, Sam had already recorded several hours of interviews in his Ohio living room.

But Sam did not think those recordings had captured the whole story. He boldly requested—and the foundation accepted—that the rest of his Shoah story be filmed in Poland "on location."

Still and video photographers had trailed Sam and Tamar all morning around town, capturing their images walking and talking, while the other pros recorded what they said. This foray to the Sodo farm, however, deviated from touch points of Sam's early life. It drew attention to revelations about what had happened to relatives who stayed in hiding throughout the war and did not survive because other Poles murdered them near its end.

Sam knew the cars and hubbub might cause neighborhood consternation, but he paid it no mind given that it was a neighbor, according to Sodo, who had told the gunmen where the Dulas were hiding on the farm. Sodo also speculated that his father had unwittingly drawn attention to himself by buying newspapers in town for his guests to read. A family of five sitting under a barn for eighteen months were particularly hungry for war news.

The crew got set up. The interviewer from Kraków, a striking woman in a velvet blazer, matching derby hat, and bright lipstick lent an air of showbiz to the scene. The cameras rolled, and Władysław Sodo, hands folded behind his back and speaking clearly, started answering the questions about how his father wound up hiding the Dula family on his farm in 1942. Sam stood next to him, jaunty in a leather jacket and khakis, and handled the mic like a pro. He praised Sodo and his family for their bravery and generosity and thanked them for all they did to try to save the Dulas.

Sodo continued in Polish on the video that I later had translated: "Then late in the war, Polish partisans came with guns one night and demanded that my father give up the Jews he was hiding." Sodo animatedly described the initial assault on their house by Polish partisans, how they knocked down the door and beat his father, trying to force him to give up the hidden Jews. "When they found the Dulas in the cavern under the barn," he said, "they marched them out of their hiding place and told them that if they cooperated, they would be OK."

Sam chimed in in English, naming his aunt, uncle, and their three adult children. "The mother, Esther, was the sister of my mother," he said.

"But," Sodo said, "the assailants never intended to spare them. The gunmen shot and killed all five Jews. They beat my father and threatened to kill him too as punishment for hiding Jews."

Sodo walked toward the hill at the rear of the barnyard, demonstrating how the Dulas were marched up the hill out back and executed.

The killers made his father strip the bodies and turn over

every stitch of clothing and every possession of the Jews. "They demanded the gold that the Jews must have had and accused my father of keeping it for himself."

I watched from the sidelines, familiar with the chain of events, and tried to fill in details for the young reporter from Akron hearing the story for the first time.

Sodo, Sam, and Tamar walked from the center of the farmyard to a small hill that was the grave for the Dulas, where they turned and lowered their heads, cameras following and capturing the scene.

I snapped some shots of my own of the thoroughly photographed scene. While everyone was watching the interview, I noticed on the periphery of the scene, some new arrivals. A young woman of about thirty with dark curly hair and a boy about eight years old stood transfixed by what they were seeing and hearing. They crept in closer. The woman listened attentively, wrapping her arms around the boy's shoulders more protectively with every sentence she heard. She looked back and forth from the man being interviewed to Sam to the people with cameras and microphones.

Her eyes widened. The color drained from her face.

The film crew had moved in for close-ups of the unmarked graves. Not needed for the shot, the interviewer approached the pair and spoke with the woman in Polish. The woman replied and the interviewer translated for us.

She said she is the niece of the Sodo being interviewed.

"At school, I was ridiculed, taunted. They said we had Jews

in the garden. But I never knew it was true," said the woman, adding that it was her grandfather who tried to save the Dulas.

She and her family lived on the property, and she looked surprised to see her uncle being interviewed. In fact, she said, he had never shared with her anything about the events he was describing on camera.

The interviewer introduced the woman, Danuta Sodo Ogórek, who was born long after the war. Slowly she repeated her revelation: "Now I understand. At school, the kids were always making fun of me. They called me Dula. They said we hid Jews. But I never knew it was true."

The boy, Dominik, seemed to be trying to understand why so many people were outside his family home. The interviewer leaned down to the boy's level and spoke very seriously to him in Polish. "Your family did something very important, very good. Always remember that."

---

Since our earlier travels to Poland, Sam had become a regular speaker in schools and on panel discussions about his survival experiences. He had emerged like a 3D version of the man who first gave me his account of his wartime experiences in halting, flat tones a decade ago. In phone conversations leading up to this trip, he seemed younger and livelier; even his hearing seemed better. I had updated him on my latest long-distance efforts to track records of Hena. He said he'd made contact with the city manager of Kazimierza Wielka, who seemed eager to be helpful.

Sam had gotten to know this official, Tadeusz Knopek, three years before while he was in town on a solo trip he dubbed his "nostalgia and closure" journey. Knopek earned Sam's trust by offering Sam some gossip: Stefan and Sofia and the Gucas struck a different tone behind his back from the friendly welcomes they offered him. Knopek said they shared with him their suspicions about Sam. They'd ask, "What's he up to? What does he want?"

Sam had told Knopek, as he had told the others, that he was not looking for anything but information about what had happened to his family members, namely Cousin Hena Rożeńka, who was supposedly still alive. Why couldn't they accept that?

Knopek had also ingratiated himself with Sam by promising he would be an ally in helping Sam get the remains of his grandmother Pearl moved from a mass grave in the local cemetery and put him in touch with those in charge of a cemetery in a nearby town where the body of my great-aunt Frymet Rakowski had been dumped in a mass grave after her remains were moved from a shallow grave at the edge of a farm field. She had been lured out of hiding and murdered by a Polish policeman who was prosecuted in the 1960s.

Knopek earned Sam's deep gratitude for taking on the task of cleaning up and repairing the defaced monument at the site of the mass execution of Jews in Słonowice.

That morning, we had a photo shoot with Knopek at the monument. Sam posed by the obelisk that had been painted to cover the vandalism with a new plaque added that detailed the Germans' execution of nearly three hundred local Jews in 1942. Knopek had preened for the film crew while Sam spoke glowingly of the city manager's efforts and thanked him for restoring the monument that recognized the great loss of the Jewish community that had once thrived here.

Afterward, the film crew peeled off, and we all repaired to Knopek's municipal office. Sam led our entourage, which included the *Beacon Journal* reporter, Tamar, and me. We entered the building and Sam announced to the receptionist in Polish that the boss was expecting us.

Knopek greeted us anew. He kissed my hand the way Stefan had and handed out stickers that bore the red shield of a ram with a sword plunged diagonally through its skull, the official logo for Kazimierza Wielka.

Knopek was not born in Kazimierza Wielka and had some outsider's objectivity. He managed to land the top job in the main city in this rural, conservative area, which was the smallest county in Poland. He was exceptionally friendly to Sam, which made me a little suspicious of his motives.

Knopek lit another cigarette and beckoned Sam to sit in front of his desk. The rest of us stood lining his office wall, watching. Knopek shared his creative plan for finding Hena. It was his idea to smoke her out under the pretext that he was a lawyer letting her know there was an inheritance she could claim.

Knopek said he had followed the original tip from Stefan that Hena "went west" and put it together with Sam's account of the reception we'd received at the vodka farm, home to the Luty family, and had tracked down some Lutys in Wrocław. One of them apparently hailed from the Kazimierza Wielka area. Knopek surmised that he had moved to Wrocław with Hena, after living next door to where the Rożeńeks were hiding. Maybe his family back at the farm had been covering for him.

Knopek suggested he telephone this Luty in Wrocław and tell him that Luty's wife was entitled to an inheritance from a relative who was recently deceased. He'd say he was calling to arrange a meeting between the heir and a representative of the lawyer for the deceased.

Sam was loving this plan. He turned to me, his eyes shining and declared, "This could be it. This could be the break we need to find her."

Knopek lit another cigarette and dialed the phone. He winked at Sam like a seasoned con man.

Someone answered the call and Knopek chatted away, laying out the scenario. He described riches awaiting the Luty family. Sam could not contain himself. He paced the office, watching Knopek and smiling back at us. It was hard to gauge what was actually happening on this ten-minute call and whether the man Knopek was talking with had a bona fide connection to Hena. Sam did not translate for us, but Knopek acted triumphant when he hung up. The man on the phone had agreed to meet us. Sam was so excited he nearly bounced off the walls.

Knopek said the meeting was arranged for Wrocław. Sam was grinning and praising Knopek for the ingenious charade. I tried to ask Sam how we knew this guy had a connection to Hena, but Sam dismissed my questions as if I was trying to ruin the caper.

Maybe, I thought, the approach of asking direct questions would not work here; maybe subterfuge was necessary. Knopek then grandly announced that he would go with us to Wrocław, a drive of three to four hours. We agreed to pick him up the next day.

The next morning, everyone else had left. Sam and I drove to pick up Knopek, which was forty-five minutes in the opposite direction from the route to Wrocław. We pulled up to Knopek's house. What a location! His house was built on land just opposite the former Rakowski residence, on the very site of the former lumberyard. Knopek had told Sam he wanted to build an addition on his house. I bet he did not know that Sam no longer owned that house. I wondered darkly whether he thought Sam could help support his expansion plans with the town.

Knopek greeted us, shaking Sam's hand and once again bringing my hand to his street sweeper of a mustache for another of those old-fashioned kisses. He shepherded us to a small parlor where he filled the table with Polish chocolates and brought in a tray of tea in tall glasses. Then he disappeared. An hour went by. Was he somewhere in the house? Had he left and gone somewhere else? Anxious to start the long drive, we waited impatiently. No sign of the man. Sam went outside and walked up to the main road. One of the Luty brothers from the vodka farm passed him on the street. A strange coincidence.

Finally Knopek returned and apologized. He could not join us on the journey. He had too many things to attend to at home.

Sam thanked him and said he'd let him know how things worked out.

Setting out for Wrocław, I was pleased that Sam had refocused on the search for Hena. But something about it all felt like we were skipping several steps ahead. Sam was so excited, he was hardly slowing down for roundabouts. He whistled off-key the whole way. He said, "This is it. I'm going to see my cousin tomorrow, maybe."

I did not want to be a killjoy, but I was not so sure. Even if we did find her, would she be willing to meet us? Did she have children? Did they know their mother was Jewish? Would it cause problems in her life to have us appear and call attention to her Jewishness? Over the long drive, my thoughts zigzagged in another direction. Hena was, we now knew, a murder witness. She had seen five people killed. And while she declined to identify the attackers at the police proceeding years ago, she might feel safer if she was never found. If we tracked her down, the bad guys might find her and make trouble or somehow endanger her.

It was dusk when we arrived in Wrocław. We checked into the Hotel Monopol, a once grand and ornate edifice on the

edge of the vast market square that had served as Nazi headquarters when Wrocław was Breslau. Now soot and age black-
ened its art nouveau and neobaroque facade. The interior
had been redone like a low-budget government outpost, with
cheap carpet and dim rooms with flimsy beds. I was washing
my hands with the caustic hotel soap when I heard knocking
on my door. I found Sam standing outside my room, looking
drawn.

"I've got bad news for you, honey."

Upon arrival, he had immediately dialed the man who
he hoped would show up with an address for his long-sought
cousin. Sam had been so excited about the prospect of this
reunion that he had ignored some red flags. It turned out that
Knopek had not vetted the guy we were meeting. He was a
generation younger than Hena, who would be in her seventies.
Sam arranged to meet with the guy anyway. But his sky-high
hopes of seeing Hena had crashed.

So much for Knopek's charade. I suspected Sam had questions before we left, but his hopes muffled his better judgment.

The next morning, we headed to meet the man at a nearby
breakfast spot and sat near the door. We waited. A guy no older
than forty entered, heading straight to our table. A polite gentleman in a wool sport coat, Tadeusz Luty turned out to be
the Luty brother who made good. He looked like he'd come a
long way from the vodka farm. Unequivocally, he dashed our
hopes. Not only did he not know the whereabouts of Hena, he
revealed that the Lutys who had been so unwelcoming did not

even live on that farm during the war. He was apologetic. He offered to show us where the Rożeńeks were buried but said the house where they were killed had been razed. He was kind and helpful but had no more to offer. Sam thanked him, but we already knew the burial site.

After Luty left, Sam looked as low as I'd seen him.

"Another dead end. No light at the end of the tunnel."

Back at the hotel, Sam tried every Luty in the telephone book (there were many) in case by chance they knew something about Hena. Sam, of course, asked about other variations on the name and described her as coming from the other side of the country. But Wrocław was full of people who had come from other parts of the country. And I wondered why he was connecting Hena to the Luty name, given that they were not actually neighbors during the war. I did not poke holes in the logic that got us here, sensing that Sam did not want to hear it.

Sam's headstrong pursuit of his agendas on his home turf seemed motivated by a mix of responsibility and redemption. But his Marine-like duty to leave no one behind, like with his steadfast efforts to move Great-Grandma Pearl and Great-Aunt Frymet's remains from mass graves or at least add markers struck a wall of reality: he had to rely on people here to carry out those wishes. These attempts to do right by those murdered relatives clearly reconnected him to our family and this long history. It was a sad end for our family and a people who thrived for hundreds of years in the garden that Poland once was for Jews. The Jews in the garden that Danuta Sodo Ogórek grew up hearing about were murder victims killed just because they were Jews. And the killers were not faraway invaders but people from the neighborhood. Getting answers from locals as outsiders under these circumstances, even for a native like Sam, had proved to be an enormous challenge.

But Sam did not acknowledge that. He clung to the belief that his family name and his own history here would hold sway and he would find Hena on the strength of those connections.

Before we drove to Wrocław, Tamar spoke of being quite moved by her experience with her father in his hometown. But she also challenged him on why he kept returning.

"There's nothing here," she said of Poland. "All our people are gone." She recalled her youth in Israel, where survivors were told to forget Poland and help build a safe place for Jews. Tamar said, "I don't understand, Dad. Why do you feel so Polish? What do you have in common with Guca and these people?"

Sam responded, "I feel a sense of belonging here. I come here and I see who our family was in the community. People liked me even if they weren't crazy about Jews. I was good-looking and strong. I got good grades and we were well off. I was the only boy in my class who was Jewish. I don't want my old house back; I have enough houses in the United States. I like coming back as a success."

Tamar asked, "Are you so insecure that you have to come back and have these Polish people look up to you?"

Sam shook his head. "Am I insecure?" He chuckled. "Maybe I am."

Eight years had passed since Sam learned the first clue about Hena. Back then, he figured he'd just come back to Poland and ask around and lean on the guy who gave him the tip and the family friend who lived close to where her family was killed. But even though they disappointed him, Sam had kept up his hopes and his trust that Stefan or Guca would come through. He'd allowed those hopes to soar. Every time Stefan steered him to another farm or promised something new, Sam believed him, and he thought that was going to be the day he saw Hena again.

The quest for Hena offered a welcome distraction from so many mass graves, but it turned out that pursuing her was revealing a lot of hidden dynamics and matters that many would have preferred to remain unspoken. That translated to a series of letdowns for Sam, whose straightforward, hands-on approach was captivating and optimistic. The balm of familiar surroundings and seeing people from his prewar life had so buoyed him. But asking those people from his early life to extend themselves for him on this quest proved to be a tall order. The war had cleaved those relationships in ways that were painful to realize.

When Augustyn Wacław revealed straight up that members of his underground organization, the BCh, had killed the Rożeńeks and that Hena had shown up later at a court hearing to identify two suspects, it seemed we were only another farm visit or two away from finding her.

If we kept looking.

We found the graves of the Dulas as a result of looking for

Hena. It seemed we would never run out of graves along this path, but we would rather find a survivor. Sam had been so excited. All the way here. I thought the scheme was too simplistic to work, but was happy to be proven wrong. Now with no reunion to fill our day, Sam said, "Let's go out and be tourists and forget this Holocaust business."

We explored the "city of one hundred bridges" on the Oder River with its Prussian eagles carved into cornices harkening to its German past.

We walked and walked. But Sam was very quiet. I could tell he was trying not to feel duped by Knopek after telling me several times, "I have a good relationship with him." Sam was also not keen to face the fact that Knopek might have other motives and Sam himself might have missed some cues. I had been immediately suspicious of Knopek when I saw the location of his house and his mentioning of plans for expanding it. But how could Knopek not know the Rakowski property, had been owned by the Polish government since the 1960s.

"It does not matter," Sam said unconvincingly. "It's a mystery."

The next morning, Sam was downstairs in the hotel breakfast room well ahead of me. He looked gray and haggard. He had hardly slept. His breakfast, the nostalgic favorite of soft-boiled eggs, sat untouched.

"Let me tell you something, young lady," he announced before I could take a sip of coffee. "I took a long bath last night and I tried to sleep." But, he said, "She came to me last night."

Speaking with glum finality, he said, "Hena came to me in a dream." He shook his head. "She told me to give it up, let it rest."

The set of his jaw and his stern look should have been withering. But his tough look just made me feel sad for all he had lost. A brother, countless bunkmates, friends, not to mention grandmothers, aunts, uncles, and cousins. He had found a way to rein in expectations and rely on himself. Not to hope too much or get too attached to something that might not happen. I had no way to dispute his dream or his resolve. But it seemed like he had found a way of managing his disappointment. He had reached a conclusion. In a line I would hear again and again, and not only from him, he said, "If she's alive, she doesn't want to be found."

Mrs. Luszczyńska describing the murders of the Rożeńek family that her father wrote to her about in detail. Her father went after the war to visit Hena in Wrocław, she says, and Hena sent her a baby present after her first child was born.

# 8

# Postwar Gift

On a sticky August day four years after Sam's declaration in Wrocław, I checked into a small Kraków hotel. On previous trips, boutique hotels in this part of Kraków would have been unimaginable. But the filming of Schindler's List in the old Jewish quarter and ghetto had spurred major renovations, creating a tourist destination. From my window, I recognized the spot where Sam had teased the cute parka seller on our first trip together.

Since Sam's deep disappointment on the last trip, the path to this one had been rocky. He had completely switched gears from looking for one lost cousin who might be alive to connecting with and guiding extended family members of survivors on trips to Poland. I was far from the only one drawn to seeing him in action on his home turf and hearing personal stories about the landmarks and touchstones of our family's imprint on that landscape. His sharing firsthand accounts was not confined to relatives. As a speaker and eyewitness he had become something of a celebrity. He had become a sensation on the International March of the Living, an educational program bringing thousands of Jewish teens from around the globe to Poland for tours of German Nazi camps and monuments, and continuing on to Israel to celebrate the revival of the remnants of the genocide from the ashes of Europe. Sam mixed jaw-dropping recollections of his experiences with deadpan humor, turning a seat on his bus into a hot ticket.

The quest for Hena, he made clear, was on the back burner, or off the stove altogether.

I brought her up on phone calls. He batted the subject away. "This is not on my agenda. It is not on my mind anymore."

I could only imagine how hard it was believing that he could rely on his "so-called friends," only to be let down again and again on trips to Kazimierza Wielka that were already freighted with emotion. The Stefans and Gucas probably knew the families of the Rożeńeks' killers and wanted to steer clear of trouble, I suggested more than once. But Sam was unmoved. He could not see it from his friends' perspective, because their position denied him the loyalty he continued to accord them and many in his hometown despite everything that had happened. I sympathized, but Sam's shutdown of our shared mission hit me hard. I should have been more understanding of his change of heart. But it just felt like rejection.

I reacted by ramping up the quest on my own. I hoped my

reporting skills might yield the clues that his friends might have shared and ultimately lead to answers and a reunion with Hena.

I was banking on building on the familiarity I had acquired with records repositories and tracing experts from earlier trips. I would just soldier on and make that reunion happen even without his help.

I'd already gone to the regional archives with Sam pursuing his birth certificate and my great-grandfather's death and burial records. We had also made trips to courthouses where we found records involving the prosecution in the murder of Great-Aunt Frymet. On my own, I had already visited the Jewish Historical Institute's genealogy tracing office multiple times dating back to the early 1990s. I had made serial requests, and offered updates over email between visits. They were very helpful, but Hena's birth name never showed up in the postwar databases. They also clued me in on how porous those records were. Poland did not conduct a census until 1951. That was six years after the war ended and seven years from the massacre of her family. Then the Soviet satellite government installed a Big Brother record system that tracked employment—everyone had to have a job—and home address. Legally, any name change was supposed to be sent to the archives where a birth certificate was on file. But practically, I learned, it was a joke. Updated records were rare.

I was accustomed to looking up documents and contacting government officials. At the height of our partnership, Sam had only so much patience for bureaucracy, particularly when it came to records of his own life. I had seen how he operated in an archive in Poland after a clerk refused to give him a copy of his birth certificate. The guy went to answer the phone, and Sam, flashing a mischievous twinkle, tore out the page with the record of his own birth from the book and slipped it in his pocket.

His reaction wasn't surprising given that he'd been ripped out of a comfortable life in a loving family. Even after he survived Nazi camps and a death march, he shepherded Jewish orphans without papers across European borders and escorte-done hundred of them in the luggage hold of a ship to what is now Israel in 1946. But without papers, he could not prove his own birth. He had trouble applying for a government-issued ID. In Tel Aviv, at a government office, "I went outside and grabbed some guys to come in and swear I was alive."

On the ground in Poland, Sam had proven again and again that he was a wild card, channeling the wits and instincts that had helped him survive. That was why whenever I got wind of an upcoming trip, I wanted to join him, lest I risk missing more impromptu capers or discoveries. But now he was freezing me out. I didn't want to be selfish. After all, by that point, I had already traveled to Poland with him three times, more than his grandchildren and many other relatives. Yet I persisted. In response, he became increasingly candid, then downright blunt. When I asked to join his 2001 trip, he said, "I don't want you to come, young lady. You are a burden."

He was tired, he told me, of having to translate for me in

the middle of a conversation. I'm sure it was also annoying for a younger relative, a reporter at that, second-guessing his moves, asking what he'd already asked and suggesting other questions after we had left the scene.

I sympathized. On these visits he was trying to assess, digest, and react to what he was hearing, and with me along to also simultaneously translate. Plenty of detached translators cannot pull it off. But when I offered to bring a translator, he said it was not necessary. He said that meant one more person he had to drive around. One more person who could not see what he saw in his mind's eye. I asked several times to join the 2001 trip. But he wasn't having it. "There's no room for you in the car," he said with finality. "And I'm not the one who rented it."

It stung, but I persisted. I tried bargaining for him to stay an extra day in Kraków. "Can't I join you after they leave? Just make a few stops and run by the property where the Rożeneks hid?" I told him I'd bring my own translator, make my own arrangements, and rent my own car. I dug in, being something of a Rakowsky.

He picked apart my workarounds and rejected the car rental. How was I going to drive in Poland? How would I find my way? How much was that all going to cost?

He may have dropped the Hena quest, but he still wanted to be in the driver's seat.

I took his questions as an opening. I backed off on the car and found a way to afford a translator on my newspaper salary. In exchange for a plane ticket to Poland, I hired a young woman from Opole Poland, attending college in the United States and related to a dear friend.

So that's how I wound up in a Kraków hotel room that I was sharing with Daga the college student in August 2001. I left her to settle in and headed off to find Sam. In a hotel next door, I found Sam in his room surrounded by several relatives. With him was an Israeli named Avi who turned out to be Sam's distant cousin on his mother's side. Sam was wrapping a package in newspapers and putting it in his suitcase. He handled it gingerly, fueling my curiosity. He turned and gave Avi his coconspirator's double wink.

Sam gushed that he'd had an "amazing time, I have had tremendous experiences and discoveries. My best trip ever, by far."

I winced. I hoped my reaction was invisible. What I had predicted proved true. I had missed out on some amazing discoveries. I summoned enthusiasm for his findings.

Slowly, with dramatic effect, Sam withdrew a document from a folder. I saw it was a photocopy of a document in handwritten Polish script. It bore an official stamp. It was, he dramatically announced, the birth certificate of Hena Rożeńka, complete with the signature of her father, Szmul (Samuel) Rożeńek.

"Wow, that's amazing," I said. "People offered different ages for her, but now we know for sure. So she was sixteen when her family was killed."

I knew I should rejoice at this discovery, another victory in the search for Hena. But I wanted to say, *Wait, I thought you quit the Hena quest. What was all that about?*

I should appreciate any progress in this quest. But Sam had gone with the other relatives to the archives and found Hena's birth certificate. Of course he did. Those wily impulses that had served him well were still firing. I felt like a child wanting to pout. Why had he rebuffed me only to continue the Hena search without me? But I mustered enthusiasm and asked, "What else happened on your trip so far?"

"Long story, but it was amazing," Sam said, his eyes shining as he leaned on his suitcase. He started to elaborate but then said, "Let's go get a *lody* (ice cream) in the *rynek* (market square)."

I trotted after him feeling like a pitiable child. We sat at an outdoor table in the square bustling with tourists, a place I remembered when it was a dreary tundra. I reveled in the chance for Sam's undivided attention. Over bowls of ice cream piled high with fresh fruit, a nostalgic delicacy from his childhood, he revealed the events of the past few days.

Sam had taken the large group to the home of Majdecki, the guy with his old dinner table. He introduced Avi to Majdecki, who recognized his relatives' names from the time when Majdecki had lived across the street from Avi's grandparents in Kazimierza Wielka. The grandparents lived in a flat in the same building as the Rożeneks' home and shop. Sam said he thought Avi's grandparents, the Ptasniks, were killed at the death camp Bełżec.

"No," Majdecki said with confidence. "They were killed in Bełżów. They had been hiding with a farmer named Pabis."

Sam said the revelation was almost as stunning as the one on the first visit to Majdecki revealing that the hidden Dula family had been murdered and buried on the neighboring Sodo farm.

Majdecki said of Bełzów, "They killed nine people there," and the murders were carried out by partisans, the AK. "There were trials after the war."

"Wow," I said. "What a huge revelation."

"So later we took the car," Sam explained, "and Avi went with me."

They drove a few miles to Bełzów, following Majdecki's directions until they got to an area without markings or road signs.

"I saw a bunch of old folks hanging around, and I drove up to them," Sam told me. "I said, 'I'm a Rakowski and we had a lumberyard on the main street in Kazimierza.' They said, 'Oh yes, we remember.'"

Sam said he was looking for Pabis. They asked why.

"I was told the Pabis family was doing good and hiding the Ptasniks. But someone came and killed them there."

An old woman said, "Pabis is my relation, but the Pabises are dead. The son is in a psychiatric hospital, and he is not in good shape."

Sam got directions to the Pabises' house further down the same road. He drove a mile and didn't see anything. He saw a farmer standing by a tractor with a younger man.

"I go through my shtick. And the older man said, 'Sam, I remember your parents.'"

After some reminiscing, Sam said, "I'm looking for Pabis's place, where the Ptasniks were hidden and killed."

The man said he did not know, but a neighbor of Pabis's was still alive. "He must know something. I'll go with you." But then he looked down and said, "I'm so dirty. I should not be in your car."

Sam told him in Polish, "You are perfectly fine. Get in."

They drove past more fields and up a driveway to a house. Sam said they found some younger people there who were "not welcoming." The farmer said, "We want to talk to the old people."

They shrugged and said the old man was sleeping.

"Wake him up," insisted the farmer.

An old man whose long beard reminded Sam of his grand-father emerged from a rear room. After quick introductions, the man said, "I can tell you the whole story."

With a willingness to share that had proved so rare, the old man launched right in. He said Pabis's house didn't exist anymore, but there he had hidden nine people, Jews from Kazimierza Wielka. They had holed up in a cowshed behind the drinking trough. The old man said the Jews had been seen at times catching fresh air after dark.

Sam said that by the spring and summer of 1944, the Germans were busy elsewhere. "The Germans were not going around looking for Jews on this farm. But it was common knowledge that they were there."

For some reason, the old neighbor said, "These people were particularly visible."

One night in August 1944, members of the Polish underground, who, he emphasized, belonged to an elite group of partisans, descended on the house. "I don't remember how many guys, but a bunch of them. They knew exactly where the Jews were."

Unlike at Sodo's, they did not abuse Pabis. They just marched the nine Jews to the rear of the barn and shot them. They dug a shallow grave in a low-lying area and buried the nine and took away all their clothes and belongings.

From what the neighbor said, Sam pieced together that the group included four or five Ptasniks and several others, including a great-aunt of Sam's on his mother's side.

Sam said, "Would you show me the place?"

"The house is gone," the neighbor said. "But I can show you the field."

The four of them walked about three hundred feet to the hay field that was the site of the graves, according to the neighbor. Only when the farmer pointed to the burial location did Sam and Avi notice he was emotional. "Over there," he said in a quavering voice, his hand trembling.

The intensity of the farmer's anger was very moving so many years later.

"The truth is when they plow here, they always come across bones," the man said.

Avi had wept, listening to the description of his grandparents' brutal execution. The only remnant of his grandparents' lives in Poland was a snapshot he took that day of the field of tasseling hay ready for harvest, on which he marked an X at the estimated site of the graves.

Sam and I ambled back to the hotel. I was hoping he had reserved some time and mojo after discovering another tragedy. But Sam had not finished filling me in on the trip's adventures.

On their way back from Bełzów, Sam and Avi stopped by the Sodo farm. Sam talked to Danuta Sodo Ogórek, the woman we had met during the Spielberg Shoah Foundation filming. He told her that the graves of the Dulas should stay put, as testament to the grim events that created them. But he wanted to remove some representative bones and take them back with him to Ohio and bury them next to his parents' graves.

Danuta agreed and her husband lined up helpers for the following day.

On the day before I got to Poland, Sam and Avi had returned to the Sodo farm and found an excavation team of locals ready to help. In an operation that was both macabre and meaningful, they dug into the mass grave and retrieved a femur and some smaller bones. Sam drove away from the Sodo farm with the remains, intent on memorializing the five brutally murdered Dulas.

Back in Sam's hotel room, his mind seemed miles away.. He sat down on the bed next to his suitcase, a seventy-seven-year-old Holocaust survivor packing bones for an intercontinental journey. He shook his head and shrugged. "It's pretty crazy."

Under Jewish law, moving human remains is quite controversial. But Sam reasoned that the murders and desecration of the Dulas' bodies warranted his actions. He was taking a big risk in hope of restoring to the family a shred of dignity, symbolic yet tangible.

I asked, "How are you going to move human bones out of the country without getting in trouble with Polish authorities?"

"Well, young lady, I changed my plans. I'm going to leave by train instead of going to the airport. On the train, they don't go through your baggage."

I could see his wheels turning, as if he was back in the *b'richa* after the war, hatching a plan for getting another group of Jewish war orphans without identity papers over a European border. Back then, he was a vigorous 21-year-old, who chose the harrowing challenges of those border crossings over confinement behind barbed wire again. Even though the armed guards at the displaced persons camp were posted for security of the Jews in, including his parents and other surviving relatives, Sam needed to keep moving.

Now he was scheming to transport a different kind of cargo. It was my turn to shake my head.

"So you are escaping Poland with the remains of murder victims by way of Germany?" I asked. "That's too ironic. And with millions of victims of German Nazis on Polish soil, you are taking bones from people killed by Poles. If they stop you, that will be a lot to explain."

"I hope I don't have to," Sam said. He nodded slowly, as if was still talking himself into the rationale and the risk.

The next day was the one that Sam had promised me. As

soon as we met, I noticed immediately that he was subdued. He brought along his cousin's son, Daniel Feldman, grandson of Sam's uncle and aunt Isaac and Sally Levenstein, the relatives Sam lived with when he attended high school in Kraków. Later in the Kraków ghetto, they were crowded together in a small apartment. When the ghetto was liquidated, the Levensteins smuggled their two small children in suitcases into Plaszów. But the Germans discovered the children and murdered them along with many other children in the camp. The Levensteins were saved by Oskar Schindler, but Sally still spent time in Auschwitz. After the war, in a displaced persons camp, despite all that she had endured, Sally got pregnant at age forty-one. Rela was their miracle child. Rela grew up in New Jersey with her doting parents, and went on to marry and become a matriarch of a family with five children, twenty grandchildren, and twenty-seven great-grandchildren. She was very close to Sam and Bilha, who were mainstays at their family celebrations. Finally on this trip, Sam had the chance to show Rela and her family around the area, sharing memories about her late parents. Her son Daniel, a student at Yale University, doing research that summer at the Auschwitz-Birkenau State Museum had joined the family trip.

Sam kept his promise of giving me that day, but he seemed distracted. Most of the time, he talked to Daniel filling him in on background and the discoveries from earlier trips. I was eager to make headway and hoped that Sam would help find new leads on Hena despite his misgivings.

Our first stop was a return visit to the farm of Adolf Poremski, the regional police boss we'd met ten years ago. I was surprised we got past the gate, given the chilly reception on our last visit. If Poremski remembered our last visit, he did not let on. He sat at a table in an outbuilding on his broken-down farm bitterly spitting out, "*Nie wiem,*" to every question Sam asked in Polish, which Daga translated for me. Clearly the man was not going to add to the grudging acknowledgment that he had sat with Hena at the police station after the war when she was asked to identify two suspects in her family's murders. He had nothing to gain by shedding any light on what we cared about. I could only hope for a miraculous change of heart. But Sam drilled him with questions about when he saw Hena and where she was staying when she was summoned to identify the suspects. Sam grew exasperated.

Finally he shouted at Poremski in Polish. "Why won't you help? Maybe you killed her."

So much for that interview, I thought after Daga translated what Sam had said. I wished Sam had tried his Columbo-style musing of possible scenarios that had proved successful in other encounters. I had never seen him get so angry. Maybe the revelations about another nine Jews murdered by partisans were just too much.

We headed to the prosecutor's office for the village where the Rożeńeks were murdered. At the counter, Sam stood asking a clerk in Polish for records by the names of the defendants we'd gotten from the partisan battalion leader

Augustyn Wacław. The clerk asked for the year of the case.
Sam answered, "Sometime after the war." The clerk said she
could not look up records that way. Sam gave the only details
he knew. "What year?" she asked again. Sam was getting frustrated, and his voice grew louder repeating that he did not
know.

A door opened and a short man with a mustache emerged.
He looked official and indeed he turned out to be the head
prosecutor for the district. He led us all into his office.

Sam explained what he was looking for. The man was cor-
dial but said he had no way of helping. He said if there was a file
corresponding to that case, it would already have been sent to
Warsaw, like all criminal cases that occurred under the German
occupation as well as those from the communist era, by orders
of the Institute of National Remembrance (Instytut Pamięci
Narodowej, or IPN).

Sam and I had this experience prior to the IPN's found-
ing when we visited a Warsaw courthouse looking for a file on
Great-Aunt Frymet's murder by a Polish policeman. On that
occasion, it was the reverse; the file had been checked out to
this courthouse in Pińczów. We went to Pińczów, and the
records we wanted were said to be in Warsaw. Chasing court
files was nothing new to me, having pursued much more mun-
dane cases in America.

We were broomed out of the prosecutor's office before I
learned what he'd said. Maybe the prosecutor would have been
willing to do a thorough search for the defendants' names or

to look for all cases over many years from the village where the Rożeńeks were murdered. Or maybe not.

———————

Sam next drove to Zagórzyce and the hilltop farm that once harbored the cousins known for their hardware store. Nothing remained of the house but a stubbly frame of a foundation on an overgrown lot. Daniel, Daga, and I scrambled through thick brush on the abandoned hilltop property, hoping for some remnant. Sam stayed in the car, hobbled by back pain. Looking down at the Luty farm, the scene of my encounter with the pitchfork-wielding farmer, I closed my eyes and wondered what Hena had seen that night.

Sam hurried us along, calling out from the car, "Nothing here. Let's go."

His trip had already been so eventful and probably had stirred up overwhelming memories. I felt sidelined, but muscled through my disappointment. I had already made plans for a number of stops with Daga the next day. I had to satisfy my own curiosity.

The next morning, Sam dropped Daga and me off at the local bus station on his way to return the rental car. "You could change your mind and come with us to Kazimierza Wielka," I offered.

Sam didn't hesitate. "Good luck, young lady," he said. "See you on the train, maybe."

Clearly his mind was on the bones in his luggage and the

perils of getting the Dula bones back to Ohio. He was taking an overnight train that night from Kraków to Berlin, where he would catch a flight back to the United States. We were taking the same train from Kraków but getting off in western Poland, where we would stay with Daga's parents. From there we would visit Wrocław and try to pick up Hena's trail.

But first I had a checklist for Sam's birthplace. Daga and I got off the bus in Kazimierza Wielka, hurrying past day drunks making lewd remarks that needed no translation. That had never happened to me traveling with Sam.

Trudging up the hill toward squat municipal buildings, I could hear Sam's voice in my head: "I am not interested in this anymore. What are you going to find? How come she never contacted anyone in the family after the war?"

But nagging at me too was my belief that something or someone here could fill in some gaps.

I hoped Daga could channel Sam's moxie. I did not expect anything to be easy. But given that many Jews disappeared into the population by marrying gentiles, I wanted to check the records of church marriages, which were maintained in Poland by municipalities and might be an overlooked resource.

In the town office, Daga asked for marriage records from right after the war. The clerk, a stern blond woman in her forties, asked for the couple's name.

"We only know the name of the woman," Daga said.

"Well," the clerk said, "you must submit an application to see any records."

Hoping to cut some red tape, I urged Daga to invoke the name of Tadeusz Knopek, the top guy in town, who had been helpful in the past.

"Hah," the woman responded, clearly piqued. "Pan Knopek. He is not higher than me."

Uh-oh. That backfired.

The advance-approved application was a barrier I had encountered before. To get any information, you needed the subject's advance permission, even when inquiring about the dead.

Daga kept talking. "We have come from so far away and we're leaving today."

Again, the clerk shrugged, walked back to her desk, and took a sip of tea.

"We have the exact date of her birth," Daga said. No reaction.

I pulled out the copy of Hena's birth certificate and laid it on the counter. The clerk glimpsed the stylized Polish script of an official document and came up to examine it. She saw the official seal of the Koszyce archives and stared closely.

For several minutes, I did not breathe as she pored over the document.

Then, her eyes widened.

"Oh, this person is from the Moshe religion. We don't have any records of those people. We don't keep records of the Mosaic people."

Daga translated what she said. Now what?

By this time, Daga was referring to the clerk by name, Ana, hoping to make some headway.

"What year did she marry?"

Daga looked at me and answered on her own. "Just after the war, '45, '46, maybe even '47."

Ana blustered, "But we do not keep records of the Mosaic people."

We stood at the counter. I offered my best beseeching look.

Ana pulled out a big book and started flipping slowly through the yellowed pages. She replaced it with another large book and flipped through it too quickly to be reading. Then Ana, who seemed to respect order and rules above all, sighed and tossed Hena's birth certificate back on the counter. If she married, Ana said through clenched teeth, the birth certificate should bear a stamp about the marriage.

Still, she did pull out more books, for 1947 and 1948. Nothing, she said.

Daga asked if she was sure.

The clerk erupted. It was as if Daga had accused her of lying. "If she married a Catholic guy and changed her religion, then she had to leave here! They would be terrorized. People would laugh at her and people would laugh at their kids. People knew who was who."

Daga, blanched. Her mother was a devout Catholic and her father was Jewish. She looked like she'd been slapped.

"I told you," Ana said. "There is nothing here." On and on, she ranted. "I would know something. I've worked here for a long time. I would tell you. I know stories. People talk here. I've never heard of this. If they were Jewish and Catholic, people knew who they were. So they would laugh at her," she spat. "Or at her kids, that they have a Jewish mother." She concluded, "Even if she changed her religion, she had to change the place where she lived. It would not be easy for them here."

Daga relayed this to me quickly in a monotone. I felt the sting of the words.

Again, Daga pleaded that we wanted to find out what happened to her and we had little time.

"I have no idea what you can do," said Ana. "Just go and ask people. They know history, they know stories. This is the only way you can get something."

We were at an impasse. We had already been through the town where the Rożeńeks hid. We had already knocked on so many doors. This must be the end, I thought.

Then Ana started looking in other files and chatting up another woman in the office. She said she knew so many stories; perhaps her pride was on the line.

Finally, she told Daga that we could visit a woman named Luszczyńska, whose people hid Hena's family. She still lived in Zagórzyce. I knew the Rożeńeks hid with a man named Radziszewski, but maybe this was the daughter's married name.

"Great," I exclaimed. "Let's find her."

Ana said the husband was dead, but the wife was still alive. "She is old," Ana said, "but maybe she will tell you something. Her husband's name was Slanisław Luszczyński." Ana sent us next door to get the address. I was amazed. This woman did an about-face from being dismissive to demonstrating how widely known this history was in small-town circles.

Next door, we found a heavyset woman in a flowery dress bustling around her office like she had a train to catch. She was locking her desk drawers and the clock had not struck 3:00 p.m. She made no secret of her reluctance to look anything up. But she took out a census book and flipped through it. She verified that an old woman named Luszczyńska was still alive and that she was born in 1923. But she could not find a current address. Finally, she told us to just go to the village and find the streets where old people live and ask someone.

We raced to the cab stand and climbed into a taxi with a flushed-face driver reeking like yesterday's vodka. For forty złoty, he agreed to take us to the village and to make sure we made it back to catch the last bus to Kraków.

Daga and I held on to each other as the cab lurched and braked through hilly backroads. Daga said the clerk had warned that the house would show no number, so when we got close, the cabbie started asking pedestrians for directions. Also, Daga explained, the place wasn't exactly a house, just a room.

The cab screeched to a stop at a clutch of houses in front of a tiny structure. A six-foot screen of pastel cosmos and wine-colored hollyhocks obscured the building. A middle-aged woman in a flowered top and checkered pants with no front teeth greeted us with such gusto I thought she'd mixed us up with someone else. Daga and I looked at each other and said simultaneously, "She's too young."

Daga asked for Pani (Mrs.) Luszczyńska, and the woman pulled the clothespin out of her mouth and asked, "Why?"

"We are here from the United States, and we are looking for some relatives, and we have some signs that she might be another family member."

"Oh yes," said the woman, moving away from the clothesline. "We have family in the United States. But my mother is on a walk right now."

Daga turned and said that she thought any woman born in rural Poland in 1923 would not be out on a walk. "I think she does not want to bring her out. Maybe if we stay, she will come out."

We did not have a lot of time to spare. I'd ensured the taxi driver would come back by arranging payment only after he delivered us in time to make the last bus.

Then our hostess said, "You're going to sleep here, right?"

Daga said we'd come from Kraków and could not stay.

Our hostess took us inside her one-room abode, which hardly fit a bed and an armchair. An ancient contraption with jerry-rigged pipes provided water and heat for a stove. Kłos said she had lived with her mother in this place since her husband died in a car accident and her in-laws kicked her out of their house, although they allowed her three children to stay with them. At my request, she wrote down her name, Kłos Erbieta, in beautiful script. I complimented her handwriting and she laughed with embarrassment.

"Oh," she said, "it's ugly. It's like Hebrew."

Daga translated this and my stomach tightened. This must be a common idiom in Polish with anti-Jewish themes so deeply embedded. Not a good sign.

Just then, an apple-cheeked old woman in a kerchief and flowered dress swept into the room. She greeted us brightly and said that indeed she had been out, delivering baby chicks to neighbors.

Kłos busied herself preparing tea and piling cookies and cakes on a plate. Daga and I whispered to each other that we did not feel right taking food from such poor people. We nibbled politely on cookies.

The bus schedule left little time for chit chat.

Mrs. Luszczyńska started off describing her experiences as a teenager during the war when she was in Germany in a forced-labor camp. Our questions focused on a young woman who would have been a teenager at the end of the war, about sixteen years old in 1944 when her parents and siblings were killed nearby.

"Did your parents hide anyone?"

"No."

"Did they hide Jewish people?"

"Oh, why didn't you say that in the beginning?" she said. "Of course, they hid Jewish people."

Daga and I looked at each other, our eyes wide.

"My parents wrote me letters about them. I am proud we hid Jews," she said.

At my prompting, Daga asked, "Did Germans kill them?"

"No," said Mrs. Luszczyńska, "Polish people killed them."

"Polish people?" Daga asked, incredulous.

"I don't mind telling you that the AK killed them."

On that cold rainy night, she said, the Jews were in the big house, which was very unusual. When they did come in the house, it was during the day when it was too risky outside because others were around. In the house, they crowded behind a big white stove in the main room. At least three could fit behind it, six if they squeezed together, she said. Otherwise, they stayed out in the forest or in the pasture.

On the night of the attack, she said, the gunmen banged on the front door. "My father went outside, because he did not want to let them in."

Her father was carrying a one-year-old baby. The assailants beat him senseless, stepped over him, and went through the house. The Jews had moved to a storage area in the attic.

"They found the Jewish people there. Then they went outside and told them to jump from the attic windows, and the AK was shooting them."

Daga asked, "There were five of them, right?"

Mrs. Luszczyńska said, "Yes, I don't care that they were Jewish. Of course we hid them. I just want to help everybody."

Her candor after our city hall experience was breathtaking. My arms shot up like we had just scored the winning touchdown. Daga and I hugged. This woman had become only the second person besides Augustyn Wacław willing to say the truth out loud: that the Rożeńek family was murdered by Polish partisans.

And I had found her on my own.

I asked Daga to thank Mrs. Luszczyńska for her family's bravery in hiding these relatives.

"*Dobry! Dziekuje ci!*" (Good! Thank you!) I exclaimed in my paltry Polish.

I hugged the old woman. I hugged Kłos. "You are good people," I said, clasping their hands and holding their gaze while Daga translated.

Mrs. Luszczyńska said that there were Jewish survivors who remained in the fields that night.

"Yes, the Jews had been hiding in a tiny shed near the forest," she said.

She said her parents had written to her about one surviving daughter who she called Helga and a young man named David, who might be a potential mate for her when she got back from Germany.

"What happened to Helga and David?" I asked.

"They went to Wrocław," Mrs. Luszczyńska said. "It was safer for Jews there than in the rest of Poland." But she said that after she returned from the labor camp in Germany, she soon got married and had her first child. Her father went to Wrocław to visit Hena, and she sent back lovely baby presents, pretty jackets, and sweaters to her. Beautiful things, Mrs. Luszczyńska said.

We told her it had been difficult to get information about the murder of the Rożeneks.

"Oh," she said, "everyone for miles around knew about the

Jews that were killed at our house. They were buried next to a big cherry tree. Each year, the tree bore fruit, but the cherries quickly turned dark. Everyone was afraid to eat them, thinking that they might be poisoned or cursed by the Jews buried below. Then the tree died."

I wanted to ask more follow-up questions, but our time had run out. We raced out to the waiting cab. The driver hit the gas and the taxi went airborne on some hills racing us back to town in time to catch the last bus to Kraków.

My heart soared. I could not wait to tell Sam.

The city of Wrocław during our 2001 visit.

# 9

# Checking Boxes

WROCŁAW, POLAND 2001

W e reached the Kraków station in time to jump on our train. Once the conductor came by and punched our tickets, we headed to the overnight sleeper cars in search of Sam.

Luckily we found Sam awake and standing by the beds talking to a man in the bunk below his. I noticed that the suitcase was occupying Sam's bed, and he never took his hand off his luggage. How was going to sleep with that bag in his bed?

Sam was surprised to see us. He tore himself away from his suitcase, and we stepped into the next train car, which had high-top tables and no people. I could hardly contain my excitement to share the revelations from Mrs. Luszczyńska about Hena and her family. I laid out everything she said, including the description of how the Rożeńeks were murdered, detailed in letters from her parents. Most significant was the new information about Hena sending baby presents after the war from Wrocław. He nodded, but I did not know if he heard what I had said over the train noise, and I was afraid he had taken out his hearing aids.

Before parting, I said, "I'm so glad we found you."

Sam said, "Found me? You found her!"

After a goodbye hug, he headed back to his precious cargo.

Daga and I got off the train in Opole, the last major city before Wrocław. Her father picked us up and her parents put me up at their house. The next morning, we caught the train into Wrocław. The city that I had last seen with Sam on our goose chase pursuing Knopek's scheme was full of scaffolding and construction. Finally the war-ravaged Renaissance-era buildings in the market square were being restored to their former grandeur. Seeing the revival of vivid colors and ornate architecture was like watching a black-and-white film being colorized. A momentous occasion was spurring the long-awaited makeover: a visit by the Polish pope, John Paul II. The church, which had allied itself with the trade union Solidarity and helped engineer the downfall of the communist government in Poland, was enjoying an upsurge in influence aided by the popular pope.

We had many places to check for clues to Hena's postwar trail.

First we stopped at the Jewish Community Center by the historic White Stork Synagogue, the only synagogue in the city that survived Kristallnacht. After the war, Wrocław evolved into a transit center for Jewish survivors returning from concentration camps and from former Polish territories annexed to the Soviet Union. Jews seeking relatives and other survivors connected by registering with the Jewish community.

Amid renovations of the nineteenth-century synagogue, other parts of the community complex were seeing a rebirth in Jewish education and religious life fueled by funders in the United States and Israel. We sat on tiny chairs in a kindergarten classroom while staff went off to look in files for references to Hena or similar names. There was no way to know how extensive their files were or to evaluate the reliability of their record keeping, but after several minutes, the helpful woman returned. Sorry, she said. No one giving a name resembling Hena's had ever checked in.

Next, we headed to the city registration office and stood in a long line to apply for information. I had a sinking feeling. It was as if we were trying to nail spiderwebs. If Hena came here with a guy named David, as Mrs. Luszczyńska suggested, she could have gone by his surname, whether or not they married. But we had no idea of his name. We tried asking for details under Hena Rożeńka and many variations on the name. Nothing came up.

We tried libraries and various other resources, including a visit to a local newspaper office, where we placed an ad seeking anyone who knew Hena, using her birth name and details. Daga's mother agreed to be the point of contact for the ad. I had developed my checklist based on what I thought we needed to do in person and what I might pursue online from the United States. But I had presumed—incorrectly—that once I scaled the language barrier, more information would be forthcoming. It turned out that records of specific people who had not consented to be discovered were not very accessible in Poland, even during this period of openness and relative transparency. They did not have a history of white pages—or yellow pages either—or digital people finders. After spending two long business days shuttling among government offices and Jewish organizations, I had nothing to show for my efforts but the satisfaction that I had checked those places. Maybe I was naïve or should have spent money I did not have on a private investigator or a lawyer instead of relying on my own shoe leather. But plenty of people I'd chased in my own country where I knew how the systems worked had proven elusive. I needed a lucky break.

Empty-handed, I left Daga with her parents and boarded a train to Warsaw. For my last night in the country, a Friday, I decided I would go to the Shabbat service at the only surviving Jewish house of prayer in the capital, Nożyk Synagogue.

I had an idea.

I had read about the uproar in Poland generated by a 2000 book by a Polish-born New York University (and later Princeton) sociology professor named Jan T. Gross. Spurred by a 1999 Polish documentary film featuring eyewitness testimonies, Gross gave a searing account of the 1941 mass executions of Polish Jews in the town of Jedwabne in northeast Poland. He revealed that local ethnic Poles, after plotting with the German Gestapo and security police, beat, stabbed, and herded sixteen hundred local Jews into a barn, locked the doors, and burned them alive. The anti-Semitic fervor that powered the attack drew from lingering sentiment from the Soviet invasion of eastern Poland in 1939. Locals claimed that Jews welcomed the Russians at the same time that Germany was charging into Poland from the west.

Official accounts and memorials had always blamed German Nazis for the grisly massacre. But Gross's explosive book, *Neighbors: The Destruction of the Jewish Community in Jedwabne, Poland*, found that the Christian Poles, motivated by deep anti-Semitism and a desire to take Jewish property, were the perpetrators in the barbaric attack.[1] The book sent shock waves through the country and challenged the national narrative of the Holocaust as one of Polish suffering and heroism, fueling an epic debate over the question of whether Christian Poles bore responsibility for the fate of Poland's Jews.[2]

In May 2001, three months before my trip, one hundred Catholic bishops in Poland had apologized for the massacre, releasing a statement saying the church felt deep pain over the killings. Two months later, on the sixtieth anniversary of the bloodbath, Polish president Aleksander Kwaśniewski issued a public apology on behalf of the entire country. The leader of the left-wing Social Democracy party, Kwaśniewski spoke at a ceremony in Jedwabne that was broadcast live on Polish television. He was quoted in a page-one story in the *New York Times*,

the year the English-language version of Gross's book was published. "This was a particularly cruel crime," he said. "It was jus-
tified by nothing. The victims were helpless and defenseless."[3]

The controversy of Jedwabne would unleash a flood of
journalistic and academic investigation. It sparked debate
that would rage for decades and a backlash that would heavily
influence the nation's politics.[4] But the unprecedented candor
and acknowledgment by civil and church leaders that summer
had inspired hopes for landmark progress in Jewish-Polish
relations.

During my trip in August 2001, the investigation of
Jedwabne by the IPN, formed in 1998 to investigate and prosecute "crimes against the Polish nation" during the German
occupation as well as the communist era, was still ongoing. On
a daily basis, the topic riveted media attention in Poland and
far beyond.

The exhumation of graves at the barn site had started
in May, testing the body count Gross cited in his book. The
scene was described in widespread media coverage.[5] Reporters
described rabbis monitoring the legality of the exhumation
process while Orthodox Jews prayed and recited psalms alongside police guarding workers and archaeologists removing dirt.

All this led me to the idea that while I was in Poland, I
might research a story about the Jews who had participated in
the rites around those most unusual exhumations. I figured my
best chance of locating those Jews would be at Friday night services. With only one active synagogue I knew of, I thought I'd

try my luck at going there to seek eyewitnesses to the exhumations and learn their stories.

I also guessed that some of those participants in the exhumation procedures were among newly discovered Jews. News stories had been chronicling the experiences of ethnic Poles who had lived their entire lives in the comfortable majority only to learn from a dying parent that one or both parents had been born Jewish, leaving them with this bombshell that had long been kept secret. Such revelations were life changing in Poland, where the Jews who remained after the war had often concealed their religious identity in hopes of shielding their families from anti-Semitism.

I thought all that through, except for the logistics of a woman attending services at an orthodox synagogue. Upon arrival, I was relegated to climbing up to the balcony, where I was marooned with a few other women and could hardly see or hear what was going on. Orthodox Jews ran Poland's Jewish community, so I knew no woman could have been involved in the burial rites at Jedwabne. So I could not get near anyone who might have been at Jedwabne, at least during the service.

Afterward, I introduced myself to the rabbi, an American, and his wife. I asked him about his participation in events at Jedwabne, and he acknowledged he was there but said he could not be quoted about it. He welcomed me, however, to join other service attendees for dinner at his house.

Soon I was looking down a long dinner table in the rabbi's house, flanked by a half dozen Poles with blond hair and blue eyes watching him intently, modeling Shabbat dinner rituals that clearly were unfamiliar. They watched the rabbi's moves and tried to join in where appropriate in the recitation of blessings over the wine and bread. I picked up from side conversations that several of the diners had only recently learned they were Jewish. Some also mentioned having participated in the Jedwabne rites. I could only imagine how challenging it was to process these experiences. What would it be like living to adulthood with the privileges of being in the majority in a homogenous nation of thirty-eight million and then discovering you belong to the tiny, reviled remnant? I hoped the rabbi would give them some tools for this jarring adjustment.

After dessert, the rabbi praised the young men for aiding the grim tasks of keeping watch over the dead. Then he launched into a long lecture warning them to be on the lookout for crackers that might contain ingredients that were not kosher. Of all the pressing problems he might choose to discuss, this concern hardly merited top billing in my estimation. What a missed opportunity.

I had not seen a spiritual leader fail to meet people where they were since the Catholic funeral I had covered in Rhode Island of a thirteen-year-old girl who died in a car crash. Those sobbing classmates drew little comfort from the priest telling them to rejoice because their friend was with God.

In Poland, the transition these newly identified Jews were facing in 2001 was overwhelming. Ninety percent of Jews had been murdered a half century earlier, and most of the remainder were purged in 1968 under communism. The NGOs and religious organizations that had streamed into Poland since the fall of communism were making headway in rebuilding a Jewish community. But the prospect of popping the news to spouses, friends, and classmates for someone who had lived as a Polish Catholic to adulthood and suddenly learned he was Jewish meant risking romantic relationships and marriages and even endangering jobs. These folks had bigger challenges than nibbling on the wrong crackers.

I offered my thanks for the meal and left the rabbi's house, chatting on the way out with some of the young men I had met. It wasn't easy, they told me, digesting their grim experiences at Jedwabne. They said they were just starting to adjust to the knowledge that they were Jewish. They were eager to learn, but it was all so difficult.

My mind spun as the conversation meandered on our walk. I had considered writing a neat little feature article that would shine a light on the remarkable experiences of some Poles at Jedwabne, but the story proved to be massive and complex, encompassing so many challenges of Poland. The thread I was pulling in pursuit of one Jewish woman who walked away from the wartime massacre of her family had revealed how much the country still struggled with the history of her tribe, an excision that some had compared to an amputee's phantom sensations of a missing limb. Tonight I had seen the anguish of the few who remained.

I wished the young men a good Shabbat and left them

without gathering the contact information I would have needed to pursue the story or leaving them with mine. I decided I would stick with chasing Hena, and all that the search for her had revealed, a big enough slice of the story of Poland reckoning with its past.

Two weeks after I returned home, where by then I was an editor at the *Boston Globe*, the terrorist attacks of 9/11 pushed the controversy over the 1941 Jedwabne mass murder in Poland far from American consciousness. But in December, Poland's IPN officially concluded that Poles were indeed the perpetrators of the crimes at Jedwabne.

Tadeusz Mleko with Sam. Mleko's parents hid Sam's family in 1942 for several months. At this meeting Judy asks Mleko how he feels about this history, which locals used to disparage his family for generations. He says he is still glad his family did something good.

# 10

# Wielding the Baton

The Dula bones traveled safely back to Ohio in Sam's suitcase. Sam buried them in a small pine box between his parents' graves in Canton, Ohio. His rabbi performed an unusual service honoring the lives of a family brutally slain in hiding.

Sam called that 2001 trip his "swan song," his best ever because he had literally dug up so much. He moved permanently to Florida and announced his retirement not only from home building and property management but also from pursuits related to the Holocaust. "Now I'm in the maintenance business," he announced on a phone call. "I'm in the business of maintaining Sam."

He created an active routine of playing tennis—"I only hit the ball if it comes right to me"—delivering kosher food to shut-ins, and helping with security in his community, patrolling as a special sheriff's deputy.

He had every right to retire. But I became surprisingly nostalgic about our earlier exploits in Poland. We'd made an odd pair, traipsing through farms and archives. He was a dynamo pinwheeling through the countryside, stopping in towns where relatives once lived or hid, and at the sight of any elderly person, he'd roll down the window and ask for directions. Then he'd throw out the names and occupations of relatives who had lived in the area and come away with fresh details that filled in blanks on his mental family tree. He was so comfortable on his old stomping grounds that it rubbed off on me. That uncanny intimacy with people from the land and life he had been forced to leave seemed almost medicinal. He'd console a widow or coax a laugh out of a farmer standing in a muddy field strapped to a horse-drawn plow. He'd move in close, showing keen interest and real kinship. His pride in being part of this place ran as deeply as the pain of having that identity stripped away.

Sam remembered every wartime kindness shown to him by a Pole, from the supervisor in the German motor pool who tipped him off about the impending roundup of Jews in 1942 to the forewoman in the metal factory where he was a slave laborer while in the Kraków ghetto who piled finished goods on his workstation, lightening his workload by helping him meet his quota. Many memories were about food because it was so scarce. More than once, a Polish driver for a Nazi officer parked at the entrance to a concentration camp when Sam's detail of slave laborers was returning after a long day. The driver dropped a sandwich within Sam's reach just as he passed by.

While many survivors would not think of returning home to Poland, Sam defended his country, pointing out that it was the only one in all of occupied Europe that did not collaborate with the Nazis. Poland's government went into exile rather than cooperate with the occupiers, unlike other European countries. And he would speak up even in groups of survivors grousing about Poland and point out that it had saved the most Jews of all occupied nations, citing the more than seven thousand Poles named "Righteous among the Nations"—the most of any nationality—by Israel's Yad Vashem, an honor for non-Jews who risked their lives during the Holocaust to save Jews from extermination.

But for all Sam's generosity of spirit toward the actions of Poles during the war, we had continually encountered stark examples that many had participated in the destruction of the Jewish population. Sam wondered aloud, "How can this happen that one day you are a normal person and you live on the same street, and the next day you are nothing? You are a dog and anyone can do anything to you that they want."

---

Three years after Sam's swan song trip, he invited me to Florida for Passover. I welcomed the invitation and vowed to myself that I'd avoid the touchy topic of Hena. At the seder, Bilha made me feel welcome by acknowledging my grandfather's role after the war in sponsoring the survivors for visas to the United States. They appreciated what Sam called our "Yankee family."

The next day, Sam handed me a translation of the original telegram from the "unknown nephew" that he wrote to Poppy after the war from Israel, where he had settled after escorting a shipload of Jewish war orphans.

> *It's difficult for me to write to you because I don't even know you and I'm not 22 years old even. I am Samuel Rakowski, the son of Józef Rakowski. I want to inform you that I had the privilege to immigrate to Eretz Yisrael. The parents I left behind in the Diaspora in Austria. My father until lately was in a hospital recovering. From our family survived your sister Lily, with her son, 19 years old, and your brother Józef, who is my father, and my mother survived.*

That correspondence paved the way for the survivors to come to America, and Poppy hired many of them in his factory.

Until he shared the telegram, Sam had not said much to me on that visit, except for telling me he'd held a service for the Dula bones to which he had invited Daniel, Rela's son. He had not invited me, even though I'd been with him on the Sodo farm when we first discovered the graves.

In his Florida living room, Sam asked me to sit down. "I want to tell you something," he said. "I want to apologize for mistakes I made over there," he said.

I gulped. I thought he might elaborate on why he had cooled on our collaboration. I had been going over and over our interactions and trying to figure out what I'd done that had bothered him.

Next he said, "I had an impact over there, for sure." He elaborated with a laundry list of information he had gathered over the years and who had given him answers to puzzles about many relatives and neighbors. I realized he was grading his own performance. Of Hena, he said, "It's a mystery." He paused.

I wanted to launch into the perennial review of what we knew and what was corroborated by whom and how. But Sam proceeded with chiding himself for not pressing Stefan and Guca harder for answers, a refrain I had already heard often and would hear many times again.

"I know how many mistakes I made just dealing with this issue and looking for this cousin. I had leads so many times, but we were just there for a few days each time. And we were always given half-truths and half-assed information." He continued, "And then you guess wrong, like in Wrocław. I held out for that man in Wrocław. The more they were telling me no, the more I wanted to go."

He should not be so hard on himself, I thought. But then I realized he was saying something new.

"Wait a minute. You did not tell me that anyone was saying Luty was not the right guy before we drove across the country," I said.

Sam raised his eyebrows and shrugged. "This does not matter," he said.

I was seeing a pattern.

So maybe Knopek had told Sam before we set off across the country that it was a bum lead. And here I thought Knopek had ditched us.

Sam pivoted back to fretting about his "so-called friends."

"If I go back now, I'll walk into Stefan's house and say, 'This is it! The end of lies. Before I die, before you die, I want to know the truth. It's not possible you don't know.'"

I wasn't sure if Stefan was still alive, but I did not believe that Sam had ever been unclear with Stefan about his desire for a reunion with Hena.

Then he said, "The biggest shock was when I saw in the telephone book in Wrocław the name Luty six more times. That was the downfall of the trip."

The downfall of that trip, to my mind, was its inception with the pretext of an inheritance offered to a guy who had nothing to do with Hena. But I kept quiet.

"When I'm over there," Sam said, "I act in a different way, not rational."

I smiled.

Like when he ripped his birth certificate out of a book at the archives. "Was I with you there or was that Daniel?" he asked.

"It was me. They wouldn't copy it for you," I said. "Then we were like criminals."

We shared a chuckle. He shrugged and tossed his head, offering a half smile, and I realized this was his way of apologizing. I thanked him even though I did not know exactly what he regretted or what he meant.

He did not share his unsettled feelings about the hunt for Hena. He still saw it framed entirely by his encounters with his local contacts. He did not believe what the daughter of the people who hid the Rożeńeks had told me. He heaped doubt on anything he did not witness. The "mystery" bugged him even though he had sworn off it. Yet he would not acknowledge that the hunt could go on without his participation. That wasn't him. He shrugged and offered me a double wink.

---

Sam had been quite successful at gathering information with his friendly approach to random strangers. But he got frustrated or fatalistic with those who stonewalled him. Then it was almost impossible to make headway. I regretted that between the language barrier and my deference to him, I was not effective in those encounters. I had experience interviewing murder suspects, corrupt officials, and protectors of pedophile priests. No approach guaranteed success, but chances improved, as with any investigation, if the interviewee had something to gain. Finding a reason for the interviewee to talk, if only to shift blame or prove a point, was something that my reporting colleagues and I would brainstorm about before an interview. Otherwise, why would anyone talk?

In the Hena search, Sam used an approach better suited to a detective with leverage. He sometimes suggested an accusatory version of events and hoped the interviewee would correct him and say what really happened.

It did not work for people like Adolf Poremski, the former policeman who had sat with Hena when she was summoned to identify her family's killers. Poremski stared stonily at Sam when he got tough with him. He just dug in and kept his mouth shut.

"I finally told Poremski, the guy with the peg leg, 'I think you killed her,'" Sam boasted.

"I know," I responded. "But that didn't exactly make him tell us anything."

Regarding interview tactics, Sam said, "This does not matter. Anyway, whatever I did gives me some satisfaction."

Regardless of the interview technique, how likely was any outsider to persuade people bound by a close-knit rural mindset and a wall of secrecy to share information implicating their own people in murdering Jews? Why would Poremski level with us when he had to live out his life in the same neighborhood as the assailants in the Rożeńek case and possibly others?

---

For Sam, a lot was on the line in this mystery of Hena, not least of which was his belief in his relationships. He'd broken bread again and again with Sofia and Stefan and the Gucas, something that would not have happened growing up when Jews all kept kosher and did not socialize with non-Jews. In the postwar visits, the boundaries seemed diminished. He liked bringing presents and talking over childhood memories. It worked, right up to when he asked for information on Hena. Following up on Stefan's tip that Hena had survived strained their relationship. By asking for help, Sam shifted back to being an outsider.

Knopek told Sam his friends smiled to his face and then behind his back asked, "Why is he coming here? What does he want?"

That wounded Sam. He was the rare survivor whose enduring affection for his native country propelled him back there again and again. Why couldn't they understand that? He still saw himself as a Pole even though his nation had distanced itself from "Poles of Jewish nationality," the official term for Polish Jews. He tried to cut his friends some slack, understanding that they had seen Jews humiliated, rounded up, shot in the streets, and deported to Bełżec, which was traumatic at the time. But over fifty years later, he expected them to accept him again as the guy they knew before the war, even if they benefited from Jews' absence.

"No one once said to us that it was a terrible thing what happened to the Jews, whether killed by Nazis or Poles," Sam said.

He did not expect it, actually. But he believed they were sincere in welcoming him as if nothing had changed in their relationship from when they were young. Their behavior around his appeals for help finding Hena signaled otherwise.

Sam had taken Stefan at his word in 1989 when he revealed that Hena had survived. He had built on that tip, with Stefan bringing us to Augustyn Wacław and Adolf Poremski, establishing that she was alive several years after the war. And he even found some corroborating value in Guca's evasiveness. But Sam struggled to believe Hena survived the war and did not reach out, seeking family. He rattled off a list of people she could have contacted and ways that they could have connected her to surviving relatives.

I countered, in a perennial go-round, that she may have considered it too risky even after the war to reveal her location. She was a murder witness, after all, and may have feared that reaching out and revealing where she lived would have been too risky. And over time, after fading into the population, she may not have wanted her children to find out about her Jewish origins.

Sam batted away my suggestions. It was as if he could not believe a Jew would not reach out to find family. "It's a mystery," was his refrain.

Sam undoubtedly judged the persistence of that mystery as a personal failure that overshadowed other successes in solving puzzles in Poland. But despite his protests and professed doubt that Hena in fact had survived as Stefan said, he clearly did not want to accept defeat. He had faith in his own iron will, which had served him well time and again. He did not come out and say it, but I understood that he could not let go of this "mystery." His approach, of relying on the goodwill of the people he used to know, had limits. He did not acknowledge it, but I thought it was a great opening for me to plow ahead like I would on an investigation for the *Boston Globe*. It was not until later that I would recognize that on that visit, we were at a crossroads. Sam had not given up on hoping for answers about Hena, he had simply run out of ways to look for her. Perhaps because of my own stubbornness, that conversation spurred me to plow back into the quest. After all, no death or emigration record had turned up on Hena. As far as we could tell, she was still alive.

I left Florida oddly fired up to find Hena. Sam was eighty years old and nowhere near as spry as on our first trip. But if I tracked her down, they could still have a reunion. I kept slogging away, chasing clues in the burgeoning supply of data that was coming online. I contacted academic experts from Poland to Israel to the United States and hopscotched contacts who might lead to answers. My most frequent correspondence was with the experts in Poland at what then was the Jewish Historical Institute's Ronald S. Lauder Foundation Genealogy Project.

The genealogy project could navigate records and databases that I could neither access nor read. I had been working for years with one particular expert in tracing lost relatives, Anna Przybyszewska Drozd, who functioned as part psychologist and part sleuth, tracking family members and sometimes bringing resolutions for people, even when it meant learning about tragic losses. The genealogy project had become better funded and organized, but I credited its success to Anna's own gifts and dot-connecting prowess.

Anna had taken on the Hena case with enthusiasm in part because she rarely had the chance to pursue a live person. She had been thrilled to receive Hena's birth certificate, and Sam's personal knowledge of people and history had been helpful to her on other searches of people in his territory.

In 2006, despite his many claims that he was done with all his "Polish business," Sam made plans for another trip, this time guiding another family of cousins on his mother's side.

"I'm going there to help them," he said. "I'm just doing a job now. I don't get emotional about it now. It's the last time," he said in a terse phone call.

I thought we had resolved our differences, but once again he declared that he was not looking for Hena.

"I'm no longer occupied with this mystery of the cousin," he insisted. Before I could ask, he said, "And there's no room for you in the car."

That stung, but I was getting steeled to his bluntness. If he had not found Hena's birth certificate on my last trip despite claiming he was no longer looking for her, I might have let his comment go. But I believed, based on plenty of evidence, that he would always be looking for Hena. At the risk of being impertinent, I pushed to join the trip.

I had just taken a buyout from an editor's position after fourteen years at the *Boston Globe* and now had more time for the Hena chase. I had stepped up my long-distance reporting, but it was slow going. To make headway, I needed to be on the ground in Poland, and Sam's next trip offered a good anchor for that reporting. Besides, journeys with Sam always turned into some kind of adventure.

But the prospects weren't looking good. Sam did all the communicating between his relatives and me. He had never been more discouraging. I did not know if they did not want me along or if Sam was telling them he did not want me to come. The negotiations got more and more awkward. I tried to eliminate the hurdles. I reserved a van large enough to hold everyone, even though I was not exactly flush with cash. I wrote to all of them, saying I could introduce them to my interesting friends in Warsaw. Radio silence. Finally Sam told me I could join them for a few days in Warsaw, and they would head south from there on their own. I could meet up with them in Kraków and visit Sam's hometown with them. The rest of the time, I was not welcome. It was like being told you could go to the prom, but no one was going to dance with you.

I ignored the tension and started making appointments for meetings in Poland. In April, I learned that years after filing a tracing request for Hena with the International Red Cross, they had just declared that the search had come up empty. My hopes focused on Anna at the Lauder Foundation. She was getting traction with help from a friend who was able to search in a special database.

"If she didn't leave the country before 1951, there is a chance to find her even if she married," Anna wrote. "I hope I will have the information, if they found something or not, after the weekend."

We scheduled a meeting coinciding with my visit to Warsaw. I knew she and her colleague would rib me for still speaking scarcely any Polish despite my repeated trips. But they could tease me as much as they wanted. Their help was invaluable. Anna did make clear that I should make time for a visit to the Central Address Bureau to request records of Hena's address. She said I needed Sam to go along as an aging relative who had known Hena. His presence might persuade the officials to waive their restrictions on applying for such information. Getting his agreement would be a challenge for me, given Sam's state of mind. I was worried he would wave me off because he had given up the search.

Everything accelerated on May 26, 2006, shortly before I left for the airport to fly to Warsaw. Anna sent a breathless email: "Believe it or not—my friends found an address and her new name: Henryka Łapińska. I just got the message, didn't check it. I don't know if she is still alive. I told them the whole story and I hope they didn't make a mistake. We will try to check it when you are here."

Heading to the airport, I wrote back, "I am delighted!!! This is so exciting!!!!!!!!!!"

I shared the information with Sam. He was ecstatic.

Just before I left, I confirmed my upcoming appointment in Warsaw with the FBI legal attaché in Poland, whom I'd been connected with through a series of contacts with longtime law enforcement sources. I figured if Anna's tip did not pan out, I had another possible path for finding Hena.

I have never been good at sleeping on long journeys, and this time, I hardly closed my eyes. But somehow when I landed in Warsaw, I was not tired. Determined not to get ripped off by the cab drivers, who always managed to change the price, I walked out of the arrival lounge and negotiated a price with a driver. Success!

I'd never seen Warsaw in June. On the drive, I was enjoying the profuse blooming trees and late spring flowers and admiring shimmering skyscrapers that finally shared the skyline with the long dominant Palace of Culture and Science, the multi-tiered mega building nicknamed "Stalin's wedding cake."

Near the hotel, the cabbie started jacking up the agreed on fare. "*Nie*," I said in Polish, repeating the number he had quoted. He pulled up in front of the Victoria Hotel. I handed him the exact amount in Polish currency. But he threw the money back at me in disgust. He kept shouting at me in Polish. I kept trying to give him the money, but to no avail. Finally, I grabbed my bags and the bills he had thrown back and hopped out. His loss.

I reached my room and heard an immediate knock at my door. I opened it and Sam burst in, reminding me of that first time we traveled together. "It's not her," he grumbled.

I asked him how he knew already.

"I got the rental car, and I was going there to the address, but I found out it's not her." He said he had talked to Anna on his way there, and she told him it turned out that Henryka and Hena were not the same person. The lead was a dud.

"Sam, after all our searching together, you headed there before my plane landed?"

He shrugged. "This does not matter. It's not her."

We met up with the other relatives and toured sites in Warsaw for the next two days. On Monday morning, they headed off. I was staying with friends in Warsaw and had meetings set up.

Trudging up the steps to the Jewish Historical Institute for my meeting with Anna, I remembered my first visit sixteen years earlier. Tables heaped with overflowing files of yellowing papers steeped in clouds of cigarette smoke had hardly inspired confidence in the keeping of records. A helpful young woman had found for me stirring testimonies about the mass executions at Słonowice, where I would later see the desecrated monument that Sam autographed. That woman afterward had escorted me nearby to a gathering of hundreds of people in the pouring rain for the annual memorial ceremony for the Warsaw Ghetto Uprising.

Now the institute was much better off with funding from international donors and full support from the liberal government in Warsaw, which held power from the fall of communism until 2005.

In a cramped office surrounded by boxes of records, I embraced Anna.

"I'm so sorry that this information about Hena was not correct," she said. We reviewed all the steps and sources she had used. I thanked her for all the time and attention, especially given the number of people from all over the world who sent plaintive appeals for help finding a trace of lost relatives. We reviewed the remaining avenues of information, and she again stressed the importance of Sam joining me at the Central Address Bureau. Only his presence could prompt a workaround.

"I'll try to persuade him, but his mood has soured," I said. His hopes had rocketed with the Henryka tip, only to crash again.

She closed her eyes and nodded. Who other than a cancer doctor had to deliver so much disappointing news? She asked where she could reach me while I was in Kraków and promised to call with any news. When we parted, Anna turned and offered such a soulful look of empathy, I teared up.

The next day, after a three-day drenching, the sun broke through. I went to see John Bienkowski, the FBI's legal attaché in Poland. We met over a beer at an outdoor café near the U.S. embassy. I told some tales about major Mafia trials and money-laundering cases I'd covered and mentioned several of his colleagues we knew in common. The expansion of FBI legats to posts in the former USSR was fascinating, but I marveled at the challenges of building new international relationships and tracking criminals who could travel with ease throughout the European Union. I laid out the details of the long search for Hena and all the traps I'd already run, including checking with Interpol and some other law enforcement contacts in south central Poland. I was frustrated.

"The communist government knew where everyone lived and worked, so I'm really surprised it's not easier to find people," I said.

Bienkowski nodded and the thought flickered that I might know more than he did about how records were organized in Poland. I knew the formal census had not started until 1951, but the secret police might have kept their own records. I realized my quest for a witness to some murders in 1944 surely did not top the FBI's priorities, but he was being very kind, perhaps because of my long tenure covering the FBI for different newspapers and our mutual connections. And I was in good company with an interest in uncovering truths from that era. The former colleague of Bienkowski who put me in touch with him told me I was "researching a noble cause." That retired agent said his parents were *Ostarbeiter*, basically slave labor in Germany, when they were whisked away from Ukraine during WWII. "It was an incredible time in the history of the world, and it should never be forgotten!"

Bienkowski said he would be happy to help, offering to enlist his Polish-speaking partner in the effort. "I also have a distant relative who lives in Wrocław, and I plan to meet him and his family in September. I will talk with him about your story and see if he has any ideas."

I left there feeling I was getting some traction on this very cold case. I needed that mojo for the harrowing process of buying a train ticket to Kraków, a task I had dreaded since my first confusing effort in the early '90s. I remembered sweating buckets over the process while images flashed in my mind of trains deporting Jews to their deaths.

This time I managed to find the right track, platform,

and, most importantly, wagon, or car, with my seat. Soon the gray apartment blocks and smokestacks of Warsaw gave way to broad, flat fields of celadon seedlings pushing through the earth. As we drew closer to Kraków, the landscape turned to rolling fields of young cabbage and beet crops. I tried to capture it with my camera, but reflection inside my window kept interfering. The photos did not match the aching beauty I saw.

The road signs flashing by were touchstones on the path my great-grandfather took in the late 1800s from his hometown of Jedrzejów to Kazimierza Wielka, the village of his future wife. Those landmarks were overlaid with a mental map of German Nazi camps, in particular Hitler's most efficient death camp, Treblinka, where many Rakowskis perished. One relative was a rare escapee from the camp, only to be murdered in his hometown. I was a kilometer away from Treblinka on this trip in 1990, but signs for the camp were scarce. Asking for directions proved fruitless. Eerily, one local after another had answered with a shrug. "*Nie wiem*," they said. Never heard of it.

As for my great grandfather Moshe David Rakowski, Sam and I had once tracked down his tombstone—he died in the bitterly cold winter of 1929—at an overgrown Jewish cemetery. We were trudging around an uncut field and I wondered how Sam knew we were in the right place. A babushka lady appeared and asked for money in exchange for help finding the invisible Jewish graves. Sam had waded into a thicket of bushes and found a cracked stone bearing Hebrew letters of Moshe David's name.

Remembering that scene while riding the train on a warm June day years later, I got a chill hearing Sam's voice in my head: "Our family was proudly Jewish, but first and foremost, we were Poles." But despite our tribe living in Poland for hundreds of years, we were never accepted as Poles. Nevertheless, this place had seeped under my skin and stayed.

It was pouring in Kraków when my train arrived. I had left most of my luggage with friends in Warsaw, but I still took a cab rather than navigate the trams. At the hotel where Sam and family were staying, I met up with them after their visit to the Auschwitz-Birkenau.

My first visit to the notorious camps in 1990, I'd gone with a young translator, a college student who was ecstatic over the fall of communism. On a snowy April day, the mood was set on the short train ride from Kraków. The empty-eyed train conductor seemed robotic, and I wondered how residents of Oświęcim—the Polish town in which the camps are located—managed to live with the history. We had joined a tour of the camp, meandering among brick barracks that looked grim but actually resembled prisons from the same vintage in the States. But then we entered a building with suitcases stacked to the ceiling, all bearing obviously Jewish surnames. I thought of the last time their owners had held the handles and wondered if they knew they would never again open them. Next we passed floor-to-ceiling bins of old eyeglasses. Then came the most chilling of all, massive piles of human hair shorn from victims upon arrival.

We walked to the vast women's camp and the crematoria at

Birkenau, with train tracks leading right into its maw. My translator read from plaques describing what had happened in this place. The victims were described—following the communist-era narrative—as "Polish citizens."

Who could fathom that one million Jews died in this place as Jews—marched straight from the trains to showers of lethal gas—only for later visitors to be gaslighted in the very place where they perished, lumped together with all "victims of fascism"?

On this 2006 trip, I had chosen to skip another visit to Auschwitz. But, I understood why no one felt much like talking or eating that night.

The next day, a visit to Sam's hometown was on tap. Sam drove into a Kazimierza that hardly resembled the one-horse town I remembered. Bustling shops and cars jockeying for parking spaces threw off Sam's mental GPS. He asked pedestrians and store clerks for directions. I followed him into one shop that was jammed wall to wall with the latest washers and dryers. But no one could answer his questions.

Next he tried a camera store and chatted with a hip young clerk with cotton-candy-colored hair. Sam told the young man that in his day, all the shopping happened on Mondays and the vendors presented all the wares, including livestock, in the market square. The salesman listened blankly to the impromptu history lesson. I wondered what he would have thought if Sam had described the main street that ran from the church to the sugar factory that in Sam's youth had been lined with stores run by Jews.

Sam took us by his former house, with its rough-hewn dark wood siding, once known as the first to get electricity. For decades, it had been held by the government. After liberation, Sam's mother warned him away from returning here after she and her sister had been attacked by locals upon returning home after the war. But at her behest, Sam had traveled in 1945 by train to the archives in Kielce, the scene a few months after his visit of a horrific pogrom. He had braved the trains, then very dangerous for Jews, and managed to get the deed to the house, which paved the way later for getting some compensation from the U.S. government. The Polish government has never compensated Jews for all the homes and businesses that were seized by the Germans and then kept by the communist government.

After a cursory house tour, I noticed Sam was heading out of town instead of making the usual stops at Stefan and Sofia's or Guca's houses. Was Stefan still around? No, Sam said. "His daughter in America called me after he died. She said her mother was now available." Sam laughed out loud.

I laughed too. The prospect of Sam and Sofia getting together—even if he wasn't happily married to Bilha—was mind-blowing. "How about Guca?"

He said, "Guca is dead. But his daughters are still around. Anyway, I'm not going to bother with these people. We're going to see the good people, the ones who hid us."

Sam fell silent the rest of the drive. Was he remembering his first time on this path when he was on foot, headed into hiding? Or was his mind drifting to the most emotional memory of all, leaving his Grandma Pearl sitting up in bed, her back turned to the wall, when he and his father were the last ones out of the house?

It was in 1989 on Sam and Bilha's anniversary trip that Sam had rediscovered the Polish people who had harbored his family. He had driven past a road sign for their hamlet and then, on a whim, tracked down the house of the township official who had arranged for their safe harbor in 1942. That impromptu visit turned into a warm reunion with the man, his wife, children, and grandchildren. My first time in Poland with Sam, visiting that family, the Mlekos, had been the highlight of my trip. I'd filled my suitcase with gifts for the grandchildren of the righteous man who arranged to hide Sam and six family members, including a toy helicopter for the grandson. Watching the children open our presents, I wondered who they thought we were and why we were there. Sam was busy comforting the widow of the patriarch who had just died. She wept inconsolably on Sam's shoulder.

The farm had become more prosperous since my last visit, and I was glad to see that finally a tractor had replaced the four-legged kind of horsepower. And Tadeusz Mleko, son of the man who had hidden Sam's family, and his wife, Barbara, looked less fatigued than before. Now only the youngest of their three children, whom I'd met as a babe in her mother's arms, was living at home. This warm reunion might have resembled any other that joined people who'd shared an experience. But this time, I asked Tadeusz if people in their community who knew the history had changed their attitudes over time about their family's generosity to Sam's family. Sipping tea at his table, I reminded Tadeusz that he had said on an earlier visit that the people in his tiny village were "not too happy with us when they found out we had hidden Jews." That was understandable during the war, given the Nazis' threat to kill not only anyone who hid Jews but also their entire village. But Sam's family left after three months, before anyone discovered them. And Tadeusz's father, not he or his children, arranged to harbor them. Nevertheless, Tadeusz frowned, the village held a grudge and passed down the stigma for generations. He said he had kept the information as private as possible. "People always suspect that we got gold from the Jews, and they think we have money."

"So how do you feel now about your father's decision back then to hide Sam and his family?" I asked.

He looked around and smiled almost sheepishly. "I'm glad that my family did a good thing and not a bad thing."

In Polish, Sam chimed in, "So am I." We all laughed.

When we got back to our hotel in Kraków later that Sunday, I had an email from Anna at the Lauder Project. She urged me to call her. When I phoned from the hotel, she said she'd learned that part of the reason finding Hena was so difficult was because a fire in a building where demographic records were kept had destroyed records. Wouldn't there be backup files somewhere? I asked. There should be, she said. That was why, Anna stressed again, Sam had to go with me to the Central Address Bureau in Warsaw.

I had been reluctant to raise this request with Sam. I knew his travel schedule would allow it, but feared he would turn me down. I thought I'd wait until after he'd seen his hometown again, particularly the wonderful Mleko family, to brighten his mood. I took him aside before dinner and told him it was Anna's idea to go to the address bureau and that I needed someone with a close blood relationship to Hena to make the request.

"No. I'm not doing this. I'm not chasing this anymore," he said.

I tried him again the next day, but he was adamant. Maybe the buildup and letdown from the start of the trip with the fresh tip had made him self-protective. At any rate, he was not leaving the door open even a crack.

The next day, I was glum heading back to Warsaw by train. But I did not want to leave without trying to get information from the Central Address Bureau.

I reached out for help from a wonderful guy whose cousin was a colleague from my days at the *Providence Journal*. Pawel was just finishing his medical degree when I first met him on a trip in the early 1990s, and he and his wife had become close with another colleague from the *Journal*, my dear friend Colleen Fitzpatrick. Back when journalists from around the globe descended on Warsaw, Colleen had moved to Warsaw for the epic story, sending dispatches as a freelancer for several American news outlets.

At the start of this trip, we'd all had dinner with Pawel,

who knew Sam through me, and Sam had introduced Pawel to the buried Jewish history of his hometown, which was a revelation for him.

Pawel answered my plea and took the afternoon off from seeing patients, meeting me at the Central Address Bureau. We filled out forms and stood in line for a very long time. Finally we were called to the window. The clerk took the papers and disappeared. Almost instantly, she returned. There was nothing in the files, she said dismissively. I did not see how she'd had time to look. Pawel was persistent. Nothing there, she said. Anna had warned me about this. Only a close relative could ask for such information *and* they still needed the subject's permission. Sam might have succeeded in getting the clerks to overlook the permission part given his age, relationship, and uncanny powers of persuasion. Despite Pawel's local standing and my sad, imploring looks, we didn't stand a chance.

We left the dingy green halls of the building deflated. "You took off work and everything. Let me at least treat you to dinner," I offered. He relented and we found a table at an outdoor café and dug into a hearty repast of roast beef and potatoes. We reminisced about my early visits and a springtime Sunday afternoon stroll with his family in Łazienki Park, a beautiful seventeenth-century palace and grounds. I treasured the many photos I'd snapped of his adorable six-year-old daughter laughing and posing with oak leaves for ears. She tried schooling me on proper pronunciation of Polish words for "aunt" and "bird."

Pawel, whose round baby face belies an earnest intensity, said he was distressed by our lack of success at the address bureau. "I want to do more to help you," he said.

His offer made me realize that after Sam's disappointing refusal to come with me, I'd become resigned to the dead ends and doors closing in my face. Pawel furrowed his white-blond brow and leaned in close. I had no clue what he was going to say. In halting English, he said, "Knowing Sam and talking to him on these visits, this has made my life worth more."

I nodded and sat back in my chair. "I know what you mean," I said. "Mine too."

The next day, I flew back to Boston. It was a long day of travel. That night at 11:00 p.m., the phone rang, waking me from a sound sleep. It was Sam. He peppered me with questions about what I did in Warsaw and whether I found anything on Hena. Then he launched into a long monologue on Poland, the trip, and Polish-Jewish relations through history. I didn't even know which continent I was on, but I told him what Pawel had said about his impact. He liked that.

A few months later, I received an email from a detective in Wrocław, Poland.

I was asked by John Bienkowski from the FBI to help you to find your distant relative. It is my pleasure. I like to help people. But...John sent me a birth certificate dated 11th of September 1935 in which Szmul Rożeńek accepted Hena as his kid. On the base of this, I found these data:

First name—Henia, the maiden name—Rożeńek, date of her birth—2nd of February 1928, place of birth village—Gorzków, Poland, father's name—Szmul, mother's name—Ita.

Then I checked in our depository where we have all people who live in Poland, even those who have already died. I don't need this woman's second name. Her maiden name is sufficient for me. I tried many configurations, and unfortunately no person who was born on 2nd February 1928 from Szmul and Ita exists in Poland.

Maybe you have additional information which will help me to find this person. Maybe I haven't read these documents correctly. I have just a copy of this.

Maybe write me once again the first name of your relative, her maiden name, date of birth, mother and father's name. Remember that we have in Poland special letters in our alphabet that you don't have.

This was exciting. Finally we had connected with someone who had access to databases and contacts that no one else had. I wrote right back and elaborated with everything I had.

In October, he wrote again, saying, "I found one woman who emigrated to Israel in 1960, but she didn't have the same data. Just a few items were the same. It is also possible that she completely changed her name and parents' name after the war. In this case I have no chance to find her."

The roller coaster had plunged to earth again. This news was crushing in its finality. I did not see a way forward. I wrote to Anna at the institute in Warsaw and told her about the Wroclaw police officer's finding. I told her I was totally discouraged. I saw no recourse. I was giving up on the search.

Her prompt answer was comforting but did nothing to change the result. "Dear Judy, I am very sorry that you had to give up to look for her. I have the feeling that we have a missing point in the whole story, that maybe one day it will come to our eyes, and we will solve the question of where she went to."

# PART III

Sam has not been able to recognize anything familiar, and then we find the wife of Sodo, whose parents hid the Dulas. She says the Dulas should still be alive. Sam's intimacy in talking with her is striking.

# 11

# Strained Truth

Cold rain shrouded a rolling checkerboard of chocolate earth and sage-colored sprouts. The hilly fields signaled our approach to Cousin Sam's hometown. I squinted at the tractors that had changed the landscape. On earlier trips, I had photographed horse-drawn wagons and farmers hand-sowing crops—scenes from another age.

I was back in Poland on what proved to be my last trip with Sam. I was traveling with my husband of five years, also named Sam, whom I'll call Sammy for clarity. When we met in 2011, we connected like fingers interlacing. We didn't just finish each other's sentences; again and again we said the same words simultaneously. One of his adult sons quipped at our wedding party that we were two sides of the same person.

Besides our personal chemistry and extraordinary fit, we

shared roots in Poland and a deep interest in the Holocaust and the region. Poland was the home that both Sammy's grandfathers left for America. In college, he had learned central European history, and in graduate school, he had studied the Holocaust. He had also delved deeply into Jewish genealogy. On our first date, he was dazzled when I thanked our Polish-born waiter in her native tongue.

We'd planned to travel here in 2016. Cousin Sam, who heartily approved of Sammy, said that if we came to Poland, he was happy to peel off from the March of the Living when the tour was in Kraków and show us around his hometown. But then Sam broke his wrist and canceled his trip. My mother became gravely ill and passed away. We shelved our plans indefinitely.

Now here I was heading into Kazimierza Wielka with Cousin Sam and my husband, Sam.

Sammy and I had started the trip in Warsaw where my dear longtime friends greeted us at the airport with a placard for my husband that said, *Sam from Dallas* a nickname he had picked up from people who misheard his surname, Mendales. They knew him from their visit to the States a few years before, when we hosted their family in Cambridge. We had opened our home to them just as they had for me on trip after trip to Poland dating back to when I met them in the early 1990s through Colleen. Over the years, I recovered at their house at the end of many trips from soul-crushing serial visits to Holocaust sites. Through the eyes of these contemporaries, I'd learned so much more about the seismic changes in the country than news reports could impart.

Our friends had grown up chatting with school friends in bread lines, something the next generation growing up in Warsaw never saw, knowing only well-stocked urban stores. Our friends saw the arrival of professions like marketing and graphics that were unheard of under communism.

In those days, between trips, Cousin Sam and I burned up the phone lines sharing good news. He was reading about all the changes in the Polish and Israeli papers, and I'd chime in with what I'd read in U.S. press reports. We breathlessly called each other, speaking cryptically. He would say, "Did you see what happened?"

And I would cut him off, saying, "I know, I know."

Along with the economic changes, Poland had created an independent judiciary and autonomous media outlets that replaced state-run mouthpieces. Prosperity and democracy seemed like they were here to stay.

When the Institute of National Remembrance (IPN) was formed in 1998, it promised to investigate crimes that occurred under communism and also crimes against "Poles of Jewish nationality." Rosy headlines abounded, with Jews around the world hoping they would finally learn the fate of lost relatives. I bristled at the phrase "Poles of Jewish nationality," as if our family had lived in Poland for over five hundred years yet remained carpetbaggers who could go "home." Sam took that slight in stride, saying, "This does not matter."

What did matter was that, as part of becoming a democracy, the country seemed to be open to facing its past, warts and all.

Sam and I had rejoiced in 2001 when the Polish president and Catholic bishops apologized for Poland's past behavior to Jews and the IPN found Poles responsible for the Jedwabne slaughter. But since then, so much had changed. Those heady days seemed not only relegated to the rearview mirror; it was as if they'd never happened.

The revelations of Poles' culpability for the Jedwabne atrocities had shaken Polish identity to its core. The backlash helped fuel the rise of the right-wing populist Law and Justice (Prawo i Sprawiedliwość, or PiS) party formed in 2001. It took advantage of the fact that Poles never had a chance to recover from the pounding they had taken from the Germans and the oppression under Soviet communism that also denied them an accurate sense of history. Both regimes distorted history at will. Hitler considered not only Jews but also Poles *Untermenschen*, or subhumans, fit only to serve as slaves to Germany. Seizing on this fact, Poland's communist regime scrubbed from textbooks and monument narratives any reference to the Reich's Final Solution for Jews. Instead, it portrayed all who perished in World War II as equal victims of fascism. Under communism, even acknowledging the former Jewish population on a town level was taboo. The Polish underground was also denied rightful credit for its substantial contributions in helping the Allies win the war.

Like other autocratic movements surging around the globe, PiS strummed those grievances, setting itself up as solely able to restore the comforting old narrative of Poles as the "noble victim," as Holocaust historian Jan Grabowski would later put it to *New Yorker* writer Masha Gessen.[1] PiS also exploited Poland's hunger for homegrown heroes. Many in Poland lapped up PiS's alternative narrative of cheering the history of the Polish underground, members of the AK, that had managed to undermine the Germans against great odds. PiS targeted descendants of Poles who were or claimed to have been heroically fighting for Poland during the war, which included most of the country.

It also pushed back on the official admission of Polish responsibility for the Jedwabne massacre, which had threatened Poland's deep-seated sense of martyrdom. Then in 2010, the president of Poland, Lech Kaczyński, and a delegation of ninety-five other top officials in the military, government, and clergy died in a plane crash en route to commemorate the 1940 Katyn massacre by Stalin's secret police of nearly twenty-two thousand Polish soldiers and intelligentsia. The plane crashed in thick fog trying to land at a military airport that lacked advanced navigation equipment near the Russian city of Smoleńsk.

That same year, Kaczyński's twin brother, Jarosław Kaczyński, lost an election for president in a campaign in which he did not mention Smoleńsk. Then, he did an about-face and alleged that the plane exploded in an assassination he blamed on Russia.[2] Polish and Russian investigations found no basis for that, but the charges would divide the public over time. The country's chief rabbi, an Orthodox American, told Israeli radio he declined the Polish president's invitation to fly that Saturday because it would have required him to violate the Jewish Sabbath, which aroused conspiratorial suspicions in Poland.[3] Ultimately, PiS benefited politically from the nation's grief over the tragedy.

By 2015, PiS had consolidated power and control of the government. It swung a wrecking ball at the independent judiciary and media. Not content to kneecap the nascent democracy, the government revived the communist playbook of sullying foes, including Lech Wałęsa, the former prime minister and leader of the movement that had slayed the Soviet dragon. PiS felled foes of its new order by implying they had once collaborated with Germans or Soviets or had Jewish relatives.

Under PiS, an obvious casualty was the IPN. Early optimism that the IPN would mount unflinching investigations into historic crimes fell flat. Even before PiS consolidated its grip on power, University of Toronto professor Piotr Wróbel, a Polish and central European history expert, told me by email in 2007, "The IPN is not a regular archive. It is a political institution deeply involved in the present political conflict in Poland. Now IPN is in the hands of right-wing historians."[4]

Once again, the interests of Jews in learning about wartime atrocities and tracking down loved ones became a casualty of the prevailing political will in Poland. The country's sharp right pivot dashed hopes for a reckoning with the suppressed history of Polish complicity in the Reich's bid to render Poland *Judenfrei*, free of Jews.

Even references to Jedwabne in theater and film struck a highly sensitive nerve. The Polish Film Institute rejected as "anti-Polish" a film inspired by Jedwabne called *Aftermath*, in which brothers learn that their grandparents took part in killing Jewish neighbors. No one said the film was untrue. Rather, the institute complained, it "chose to overlook acts of Polish heroism and compassion shown toward Jews during the war," according to the *Hollywood Reporter*.[5]

If Jedwabne was the only massacre of Jews by Poles to emerge, the intense backlash it generated might have closed the door on the broader topic. But after communism fell in 1989, scholars and journalists who had finally been able to access archives and records about Poland's wartime past learned about more Nazi crimes and Polish complicity as well. Poland's government proudly never collaborated with the Germans, but this generation of graduate students operating with newfound intellectual freedom discovered that many ethnic Poles themselves were active in persecuting, exterminating, and dispossessing Poland's Jews. In response, the right-wing government, media, and academics pumped out propaganda, heaping skepticism on emerging disclosures and disdain for those who made them.

The day after we landed in Warsaw, our friends put us in an Uber headed for the annual Warsaw Ghetto Uprising commemoration ceremony.

While it was my third time attending this poignant event, I saw it through my husband's fresh eyes and framed by a new political backdrop. We managed to move through the large crowd and get close to the massive monument, a two-sided sculpture erected in 1948 on the ruins of the ghetto. The dramatic tableau on the front of the bronze *Monument to the Ghetto Heroes*, created by Warsaw-born sculptor Nathan Rapoport, pays tribute to the leaders of the seven hundred young Jewish fighters who fought boldly against over two thousand Germans equipped with mine throwers, tanks, and more than two hundred machine and submachine guns.[6] The monument depicts seven fighters gathered around uprising leader Mordechai Anielewicz. He stares straight ahead, his bandaged head held high, clutching a grenade in one hand. A fallen fighter lies at his feet. A firestorm swirls in the upper part of the scene, surrounding a mother and child whose hands stretch up in despair. The back side honors the more than three hundred thousand Jews who suffered and died in the ghetto and in the gas chambers at Treblinka.[7]

We watched the official Polish ceremony with a procession of soldiers marching floral wreaths to display before the monument. "That's weird," Sammy said, shooting the scene like the expert photographer he is. "Military honors at a monument to rebellion."

I noticed a different vibe this time. Sammy's photos captured the scene of scores of Poles gathered for the ceremony wearing on their chests the signature paper daffodils that echo the yellow Star of David that Jews were forced to wear on their clothing. This outpouring of symbolic solidarity was heartening. We also noticed many far-flung tourists on hand for visits to the new POLIN Museum of the History of Polish Jews, built opposite the monument on former ghetto land.

The very name POLIN was chosen purposefully. In Yiddish and Hebrew transliteration, it means "you will rest here." The term is rooted in a legend dating back a thousand years to when Jews were fleeing persecution in western Europe. Hearing birds singing, "Po-lin! Po-lin!" they took it as a sign from the almighty to stay. Over time, it was adopted as the name for this place: Poland. The name also signaled that this museum, a national, city, and private partnership that took more than twenty years to complete, was aimed at audiences with shared interests in the history of all Jews in Poland, not only descendants of the vanquished population.

After the ceremony, we took a guided tour that our friends booked for us. We sank our minds and senses into remarkable exhibits depicting the long, rich Jewish cultural history of this land. We walked out shaking our heads. Sammy said, "We were woven so deeply into the fabric of this place for so long but never accepted."

"So easily discarded," I said.

Afterward we walked around Warsaw for hours and noticed Poles from the ceremony still wearing the paper daffodil. One couple with daffodils on their coats pushing a young girl in a stroller looked at us intently.

Sammy said, "Did you see that guy? His look of defiance?"

"I don't think they were Jewish," I said, realizing my daffodil had fallen off. I wondered if he had identified us as Jews or maybe he recognized us from the ceremony.

"Maybe they are wearing them because they care about what happened to the Jews," Sammy said. "Or they are still wearing them as a sign of resistance to this government."

We walked a little farther.

Sammy stopped and said, "If young families are willing to show up and be counted, that gives me hope."

"Yes," I said. "But this is liberal Warsaw, not the countryside where the government is very popular."

---

The next day, we headed to the main train station, bound for Kraków. The first time I saw the station, it looked like a hangar for the Goodyear Blimp. In the 1970s, it was built as another Soviet mega project showing the awesome power of the state. Decades later, it looked less impressive wedged between mirrored skyscrapers and neon banners.

In the cavernous interior, I was scanning the big board for our platform number. Sammy looked a little dazed. "It's incredible," he said.

"What?" I asked distractedly.

"That shiver when I see Białystok listed on the board along with these other towns where my family came from. I hear the voices of the older generation. They told stories about these places." He surveyed passing travelers. "A lot of people here look like the guys who chased me growing up in Queens and called me Jew, and a lot of them look like members of my dad's family."

I agreed. "You experience things that hit me on my early trips, and now I notice what has changed over time."

The trains themselves had a big upgrade. Compared to the clunky old wagons, we boarded spaceships. While speeding south, we sipped hot tea and nibbled biscuits delivered by an attendant rolling a cart past our seats, enjoying how an infusion of European Union cash had transformed Poland's railway system.

In Kraków, I had booked a hotel walking distance to Cousin Sam's and had lined up a driver and a translator. With Sammy's expertise, I no longer had to rely on my amateurish snapshots to follow our steps. I figured we'd steer away from the people who had deeply disappointed Sam in his pleas for help finding Hena. We had developed good connections with the outsiders, descendants of Poles who hid our relatives. I did not tell Sam I was always still looking for Hena. On some level, he knew that. But he was intent on doing a good job on the March of the Living, bearing witness as one of a dwindling cohort of Holocaust survivors.

We had plans to meet Sam at the hotel where he was staying with scores of March of the Living participants. In the three days since we landed in Poland, I had not reached Sam by phone or email. I knew the march kept a tight schedule with

the need to coordinate movements of so many buses full of visitors. I tried again after we checked into our hotel. Still nothing.
Now I was worried. We walked to his hotel, just blocks from
ours. Lots of people from the march were hanging around on a
Saturday, with no programming on Shabbat. We asked around.
No one had seen Sam. I finally persuaded someone to help us
get his room number. We headed upstairs and my heart was
pounding as we approached his door. We knocked for what
seemed like an hour. After all he'd been through, I could not
bear to think that something might happen to him in Poland
and on his eleventh March of the Living.

Finally, Sam opened the door. His shirttail was out and he
was blinking like he just woke up. "Oh, good to see you guys,"
he muttered. He had been napping, trying to recover from a
cold that turned into bronchitis. He hadn't heard the phone
because he wasn't wearing his hearing aids. And he was not
checking email on his phone. I tried to act like it wasn't a big
deal. But what a relief. After all, he was traveling alone at age
ninety-two.

The next morning, he said he felt better. Our driver,
Derek, a relative of a Boston friend, picked us up wearing
reflective sunglasses on a rainy day, his van pulsing with
Europop music. Sam rode shotgun. Sitting in back with us
was Gosia, a bilingual college student serving as our translator. With her along, I would know in real time what Sam was
saying to people here.

Sammy had brought his sophisticated camera, poised to

capture the beauty of the countryside and Sam's interactions with the characters from his hometown I'd described.

Wheeling across this landscape on my seventh foray into this land, I felt affection for this place my grandparents left. The scenery was still striking. The fields, ribboned with spring green, looked like strips of mint ice cream. All that I'd learned over these journeys complicated the fondness I felt for the lush beauty of this land, knowing it belied a dark history and the remains of so many murdered relatives. Layers of silence like seams in a mine protected the killers and suppressed the crimes until they beggared belief.

Up front, a subdued Sam chatted with Derek in Polish. We reached his old turf, where he once knew every bend in the road. But so much construction had taken place. Besides the rise of new homes and commercial buildings, new roads spliced familiar farms. Sam's mental map predated the additions, obscuring the remaining houses and barns built with Rakowski lumber.

We crossed a road that Sam thought was our turn, but he did not tell Derek until we were well past it. The van pulled an awkward three-point turn. Then it happened again. Sam made a hand gesture for Derek to turn after it was too late. Another U-turn. A little farther along, Sam said, "*Prawo, prawo,*" meaning turn right. Then he said, "I mean *lewo, lewo,*" meaning left. Derek nudged to the edge of the road, which had no shoulder and a steep drop. He turned off the music and took a deep breath.

By old habit, I had expected the wily Sam from the early trips with his uncanny sense of direction and street smarts to find the Sodo farm. It wasn't really fair, in fact, to expect him to remember sixteen years after our last visit how to find the place.

Sam had high expectations for himself too. He was growing frustrated. "Forget about it," he said. "Let's give it up."

"No," I said. "We'll find it."

We pulled into a drive that Sam thought he recognized. A thick metal gate blocked the drive.

"This isn't it, Sam," I said. "They never had anything like that. Maybe Gosia can help. She can go and ask for directions." I handed her a photo of Sodo.

Before Sam could protest, Gosia jumped out and went to the gate. She raised her voice to be heard by a man standing at the gate over the cacophonous dogs. She showed the photo. The man frowned and peered into the car. He said he did not know, and why did we want to see him anyway?

"We should give it up," Sam said again. It was so unlike him, I thought. His cold must be really bad.

At the next stop, there was no gate. Gosia showed the picture to an old woman and then rushed back to the car. The woman wanted to talk to Sam.

Sam tottered out, looking his age. But when he started talking with the woman, he straightened up. He came alive. They embraced. She put her head on his shoulder. He stayed close.

"Do you see how he talks to people?" I said to my husband. "He's like a different person over here."

Lowering his window and raising his camera, Sammy said, "Let me get it." The shutter clicked away. The images captured the intimacy.

Several minutes passed. They continued talking. Sam was slow to leave her.

Gosia said the woman had just lost her husband and that he was the man in the picture she showed him.

"Oh, wow," I said. "That's Sodo's widow. Let's go." I hopped out with my recorder and trotted over to listen. Gosia joined me.

Sam was telling the woman that he had been to the Sodo farm several times, and the people killed there were his cousins.

She nodded. Then she said, "You see, they should be alive, all the people there. But they did this. They killed them all."

I could hardly believe my ears. We only heard this regret about Jews from rescuers.

Back in the car, Sam was energized. He had tenderly comforted the widow of Sodo, who had died at age eighty-three of lung cancer. He had made a connection. She remembered him and his family. Suddenly, the trip was worthwhile.

I said, "I thought when we first saw Sodo in 1991, he was living on the farm."

Sam said, "I know, but she said they lived here since the '60s."

No wonder, I thought, that his niece was surprised to see

him in the farmyard that day talking to the film crew. Sodo had
arranged the on-site interview without telling his niece and
family who lived there.

So many secrets here.

With the Sodo widow's good directions, the driver headed
straight to the family farm. We pulled up, but Sam did not recognize it. "No, no. This isn't the place," he said. "I've been here
before."

Gosia jumped out and showed the photo of Sodo to a
woman standing in the front yard. She said that indeed the
man in the photo was her uncle and she was Danuta Sodo
Ogórek. She came to Sam's window and peered in. "I know
Pan Rakowski. He has been here many times before."

"Sam, it's her. We found her," I said. "It's the woman with
the son from before!" I prodded.

Sam climbed out and they embraced. She invited us into
the new house that she and her husband had built where the
driveway used to be. That change must have confused Sam.

Over tea and cookies, she recalled our previous visits. I had
not seen her in twenty years, but we soon were chatting like old
friends.

"I remember the shock on your face when your uncle was
being interviewed," I said, smiling.

Her eyes twinkled. "I remember," she said. "I remember
everything, and I remember you."

I introduced my husband and got her permission for him
to take photos.

We talked about our first visit when Sodo, the soulful man we had found in the farmyard that first day, had said what happened on the farm was "a tragedy for your family and for mine."

"He didn't even live here, so I didn't know why my uncle was here," she said, sounding angry. I asked Danuta why he had been secretive. She shrugged and looked away. She said it did not matter now.

I asked, with Gosia's translation help, how the Dulas came to hide here.

She said her grandfather used to transport materials for the Dulas' textile store.

"They were kind of friends," she said.

"A very brave man," Sammy said.

"No one was prosecuted, right?" I asked, remembering that Majdecki said there was an investigation. Danuta said she did not know.

Cousin Sam turned to Gosia and explained in English, "That's a big story here. They were hiding my family for eighteen months, and they were killed and buried in the cellar there. I dug out some remains and took them in a suitcase to America."

I asked Danuta, "When you were young in school, people said you hid the Jews, right?"

Sam interrupted, "No, she didn't say that. She said they were laughing at her."

I turned to him and said gently, "Sam, why don't we let her answer? I want to hear what she remembers."

Danuta said, "When I was a child in school, other children told me that in my garden, there were Jews in the ground. Jews in the garden. They were killed and now they are in the ground." She came home and asked her father about the taunts. "He told me they were hiding there, but, 'No, they are not here anymore. They got taken away from the garden. And I will tell you the whole story when you are older.' But he never said more about it." Her mother died from illness when she was nine, and her father died when she was eighteen.

Danuta assumed that her relatives were protecting her from a truth too ugly to share with a child. Her father never told her the names of the people who had hidden there. So when schoolchildren called her Dula, she did not know it was the name of the dead Jews. Her father told her only that the family had two daughters and a son.

"Dad told me that he had a crush on one of the girls."

Her grandfather, Kazimierz Sodo, had built a place she described as a "dungeon under straw" where the Dulas hid from the fall of 1942 to the spring of 1944. "Grandma cooked in big kettles and took food out to them at night."

When neighbors came to the house, they'd ask her, "Why are you cooking so much food?"

Her grandmother would say, "I want to have food for a long time." During the war, when no one had anything extra, that was suspicious.

"When the front was coming, and liberation was close, the Dulas started going out at night to breathe some fresh air,"

Danuta said. "It is sad to say, but our neighbors blew the whistle on them."

She described the attackers as Polish partisans. Of all the people we had talked with over the years, only the rescuers—the Sodos, the Pabises, and the daughter of Radziszewski—along with Augustyn Wacław, the former farmers' partisan leader, would say so out loud. By doing so, they defied the enduring code of silence among Poles.

Danuta volunteered, "We all know that these killers were not Germans. My dad told me that they beat Grandpa Kazimierz really hard. After they killed the people, they made him dig the pit and put the bodies in the ground. They threw him in this pit on top of the bodies and threatened to bury him alive."

As a result, Danuta's grandfather suffered "a big psychological shock. After this, he never snapped out of it. He died very soon."

Danuta's detailed knowledge of the events resulted from conversations she had with her uncle after Sam brought the film crew in 1997. She pieced together memories from remarks her father had made.

He rarely brought it up, she said, because villagers looked down on her family. Her father tried to shield her, but the village's ire did not diminish over time. "They were angry at my grandmother, my grandfather, and my parents," Danuta said. "They accused us of putting the whole village in danger" of German reprisals if they found the hiding Jews.

How had the village reacted to the film crew?

Neighbors still gossiped about it decades later, she said. Every time the Sodo Ogóreks bought a tractor or built anything, neighbors said the money came from gold left by the dead Jews or money from the Jews who had visited from America. That would be us.

"How awful for you," I said.

"I don't pay attention to them. I don't talk to them anyway," she said, turning to her husband. "My husband works construction now. I don't have to account for my money."

And how had this affected her son?

When Dominik was young, children made fun of him in school too. But after the visit with the film crew, Danuta said she talked a lot to Dominik about what had happened. "He was so proud! I remember he had a contest in school, and he wrote a paper about it," she said, including that Poles were the killers. "People did not believe him, even teachers."

She ignored the bullies and gossips. Her grandfather had acted in a way that made her proud and had, in the words of the interviewer with the film crew to her son, done something good. Her strong Catholic faith guided her. "I am a deeply believing person, and these things are important. It was obvious," she said. "These Jews, your family, they just wanted to live."

Her words made me shiver. No one else, including Sam's old friends and others we'd met, had said that. It was bad enough that so many Jews had huddled in dirt caverns, in sheds, under a barn, behind a stove, and still did not survive. But we had seen again and again a big shrug from those who remained here for generations and took these wholesale murders in stride.

I tried to swallow the lump in my throat.

Sam had been talking in Polish with Danuta's husband about the time he came in 2001 and the guys helped him dig out some of the Dulas' bones.

She and her husband looked at him with tenderness like he was a treasured relative.

Danuta smiled. "I was asking people about him, wondering if they knew how Mr. Sam was doing. I'm glad to see him."

The warmth in Danuta's kitchen, rooted in carnage from more than seventy years before, flowed from the way her uncle had welcomed us on the first visit. Sodo's sincerity and Sam's gratitude for his family's efforts helped forge a bond that outlived Sodo. Danuta saw the importance of facing the history, however grim, of what had happened on her farm. She had bonded with us in defiance of those who tried to shame her family for acts of selflessness.

The community had shunned her family, not only punishing her grandparents for trying to save five lives but holding a grudge against them for three generations. She brushed it off. It said more about them than her family, she said.

Danuta and her husband lived on this property with the ever-present reminder of the Dulas' graves. In fact, they built the house where it was because of the location of the graves.

She said they had wanted to put some marker at the grave

site, but Cousin Sam thought it might draw vandals. "Mr. Sam said we shouldn't do anything or build anything, just keep them as a reminder of what happened."

Sam nodded slowly.

Soon, it was time to leave. Sam said, "I'll meet you in the car."

He knew where we were going.

In a cold drizzle, Danuta led my husband and me across the farmyard. She walked with a halting gait from chronic back pain, the result of a lifetime of grueling farm work. She led us to a raised mound of soil framed by fruit trees blooming in the mist. The tree trunks were painted white, a local agricultural practice for warding off pests. They looked like white pillars, thin sentries guarding the graves.

The burial site took me by surprise. I thought the place would be more familiar, but the farm was always changing. The first time here, it had been curtained off by drying tobacco leaves, a crop not grown here in years.

I scoured the ground for a small stone to place on the graves in the Jewish tradition. I found only some clots of hardened mud. They would have to do. Bowing my head, I shot my husband an apologetic look for this stark introduction to Poland. He rummaged in his pockets and found a yarmulke to cover his head. We murmured together, "*Yitgadal v'yitkadash sh'mei raba*," from the Kaddish, the Jewish prayer for the dead. Tears choked my chant. I glanced back at Danuta. She smiled warmly. She nodded.

The drizzle turned into a steady rain. I knew Sam was in

the car waiting, probably impatiently. His emotions about this place were in check. He had already paid proper tribute and had gone out of his way, risking legal trouble by removing bones from the country. He was secure in the knowledge he had done right by the memory of these murdered cousins.

Danuta walked Sammy and me to the van. I turned to her. "Tell me. What do you think of Sam coming back here so many times? And I've come back a lot too. Do you find it strange?"

Defiance shone in her coffee-colored eyes. She declared, "Of course you come back. Why wouldn't you come back? Your people are here."

I shivered. No longer was I a tagalong or bystander. This land, these stories, were part of me now.

---

I could not help but try one more time to see if Sam's presence might be persuasive with someone very likely to have knowledge of Hena's fate.

We parked outside Guca's old house, a brick split-level that no longer stood out from others on the street. We knocked, but no one came to the door until Andrzej Anielski, the physician married to Guca's older daughter, finally answered. He recognized Sam and invited us in. The house had lost the gloss I remembered. Some showcases containing cut glass goblets and tchotchkes remained, but the grandeur was gone, leaving the stale feel of an elderly person's home.

Guca had died seven years ago at the age of ninety-eight,

said the son-in-law. Guca's daughter, our host's wife, Janina, had died two years ago. Their daughter, Monika, the one who had wowed me with her Beatles collection so many years before, was a local schoolteacher and still lived at home.

Our translator, Gosia, had gone on a scouting mission in search of Guca's other daughter, knocking on the outside door to the other apartment in the house and asking neighbors on the street to tell her that Sam was here.

Andrzej said his sister-in-law Maria probably went to the hairdresser; she was not answering her cell phone.

Even though Sam was sitting there, I asked Andrzej what the family thought of his making so many visits.

"He was a friend of my father-in-law. They had a business before the war. They were friends, my father-in-law, Wojciech Guca, and Mr. Samuel. He was always happy to see Mr. Samuel. They had common memories."

"Do you know what happened to the lumberyard?"

Andrzej said, "My father-in-law told me that during the war, Germans took away all the wood." Shortly afterward, the government seized the entire business from Guca.

Sam asked Andrzej where he came from originally. He said a town not far away, Skalbmierz.

Sam's cold and his advanced age melted away, spurred by memories of his thriving family business. "We had a lumber-yard there. Near the train station."

Andrzej said, "Oh, I know. It is not far away, about ten kilometers from here. But there are no more trains in Skalbmierz."

Sam asked what had become of the sugar factory. Now it was a shopping center.

Gosia, meanwhile, was going down a list of contacts with phone numbers from previous visits. She phoned the daughter-in-law of Majdecki, who still lived in the house near the Sodos' where visited Sam's table. She told Gosia that she remembered Samuel Rakowski very well. She said she was not feeling well and was not up for a visit from us. She added, "You know it's a funny coincidence, but we have Mr. Samuel's old dinner table."

Just then, in walked Maria, the daughter who years ago had greeted Sam in her blazing red dress. This woman of eighty-eight had painted her lips bright pink and had her buttery blond hair freshly coiffed. She swept into the room out of breath.

"What, were you shopping or in church?" Sam asked, his eyes twinkling and his face filling with color. "I always want to see you when I come to town," he said.

My jaw dropped. He was flirting.

Maria said, "I went to the hairdresser, but I saw through the window that someone was knocking on my door so I came here." Then she turned her head away from my husband's camera aimed at her and Sam. "But I do not like photos."

Gosia, with no prompting, told her she looked great. She told Maria that Sam had revealed that he had a crush on her when he was fourteen years old.

In response, Maria turned full coquette. "It was him?" she

asked, as if she were surprised. "I remember there were two boys, Rakowski and the other one, what was his name?"

Sam said, "He was Sam Banach, and he was three years younger than me."

Maria said, "Yes, Banach. I remember you were cousins. But are you sure you were in love with me? Because I remember only Banach offering to marry me. And my uncle really wanted me to marry that Banach boy. Is he still alive?"

I burst out laughing. She was teasing Sam, dissing him in favor of his very handsome late cousin. It was like a scene from a high school reunion in which grads totally reimagine the romantic histories of classmates. Of course, seismic events back then made none of what she was saying remotely possible. But how wonderful for Sam—who had been an onlooker everywhere else he lived, in Israel, Ohio, and Florida, watching others enjoy reunions—to hark back to routines that had been wrested away and replaced by reunions of members of concentration camps.

Sitting on a couch together, they shared youthful memories from back when Sam and his father spent a lot of time in Maria's house in Zagórzyce. Maria's family lived with her aunt and uncle. The uncle was Sam's father's business partner in the timber business, Guca's brother-in-law. Sam had visited that house many times. It was located doors away from where the Rożeńek family later hid. In fact, Maria had played with a girl in that house during the war. They used to giggle, Maria had previously told Sam, about a secret she was not allowed to tell. In all the visits to the house where we were now, Sam had begged for more clues to the whereabouts of the surviving Hena, to no avail.

Now Sam, just as I suspected, despite all his claims of having given up on finding out about Hena, popped the question: "Do you know Radziszewski from Zagórzyce?"

"No. I can't remember Radziszewski from Zagórzyce," Maria said of the family in whose house she used to play as a girl.

For some reason, she chose not only to say nothing further than before, but also to snatch back the one helpful memory she had previously shared. "I never said I was giggling with the daughter in that house," she said. She turned and snapped at my husband. "Please tell him that I am too old for photos, and when somebody is taking photos of me, I look horrible!"

Gosia protested, "But you look great."

Maria's mood shifted. "I got it from my father. In my family, we live a long time. When my father died, he looked so good."

"Do you remember your father's reaction when Sam came back again and again?"

She beamed at Sam. "They were good friends. Even now, when I heard that you are here, I said to the hairdresser to hurry up because I want to meet you."

I tried to make sense of Maria's reaction. She was clearly eager to see Sam, but even at this advanced age, she would not acknowledge what she had previously said about a wartime playdate.

Heading away from the Gucas' house, I realized that the

family never acknowledged Sam's frustration with their refusal to help him find Hena. He felt he had pushed them hard or as much as he could without fraying a fraught relationship. Why not help the prince of the city find his lost cousin? Did they really not remember, did they not care, or was the taboo on such subjects stronger than anything, even empathy for an old man? What did they have to lose?

I would later learn that the dynamic we observed in this village was quite pervasive. Something referred to as a "conspiracy of silence" regarding Polish-Jewish relations under communism has erected an impenetrable wall of memory resulting from the traumatic events and the sustained communist suppression of the discussion.[8] Talking about it was not an option.

Put another way by an ethnographer in Poland familiar with the facts, "They might want to help, but their primary instinct will be to protect their own community. The fact that some of them started talking and then stopped makes me think that there might be some sort of self-regulating spoken or unspoken solidarity that favors silence, rather than testimony. As they say in ethnographic research, the 'source' is half-open."[9]

In Kraków, we ate an early dinner with Sam, who was scheduled to speak to hundreds of attendees of the March of the Living that night at Plaszów, his first concentration camp. His deep cough was concerning, and I urged him to rest and skip his speech. "Oh no," he said. "I can't do that. I am an eyewitness. They need to hear from me."

Sammy and I were too tired to move. I had already seen

Plaszów with Sam. We returned to our hotel where I saw an email from Sam's wife, Bilha, home in Florida, written on their shared account. Bilha was worried about Sam's bronchitis. "I hate Poland!" she wrote in an email she knew Sam would read. "It is like a magnet for him, and it is too much for his health."

I replied, "His cold is getting better. We had a good day, meeting with some really good people. You are right, the magnet is strong!"

Reflecting on the day, I marveled at the references locals were making to potential romances between Poles and Jews in the war era, as if they forgot that such relationships were taboo back then and not exactly welcomed since. But Guca's daughter Maria had flirted unabashedly with Sam on earlier trips, and that very day, she had needled him with the boast that her uncle wanted her to marry not Sam but his cousin. Perhaps this fiction was a way of seeming accepting of Jews. Danuta said her father had a crush on one of the hidden Dula daughters. The third had come from Mrs. Luszczyńska, formerly Radziszewska, who said her father wrote to her when she was in Germany naming a Jew, David, he was hiding as a possible suitor for her. None of this jibed with the Kazimierza city clerk's description of how impossible life would be locally for anyone in a mixed marriage. After the Jews were gone, did the remaining monoculture muse about the prospect of romance with Jews, still clearly forbidden, as something exotic?

The best result of the trip was Danuta connecting me with her son, Dominik. He had left the farm life for university and become an engineer. An aluminum foundry in eastern Poland hired him, and he moved some distance from his family. I got in touch with him by email, and he sent a warm note, saying he remembered meeting me from the time the film crew came to the farm when he was a boy. He said he was happy to be in contact and very proud of his family for their efforts to save the Dulas.

When he was young, he wrote, after learning what happened to the Dula family, he tried to find out more details about their murders.

"But I had a big problem finding information," he said, despite looking at sources on the internet and in records and books. "It was a taboo topic in Poland, and nobody spoke about it officially for many years. For me it is very important not to forget about it, even though the history is very tragic," he wrote. "Everyone close to me knows this history," he said. "I would like to keep it in my memory."

I told him how sorry we were that his family had suffered for trying to save my relatives.

"I personally remember only one situation when children bothered me and laughed, but my mum had more of these situations," he said. "And my grandfather had really big troubles over many years. People from our village had great regret that he dared to help." Dominik said, "The murderers who killed your family and also killed my great-grandfather" the shock his great-grandfather suffered led to his early death—"were judged after the war and sentenced to death, but after a few years, they left the prison because Poland announced amnesty."

This was a revelation. Majdecki had made a passing reference to prosecutions, but this was far more definite.

Dominik also said he believed the stigma his family had suffered was ebbing. Times had changed, he said. "In my opinion people think differently now, and they understand more."

I hoped that was true.

Two views of the rich, fertile land that conceals many secrets.

# 12

# Fake Partisans

Sam was not the only survivor who regularly returned to Kazimierza Wielka, reminding locals of their bygone Jewish population. Ray Fishler was a daring prisoner in Plaszów who had successfully bluffed about having the skills to produce Nazi uniforms. It helped him survive, the only one of the six children in his family. Like Sam, after building a life and business in the United States, Ray liked to return regularly to his hometown.

Ray and Sam shared a resilient optimism but processed their experiences differently. Ray was like a poet, remembering color, sounds, and smells. Sam worked through his memories like an engineer, focusing on action, like jumping in line with the gentile Poles on the death march.

Ray recalled a time when his packed cattle car stopped at a railroad crossing. He peered out at a Polish couple walking arm in arm, enjoying a lovely spring day. "I thought, *How can this be? Life is going on as usual for other people.*"

Ray told that story when he and Sam and their wives attended a reunion in 1995 at Sachsenhausen, Sam's last concentration camp. Sam had joked when we were making arrangements for that trip that any hotel we stayed in would be a step up from his first time in the city.

I'd arrived at the Sachsenhausen reunion to find Sam and Bilha at a huge reception of prisoners from across Europe. Sam greeted me, saying, "I'm glad you are here." Then he took off schmoozing from table to table. The atmosphere resembled a reunion of schoolmates or soldiers. But the shared experience of this assembly was one of surviving internment after being forced together at gunpoint.

The depth of Ray and Sam's friendship drew from their shared love of their hometown. Ray returned regularly to Kazimierza and made a deep impression on a local pensioner named Tadeusz Kozioł. From meetings with Ray, Kozioł became so curious about the history of local Jews that he wrote a locally published book in 2017 on the "martyrology and the Holocaust" of the Jews in and around Kazimierza Wielka.[1]

Kozioł had interviewed elderly area residents who remembered when the Jewish population was persecuted and destroyed. A month after we returned from Poland, Dominik sent me the sixty-three-page book, which included fresh information about what happened on his family farm. I started at the Polish text, eager to understand it.

Psychologists, anthropologists, and sociologists have studied the reliability of memory and selective recall and how trauma affects it. Historians long rejected eyewitness and survivor accounts for their subjectivity unless they could be corroborated. But journalism and courts routinely rely on firsthand witness accounts, with corroboration, as sufficient to imprison suspects and destroy reputations. In a local landscape where little official interest had been shown about these historical events, Kozioł took on an outsized role. Only Kozioł was interviewing aging eyewitnesses to the massacre of the Dulas and doing it as a trusted insider. His accounts and assessments came without the rigor or objectivity of scholarship but mattered as pieces of a puzzle that was far from complete.

I immediately sent Kozioł's book to Sam. He gobbled it up in one sitting.

On a phone call, I asked, "What does it say, Sam?"

"There are stories about what happened to some people, but I already knew about it. And they mention my house is the last Jewish house still standing there."

"Does it talk about the Dulas?"

"Nothing new. We know all this," he said once again.

I had to know for sure. Sam, now ninety-two, increasingly swatted away new accounts I shared only to take a different tack later.

The next day, my cell phone rang. I answered and he switched to FaceTime, providing visual cues for better hearing. "It's interesting what he has here," he said, swiveling in his desk chair, before a wall full of historic photos of him and family members in Poland. "We didn't know some of this. He has a guy saying that the Polish police came by after the killings and removed the bodies from the grave."

"So there was an investigation of some sort," I said, "which matches what Dominik said. He learned there were prosecutions, but the killers later got amnesty."

I added that I was paying someone to translate the book.

"I read it already," he said.

"I know," I chuckled. "But I need to know what it says."

Fortunately, over the years through Boston's academic community and beyond, I had built some Polish-speaking connections, including a woman who wound up living two blocks from me in Cambridge, who coincidentally had handled my International Committee of the Red Cross search request for Hena decades ago. Regina Swadzka, a Polish-born career employee of the ICRC, had ultimately sent the letter of regret that their researchers had been unable to turn up a trace of Hena. Regina had spent her career as a globe-trotting trainer of aid workers operating in the world's hottest conflict zones. She introduced me to her Polish-born son, who had a strong knowledge of English after attending high school in Massachusetts and university in Canada. He also had keen interests in Jewish history and the Holocaust in Poland. I hired him to help with Kozioł's book.

Przemek Swadzka dug in and reacted with some emotion. "It is quite difficult because their Polish is archaic, the language of old country people, and also what they are saying is terrible. I know this history well, but reading it while I am in this country is something, I can tell you."

Kozioł was not an academic or formal researcher, simply someone who was curious about the history of his hometown and saw time running out on the chance to learn from locals with eyewitness accounts of the destruction of the Jewish population in the area. Kozioł acknowledged that his work was "fragmentary and deals only with a few factors of very complex aspects of Jewish society." But, he wrote, "These are the last moments to complete this work in my own capacities and means."[2]

His efforts to record details of what happened to the Jews in Kazimierza are an important addition to the historical record of my family's hometown. He reported that based on the local Jewish community's tabulation—one that Sam was involved in as the keeper of lists at the time—the Jewish population in 1942 was 530. Taking survivor testimonies and other reports into account, only twenty-two survived the war. The trains from Miechów carried 186 to Bełżec, and a week later, the Germans shot another 210 at Słonowice. Kozioł accounted for the killing of sixty-five others, leaving a gap of sixty-nine.[3]

His introduction, when he summarized thousands of years of Jewish history, was less precise and objective.

"After Jews arrived, they were followed with the stigma of being responsible for killing Christ fueled both by Catholic and Protestant circles, which did not improve their esteem in the eyes of the local population. That is why regularly their liberties were limited, and they have been prosecuted."

Kozioł went on to write, "There were many attempts to limit what they could be doing, with various outcomes and results." He quoted an area woman who said in a family memoir, "We got rid of Jews running bars and gave them to Catholics, but it was scary what followed! Each bar owner became a drunk, and they [the bars] have become even more immoral places, worse than when the Jews operated them."[4]

I called Sam and griped about how Kozioł framed the history of Jews in Poland.

"He excuses everything that happened because of the canard that Jews killed Christ," I said.

"This does not matter," Sam said.

"What do you mean?" I said. "Everyone reading this will believe him."

Sam replied, "Did you see in there he mentions my house and he describes where the synagogue and the mikvah were? And not only that, he talks about the stores along the main streets," Sam said. "He has a lot of facts about how we functioned as a community during the war and lists the businesses that used to be there."

"Yeah, that's good," I said. "But he seems pretty intent on whitewashing the role of Poles in the Holocaust."

Indeed, Kozioł wrote, "People often displayed very negative attitudes towards the Jewish community. The trigger was the Second World War and extreme anti-Semitic legislations introduced by the German occupier that led to the Holocaust-extermination of Jewish society. Regrettably it took place on Polish soil, but I want to underline that it was not committed by Poles."[5]

His heavy-handed point of view made it difficult to determine whether he influenced his interviewees or if they were presenting the shared local perspective. But he repeatedly referred to members of the underground implicated in killing Jews as "fake partisans" or "so-called partisans."

Most important to me, however, were the accounts he offered from conversations with locals on the Dula slayings on the Sodo farm.

The fullest one came from a ninety-two-year-old man named Tadeusz Nowak, who said that in May 1944, he had run away from a German forced-labor camp.

"We were billeted in Witowo, but often Germans were taking some of us to assist them in their activities (extermination). We worked the entire week; on Sundays we had permission to go home, but we had to be back on Monday morning. I ran away from there and I was hiding."[6]

He was sleeping at home when his aunt woke him up and said something was happening in the village. Shots had been fired. Fearing discovery as a runaway from the camp, he darted out and hid in a briar bush for the rest of the night. The next morning, he saw a neighbor pass by. He asked what happened. The neighbor told him Jews were shot at the Sodo farm. The neighbor said it was the Dulas, a Jewish family of five hiding there.

"In the night, some people came to the village and claimed to be partisans, took the family out of the barn and killed them: parents, two daughters and a son—five people—an entire family," Nowak told Kozioł.

Nowak said Polish police came to investigate and had the bodies removed from the graves and laid out in a field. Then the Polish police ordered the bodies returned to the "potato hole."

Nowak recalled that his younger brother used to go to that farm and the father would be measuring potato soup to take to the dogs, which drew his suspicions. The Jews had hidden in a bunker in the barn, and Nowak thought it was strange that in a densely populated village with houses built very close together, no one had noticed anything before.

Nowak immediately zeroed in on the robbery motive. The killers "probably were not gaining anything by doing it, because if this family had any money, they would not have kept it with them but with some trusted people, or they would have hidden it well," Nowak said.

"Those bandits who killed them claimed to be partisans, but it could not have been true because real partisans did not behave like that." Nowak went on to speculate about where the murderers came from, acknowledging they were Poles. "The killers for sure were from a neighboring village. How else would someone from far away know they were there?" He did not refer, as the Sodos had, to the fact that one of his fellow villagers had tipped off the killers to the Dulas' location.

But Nowak went on to say that some of the bandits after the war "got long prison sentences," but, he said, "nobody knows for what reasons." He added, "I cannot understand how one human can do that to another human, maybe a German, OK, he is the enemy, but a Polish to a Polish? Because while yes those people were Jewish, but they lived in Poland, we knew them, we were going to their stores in Kazimierza."

This was a rare acknowledgment that Jews in Poland were not "Poles of Jewish nationality." Their nationality, as Sam proudly has proclaimed, is Polish.

Kozioł also talked to Stefan "Wilk" (Wolf) Grudnia, age eighty-nine. He said he belonged to the underground peasant organization, the BCh, the same organization in which our interviewee Augustyn Wacław had held a leadership position. "One day I was going to Stradlice, the base of our group under the command of Stefan Biela," and he learned about the Dula murders. He said the people who had killed the Jews in hiding at the Sodo farm "were pretending to be partisans, but it is not true." Wilk, who like Nowak was interviewed in 2014, voiced a belief that clashed with the rising right-wing political narrative. "When I think now about those times, I realize that Poles could have done more for Jews."[7]

The author disagreed. "Some people accuse us, the Poles, of not doing enough to help to save Jews during the war," wrote Kozioł, who grew up after the war. "What else could we have done?" He said that Germans killed his wife's grandfather in another part of the country in 1943 for helping Jews. "Our lives, those of our families, neighbors, and even innocent bystanders...constantly were in danger." Kozioł acknowledged, however, that incidents of Poles killing Jews had been deeply suppressed, saying, "I know this history and I know people are quite reluctant to talk about it." He continued, "I do not know why, maybe some stupid jealousy. People more easily forget and forgave those who participated in killings and pogroms instead of those who endangered their lives to save others. But probably only Poles can act like that."[8]

Kozioł clearly struggled to come to terms with this history. His book made frequent references to "fake partisans" or "people who claimed to be partisans" while offering a window into local attitudes.

But it was Nowak's reference to our visits to the Sodo farm that jumped out at me. He told Kozioł that the Sodo family was rightly ostracized for endangering everyone in the village by hiding Jews. Nowak said, however, that he sympathized with the Sodo family because of the position that we outsiders had put them in when we showed up for a visit.

Nowak said, "About ten years ago, some Jews came over here and were asking about it, they took some photos and left, and this poor family is still buried there without any sign or a stone."[9]

How ironic, I thought, that Sam had come back to Kazimierza as a returning son only to be viewed as a Jew imposing on the Sodos. Nowak reasoned that we were supposed to somehow move the Dulas' remains after the Polish police had returned them to a mass grave. Why, if there were prosecutions, had nothing been done about exhuming and moving the remains?

This pretzel logic was stunning.

Despite Nowak's diss, his mentioning our presence made me smile. My own footsteps here had made an imprint.

Judy watching Sam reading Polish documents.

# 13

# Documented Evidence

Dominik sounded optimistic about Poland being ready to view its conduct during the Holocaust with clear eyes after the subject had been taboo for so long.

I had no delusions. It seemed like decades of suppression of facts and enduring self-interest of those who benefitted from Jewish property had sealed off this dark history.

During the time Dominik and I were corresponding, I'd found a reference to a sad chapter in American history that resonated with me. I came across a historical pamphlet written about Allen County, Ohio, where Indigenous Americans once flourished. "After the removal of the Shawnee Indians," started a line that jumped off the page at me. The phrasing belied the violence of that removal and the willingness of settlers in 1831 to rid the land of "those sanguinary savages."[1] The tribe's name in my hometown signaled something entirely different from that history. Shawnee was the name of the exclusive country club with the area's best golf course, a verdant landscape shaded by mature trees where a lot of business got sealed on the back nine. The history of the Shawnee was lost on this country club that excluded Jews and Blacks until the mid-1970s. Our family was one of the first Jewish families admitted. I did not want to join or swim on the team of a club that did not want me, but my parents decided we should try to fit in and perhaps help change minds.

Of course, our experience was not on the scale of a life-or-death calculus in Europe in the 1940s. But the memory of the Jews of Poland, though far more recent, and how many of them disappeared and at whose hands seemed to be as ephemeral as the Shawnee.

Perhaps my parents' attitude about joining Shawnee was similar to Dominik's hopefulness. After growing up picking cucumbers in a politically conservative hinterland, Dominik saw Poland on a positive trajectory. People like him were growing up, getting educated, moving to cities, and living more comfortably than on family farms. In the postcommunist era, the country had become prosperous, and Poles enjoyed freedom of movement throughout the European Union. He aligned those trends with hopes that Poles were becoming more broadminded, willing to face history in an open and forthright way.

He was encouraged by Kozioł's book addressing the fact that five murder victims were buried on his family's property. In his lifetime, the topic of the Dulas' fate had never come up for open discussion with neighbors or even with his parents until Sam and the film crew showed up to interview his great-uncle. Mystery still shrouded the question of whether anyone was ever held accountable for those murders.

I was struck by the gap of sixty-nine Jews in Kozioł's accounting of the fate of the local Jewish community in Kazimierza, which meant clearly there were more unreported murders of Jews and perhaps more untraced survivors like Hena.

The attitudes of Dominik and Przemek, who shared an expectation that these questions could be answered stirred my hopes of finding documented answers to what became of Hena and whether anyone had ever been held accountable for the murders of her family or the Dulas.

Przemek approached contemporary Polish attitudes with more skepticism. I chalked it up in personality and life experience. Dominik was younger, and after growing up in the countryside, became educated and moved into a professional job. Przemek was not surprised that Kozioł repeatedly questioned whether Polish partisans participated in killing Jews in hiding, in part because he was familiar with the revelations from his connections with the Jewish community in Warsaw and other organizations.

Przemek became motivated by the quest for Hena. He grabbed the baton and started setting up appointments with foundations and associations and submitting requests for documents. I hoped that more records were becoming accessible, with databases coming online promising new possibilities, since my repeated efforts over the years of knocking on doors of government offices, visiting courthouses and archives, and filing formal requests at all levels of government. I had worked through genealogy experts and local and international members of law enforcement, and I had queried academics around the world, not to mention working contacts in the area where Sam grew up. I welcomed Przemek's approach as a native and the tack he took toward seeking help from advocacy and community-based organizations.

Przemek fired off email requests, made calls, and showed up at offices from Warsaw to Wrocław in pursuit of files and leads. He followed procedures to get files from the IPN, which was in charge of vast archives, focusing on its goal to investigate crimes committed under totalitarian oppressors since World War II. [2]

Przemek pursued organizations like one devoted to finding and commemorating the "hundreds or even thousands of forgotten, unremembered graves of Holocaust victims in Polish towns and villages." The group also worked on "supporting local communities in coming to terms with the past and dealing with the difficult heritage of World War II."[3]

Their website language signaled the massive scale of the task they undertook and forecast the steep odds against this bid to track down one ghost survivor. Indeed, Przemek's hunt for Hena hit the now-familiar obstacles. Not long after he started, he wrote, "On the front of looking for traces of Hena, I am experiencing some difficulties." One organization that he expected to be open and helpful turned down his request. "They do not want to give me access to their database. They say they cannot do it. I do not expect to find her name in there, but knowing her date and place of birth is why I need to look in there. Of course, that takes longer."

His energetic drive salved my flagging hopes of ever tracking her down or learning whether anyone was held accountable for the Rożeńeks' murders.

Przemek had not been under any delusions about his country's posture toward this history of ordinary citizens and underground combatants killing Jews. But his pursuits coincided with a rising right-wing backlash against "anti-Polish" history, throwing additional obstacles into his path.

The national discussion of the part Poles played in the Holocaust had resurfaced and was quite topical. Przemek wrote, "The problem in Poland is that the majority of people, including the political elite (government and opposition) continue to support and sustain the mythology of 'good Poles/ Poland' and victimhood."

The PiS government, leveraging what critics have called the "politics of memory," was pumping up a narrative of false equivalence of wartime victimization of Poles and Jews, and wildly overstating the number of Jews saved by Poles, winning points with the party's rural political base.

That insistence on a Pollyanna view of Poland's wartime behavior toward Jews was up against a burgeoning body of academic scholarship and journalism relying on documented testimony and eyewitness accounts that had started early in the century with the revelations about Jedwabne.[4] Respected scholars who later became known as part of the new Polish school of Holocaust research, were revealing accounts of Polish complicity in the Holocaust that ranged from ordinary Poles denouncing—reporting the whereabouts of Jews in hiding to Germans, leading to their executions—or taking matters into their own hands and murdering Jews.[5] These authors and journalists persistently drew strong rebukes and criticism from the government, state-controlled media, and PiS supporters.

I discussed these news reports and sent lots of them by email to Sam in Florida. Our conversations would be indecipherable to anyone who was not so steeped in the latest news out of Poland. We spoke in terse shorthand. Sam was not only a news junkie; he was also able to read the Polish, Israeli, and U.S. press daily.

He noted the uptick in tributes by the government and its supporters to deify the Polish partisans as pure heroes of the war. That shift did not bode well for government openness to revealing records about incidents involving Polish crimes against Jews during the war.

Nonetheless, Przemek's on-the-ground sleuthing led to a breakthrough in 2017. Over the summer, momentum seemed to be building. I opened every email from him with anticipation I had not felt in years. I read his updates aloud to my husband. But I rarely forwarded them to Sam in Florida, fearing he'd throw cold water on my fragile optimism.

Przemek got a promising note from a foundation he had queried: the material he sought would be available soon. He had filed multiple requests and did not know which one was being fulfilled. Would it be about the murders of the Rożeneks, a trace of Hena's whereabouts, or material on the Dulas' murders? Two months passed. Finally, he received a huge electronic file.

"I have not had a chance to look at it yet, but it is here!" he emailed. Then he sent me the file, and I downloaded it— 276 pages of an official court case from the IPN.[6] The familiar names of Dula and Sodo were all over it, and I could see it contained the names of many defendants. I took a deep breath. At last it was clear that someone had indeed bothered to investigate and prosecute perpetrators for killing five adults in the Dula family.

I promptly dialed Sam in Florida. This guy born in 1924 had figured out email, the iPhone, and FaceTime. But this challenge was on another level. Getting him the file was the subject of multiple calls and emails. The following week, I saw him at the wedding of his granddaughter in San Francisco. I figured I'd show him a printout there, but once again, Sam showed his pragmatic resilience. He surprised me a few days before the trip.

"I read half of the file," he said. "Most of the information is not relevant."

By this time, I had come to expect Sam's habit of dismissing what I'd shared only for him to later change course and find value in the material. What once had stung like a parent's rejection now made me chuckle. Perhaps he needed a defense mechanism to brace against disappointment and loss after enduring so much of it. But even at his advanced age, he still showed boundless curiosity for muscling through obstacles.

Between wedding events in San Francisco, I lugged the thick file to Sam and Bilha's hotel room and watched Sam pore over the pages. The official stamps and docket listings were familiar to me from court cases I'd covered, but I could not decipher the Polish text. Sam flipped through pages, reading and nodding. I watched, eager for his decoding. "This is very interesting," he said. "We did not know all of this."

On the one hand, I could not imagine a case file this size that clearly centered on the Dula murders would not yield significant revelations. But Sam did not easily cede credit to me for adding to his findings about relatives in Poland, so his acknowledgment was big.

He saw references to ranking members of the AK underground group and others being charged, convicted, and sentenced to prison for killing the Dulas and others.

Sam turned and looked me sternly in the eye. "You are going to write about this, saying partisans killed these people? You know what's going on in Poland? They are not going to like this."

"But it's a court file," I said, ever the American journalist believing in official records and the legal protection they afforded to publications.

"Whatever, honey," he said. "This is not popular to say in Poland now."

"But, Sam, at least we have an official record of what

happened to one group of cousins, and that tells a lot of the story for the others."

I was boarding my flight home from San Francisco when Przemek emailed me the first translated portion of the file, the interrogation of Danuta's grandfather, Kazimierz Sodo, on July 7, 1950, six years after the Dulas were murdered.

The interrogation began with Sodo describing the sequence of events resulting in the Dula family hiding on his farm. First he met Kalman, whom Sodo apparently knew from the family store. In the autumn of 1942, Sodo said, he agreed to hide the family from the Germans in his house. A week later, Sodo drove his wagon to an agreed-upon location in Kazimierza and picked up the family. He took them to his house, where he had prepared a hiding place in his barn under the haystack. He testified that they lived there for a year and a half.

On May 3, 1944, Sodo testified, around midnight, a group of men armed with various weapons showed up at his house.

"One of them, I assume the chief of the group, demanded that I give up the hiding place of the Jewish family. I did not want to give them up because I was afraid they would be shot. After my refusal, the commandant ordered his men to hit me. Two of them started to hit me with sticks and rubber." Others in the group were searching his house, the barn, and the haystacks. "When the bandits realized that beating me and searching my house was not bringing results, one of them went to the village. When he came back, he went straight to the barn, leading the rest of the gunmen. They took me to the barn with them. After removing a few wooden planks, they ordered me to enter the hideout and move out all the Jews. I entered the hideout and told the Jews that they have been given up and now must come out."

I was reading this on my phone on the plane, crossing the American continent with my mind on the Sodo farm. How hard it must have been for Danuta's grandfather to enter that barn where he had sheltered and cared for these five people for eighteen months. Did he look into their eyes? Could he bear to do so, knowing they were doomed?

Sodo's testimony continued. "Outside the hideout, one of the bandits told one Jewish girl to give him her watch, which was on her wrist, and her ring, which he then put in his pocket. They ordered the Jews to walk in front of them toward the orchards.

"They took me along with the Jews. Once we reached the orchards, I was told to move to the side, while five men armed with handguns and machine guns approached the Jews and ordered them to turn their backs and put their hands in the air. Then they put their guns next to the heads of the Jews. Following the order, they shot. All the Jews fell on the ground face-first. They ordered me to bury them at this spot and remove all signs of blood.

"Afterward they came back to my house and ordered me to give them bags to take all of the Jewish belongings. Once they packed them up, they left. The next day I buried the bodies."

Asked by the interrogator if he knew anyone involved in

the killings, Sodo said he recognized one man who had held a gun to his head. The same man returned several times after the slayings to demand money and other valuables that he presumed Sodo had kept from the Dulas.

Some passages in the file settled old rumors we had heard around the Sodo farm. They revealed the name of the villager from whose house the attackers came and to whom they returned when their first search came up empty. It was a neighbor named Edward Kozioł, unrelated to Tadeusz Kozioł, who penned the book that referred to the slayings.

According to the file, "The investigation has revealed that it was he who informed his superiors that there was a Jewish family hiding at Sodo's in Chruszczyna Wielka where he was living and was native of. Also, not only has [Edward] Kozioł revealed the fact of his neighbor hiding the Dula family, but also took the KB [executive body ruling the partisan groups] to the farm, and finally revealed the exact hiding place in the barn, while he was aware of the fact that the purpose of finding this family was to kill them."

The court sentenced Edward Kozioł to seven years in prison for the role he played in ratting out the Dulas.

Just like the original discovery of the Dulas' graves, this remarkable cache of information about their murders stemmed from Sam mentioning his cousins' names to the owner of his old dining table. Both were byproducts of the search for Hena.

It came from pulling the thread of the case of the Rożeńeks, another family of Sam's maternal cousins, who were also killed in the spring of 1944 on the Radziszewski farm a few hamlets away. Chasing Hena had led—almost by happenstance—to the Sodo farmyard. It all started with Sam pressing Stefan to say more about the lost cousin who got away from the murder scene of her family.

Up to this point, we had Majdecki saying someone was prosecuted in the Dulas' case and Kozioł's book referring to Polish police appearing on the scene the morning after the shootings. But the Sodo family, who the villagers had shamed for generations for hiding the Dulas, had seemed to think it was an event that few knew about and hardly remembered.

But it turned out that the Dulas' murders on May 3, 1944, were probed in connection with a total of twenty victims in a wide-ranging investigation from 1950 to 1954 that resulted in charges against twenty men, some of them high-ranking members of Polish military underground organizations. As I read the files, I did not find any reference to the Rożeńeks, but the timeline and similarity of modus operandi made me suspicious of some overlap.

Eleven years had passed since I learned from correspondence with the Polish Academy of Sciences professor Dariusz Libionka, an historian and editor in chief of the Holocaust studies journal *Zagłada Żydów*, that he had researched incidents of partisans prosecuted for killing Jews in Lublin and that separate research of similar cases had been done by other academics in incidents in the region around Kazimierza.[7]

I wrote to him in 2006 at the suggestion of Yehuda Bauer, a

world-renowned Holocaust expert, author, and longtime advisor to Yad Vashem in Israel who said that no one had done a major study of the "many accounts of AK murders of Jews. The AK was composed of different groups; sometimes these were friendly to Jews," especially the groups aligned with socialist underground groups, and sometimes with the peasant underground, he said in an email. "Things changed in 1943 when the extreme radical NSZ, an antisemitic fascist group, joined the AK. They killed Jews wherever they could, and some of these crimes were later committed by them in the name of the AK."[8]

He connected me to Barbara Engelking-Boni at the Polish Center for Holocaust Research, who said in an email that after the war, "there were hundreds of cases of Poles murdering Jews in hiding. There were hundreds of trials on Poles disclosing to Germans (more frequently) or murdering Jews. Some of them were sentenced to death. There were also thousands of trials against Poles collaborating with Germans."[9]

Libionka was the only one with specific knowledge about the area around Kazimierza Wielka. "It is not easy to discover the identity of the murderers," he wrote. He also said he knew of similar cases elsewhere. "Unfortunately," he said grimly, "I have knowledge about the Kraków district," referring to the area of our concern.[10]

The article Libionka had completed in 2005 was based on "an analysis of hitherto unused trial records related to the so-called August Decree" of 1944,[11] which was one of the world's first laws on liability for crimes of World War II used against

Germans and their collaborators. The August Decree was the legal rubric under which members of an alphabet soup of partisan organizations were prosecuted,[12] some of them politically motivated by the communist government in the postwar years in an effort to settle scores against underground groups that had been allied with or carrying out missions in support of the Germans.

Now I had a case file on the five Dulas with charges against twenty men linked to at least twenty murders, including the five Dulas and nine Ptasniks and Czosneks. The defendants belonged to various bands of partisans in the Polish underground and were charged with carrying out the organized killings on May 3 and May 4, 1944, in Chruszczyna Wielka and the nearby hamlet of Bełzów (the scene Sam had visited in 2001 with the Israeli son of a Ptasnik). And some of the same defendants were accused of "assassinating" two members of a communist underground group. That offense might well have motivated the entire case. At the time, the communist government was pursuing former partisans belonging to right-wing bands in the Polish underground, using their killing of Jews as an excuse.

The case file even included what might be considered a primer on the various partisan organizations, their cooperation, and conflicts during the war in that part of the country. According to the prosecutors, by the summer of 1943, the right-wing factions of the BCh and several smaller underground organizations were all put under the command of the AK. The executive body of those groups, the records showed, was also participating in numerous killings of operatives in left-wing underground organizations as well as of Polish citizens of Jewish nationality.

Over the weeks that followed, Przemek translated the file in batches, sending me emails both revealing and upsetting, which I read on my subway ride home from Boston to Cambridge. Around me, other riders were playing games or listening to music on their phones. I was the one grimacing, reading about grisly scenes, and feeling like I was rubbernecking at the scene of a catastrophe.

The picture that emerged from the file was of a time late in the war when these underground soldiers were operating with impunity. The attacks were not staged by a few violent anti-Semites killing Jews to prevent reclamation of their businesses and homes after the war but by multiple teams of paramilitary members operating on a considerable scale. With soldiers from several different units using machine guns, according to the testimony, the attackers did not seem worried about alerting Germans to their presence, even though the Sodos and Pabises would be punished for generations by their neighbors for endangering them with their charity.

In interrogations, the dozens of suspects and witnesses used military references, describing setting up security perimeters and referring to the killings in terms of following orders from superiors. Many references were made to demanding money from the Poles who had hidden the families, stripping clothing from the bodies, and stealing jewelry and other goods.

The description of the Pabis farm killings was even more chilling than the massacre of the Dulas. The commander of one partisan unit, Slanisław Stasik, the rare defendant who admitted an active role, testified that "our band took part in one more liquidation action; it was in Bełzów, where nine persons of Jewish nationality were killed." Stasik testified to authorities that his team had assembled and he "finished distributing weapons to all members of our group." Then, he said, the commander told them "their mission was to go to the village and eliminate a Jewish robbers band, and that the objects that we will recover will serve the purposes of our organization." Ten of the partisans started walking toward the farm. Another ten underground soldiers from a different group joined them along the way. A third squad participated, riding in a horse-drawn carriage. "We surrounded the farm inhabited by an older woman who did not want to give up the Jews." A search of the property revealed ten frightened people hiding near the pigsty.

"They were taken out and placed next to a hole that was already there. We told them not to be frightened because they will not be killed, and not to run away because we are the Polish Army. We only demand to be given all the valuables which are needed for operations of the Polish Army." The leader of the operation, identified by his code name, then collected watches, rings, and money from the victims. "After the valuables were collected, the Jews realized what was going to happen. They started to talk among each other and then they started to run away." He testified that, "in the beginning, it was difficult to shoot at them because they mixed with members of our group. Once they passed us and entered an empty field, we were able to shoot at them, and we killed them all." The leader of the operation commanded the partisans to bring the bodies from the field "and place them in the hole where they had been hiding previously, and placed all the valuables and found objects on the carriage."

As a journalist, I have covered many criminal cases for decades. I logged hundreds of hours covering trials in state and federal courts that handled murders by several crime families in the Mafia, Asian organized crime, and drug gangs of many stripes. I also chronicled a court-martial of a U.S. Navy-enlisted man who killed his superior officer at sea and civilian murder trials that dealt with insanity defenses, including a John Hancock executive who killed his wife, then impaled her heart and lungs on a stick in the backyard. Every organized crime and gang defendant I encountered displayed ardent loyalty to their organization, sharing a strong sense of commitment and identity with that association. Even the Hancock executive seemed to think his station in business would provide protection from accountability. But once accused, defendants universally turned into amnesiacs regarding their own behavior, scarcely able to recall their own names, only their unwavering loyalty to their tribe.

I once described my career as a crime reporter as continually trying to understand the answer to the question, "How could they?" This Polish case, however, offered extraordinary denial of responsibility, including defendants who acknowledged they were in charge of a particular band of partisans yet nonetheless blamed underlings at the scene for giving the orders to kill.

For example, Slanisław Kozera testified that he was ordered by his commander to meet men under his command, all armed, near the Sodo farm, following a tip that fit their mission to look for Jews in hiding. Kozera said that after the hidden Jews were discovered, he turned to the head of another partisan group, "asking him what they planned to do with them, to which I received the answer that their orders were to eliminate them, i.e., to shoot them. To which I was unwilling to agree." He said he was not one of the shooters, "because I had only a revolver. The rest of my people went to the Jews and led them into the farmer's garden, after which shots were fired. Who gave the order to fire, I am not aware, and who directly shot the Jews, that I do not know."

To a man, none of the twenty charged in these immaculate executions saw anyone fire a shot. Nearly every defendant claimed they had been merely setting up a security perimeter around the property, conjuring an image of multiple guards with no one anywhere near the victims who somehow wound up dead.

Another Polish Holocaust scholar would later analyze these same documents and the testimony of Kozera, a member of the sabotage unit of the 106th Infantry Division of the AK in the Kraków district, and describe this form of testimony as "affective ignorance," a way of excusing the speaker from going into details of a crime.[13]

The same description applies, according to Professor Joanna Tokarska-Bakir, to the testimony in the case file I had from Edward Szczesny, who reassured the Ptasniks and Czosneks at the Pabis farm that "the Polish Army would not harm them as long as they surrendered their money... He denied having been in charge of the shooting and talks like a bystander who found himself on the scene by chance. Particularly telling are elements of cynically 'affective ignorance': 'out of interest, I went closer,' 'I asked whether the operation had been successful, and at which I received the answer that it had been successful,' 'shortly afterwards in the villages, I heard that some Jews had been killed in Bełzów. I went to tell this news to Commander Wojnar, and he was surprised.'"

Tokarska-Bakir goes on to say, "The average testimony of a perpetrator of the murders in Chruszczyna or Bełzów states that somewhere in the world a disconnection, interference in space-time occurred, and the testifier remembers nothing... He turns his eyes away, but cannot control them. A moment's distraction and the eyes are back where they began, The perpetrator attempts to reconcile their self-knowledge with their self-assessment: the effect is a deepening sense of disorientation... This was also the line taken by commanders, leaders of AK sabotage units, and Popular Security Guard commanders. After the war, many of them joined the regular Communist police force."[14]

Aha, I thought of Poremski as one of the people we had

approached who might have been nervous about other activities during the war that helping us with Hena might have shed light on.

The testimony painted a clear picture of the suspects' utter disregard of Jews as people. I understood that by 1944, the Polish population had been under German occupation for five years, longer than any other country Hitler victimized. And we knew from Tadeusz Kozioł's book that one of the elderly residents he interviewed had run away from a forced-labor camp for Poles where he said the internees had been forced to participate in the Germans' liquidation actions.

The Germans had brutalized and starved the non-Jewish Polish populace. From the start of the war in 1939, Polish intellectuals were rounded up and killed or sent to concentration camps. The Germans constantly looted businesses, seized livestock and crops from farmers across the country, and made no secret of regarding the Poles as not far above Jews on the ladder of *Untermenschen*. But reading the case file made me think that these underground members had a serious case of Stockholm syndrome, because they adopted the goals and even the methods of the Germans they had taken up arms to undermine.

The testimony also included references to a purported security threat posed by these stranded hunted Jews, finding a rationale for attacking them. One defendant claimed their unit's purpose was searching for Jews who were "responsible for oppressing the local population." Dehumanizing the victim is an old tactic. But in wartime Poland, these killers had an extra motive to act because murder enabled them to steal Jews' possessions and divide the spoils among themselves.

In this case, the Polish communist government at first took a harsh posture. In 1950 and 1951, the courts convicted twenty men of crimes related to the deaths of fourteen "Polish citizens of Jewish nationality who were oppressed by the occupier on a racial basis." Six of the suspects received two death sentences, one for killing Jews and another for the slayings of two left-wing activists and a member of a leftist band of partisans.

But no sentences, for life or for death, were ever carried out. After exhaustive state-funded appeals and heavy lobbying by political officials, the death sentences were reduced to twelve years, and many defendants were pardoned or released after much shorter terms. A few managed to postpone serving their sentences due to illness, one of them indefinitely.

Generally the partisans' appeals paralleled arguments I'd seen in the States—alleging they had been nowhere near the actual murder scene and had not participated in any wrongdoing. But the decidedly political flavor of the appeals—citing eagerness to help build a strong socialist republic and begging top party and government members for leniency—spoke to the political nature of the prosecutions. One defendant claimed to have harbored Soviet officers on his property during the war, while another professed—with no supporting evidence—that he had saved a family of Jews who made it safely to Palestine, and therefore he could not possibly have been engaged in an operation to kill other Jews. Another defendant facing two death sentences had a witness argue for leniency on his behalf in a blatant appeal to a communist judicial system that he had been defending area peasants from landowners belonging to the nobility. Yet another defendant appealed his death sentence on principled grounds, seeking clemency because of his social class background and "devotion to the Communist party and the ideology." During the war, he said, "he was a simple soldier fighting for liberation of his homeland from the German occupier." He never mentioned how that related to killing Jews.

In chopping years off the sentences of eight defendants, a court in 1958 acknowledged their special circumstances at the time of their crimes: the convicts "had no opportunity during the Occupation to learn about left-wing ideologies and to understand criminal activity."

Only one defendant admitted after indictment to the accusations and expressed remorse, which persuaded the court to halve his ten-year sentence. But others got equal breaks without acknowledging responsibility.

One case was in a class by itself. The defendant was Włodzimierz Bucki, whose underground moniker was Dym, meaning "smoke," which was apt because he did everything in his power to vaporize his presence at two scenes and charges that he was involved in the murders of fourteen people. Przemek had his work cut out for him following the long saga of Bucki's case from his original testimony through many pages of court records covering decades of appeals. A "soap opera," he called it.

When Bucki was arrested in March 1950, he was working as a shopkeeper in a small village and had joined the communist party. In his first interrogation in June 1950, he admitted that one of his unit's objectives was "the elimination of all Jews hiding in the region," and he acknowledged participating in the attacks on the Sodo and Pabis farms. He testified that he shared in the loot from the Pabis farm victims, namely by taking a pair of leather shoes. He was behind bars for nine months until his conviction the following January for participating in the murders of all fourteen Jews. He was sentenced to twelve years in prison.

Bucki proved to be a wily litigant. He was sentenced in 1951 but was allowed to defer serving his time due to falling ill with tuberculosis. He flooded the courts with letters from doctors and the sanatorium where he was being treated. His conviction was upheld in 1952. Six years later, when the Supreme Court reduced his sentence from twelve to eight years, he still had not set foot in prison, because every six months, he renewed his assertions that prison would threaten his fragile health. Further, he asked the court's indulgence because he had two small children. In 1959, Bucki changed course and asked for a pardon, admitting he had committed crimes but alleging that because he was a young man at the time, he was unaware that what he had done—participating in the murders of fourteen people—was wrong. He continued to cite his ill health. The regional court looked favorably on his request, noting the context of the times in which he committed his misdeeds and acknowledging that he had been a good citizen ever since. The ruling was sent to the general prosecutor's office in Warsaw. On January 20, 1960, the national prosecutor's office pardoned Bucki, and a court allowed his reprieve two months later.

But Bucki, who had not been jailed since his pretrial arrest, was not satisfied. He turned to maintaining for "reasons of honor and ethics" that his conviction and sentence should be vacated and his record scrubbed clean. Taking advantage of new laws enacted in the postcommunist era, he argued in 1995 that as a member of a Polish paramilitary organization operating in support of the independent Polish state, he never should have been charged, convicted, or sentenced at all. That contention worked. In 1997, the regional court annulled his conviction and directed that the government pay all court costs.

Later in 1997, only shortly after Danuta Sodo Ogórek and her son had seen the film crew and learned for certain that five adult Jews had been murdered on their farm, an appeals court handed Bucki a setback in his bid for an annulment. His request was sent back to the lower court for review. At that juncture, Bucki, in a now-familiar feint, declared he had no idea why he was on hand in May 1944 at the Sodo farm. He further asserted that he did not know there were Jews there. He said he heard shots coming from the buildings, despite the fact that no evidence had ever been presented that anyone was shot inside a building, and he blamed everything on his commander. Further, he stated that everything he had said in earlier testimony had been coerced by police under the former communist regime.

Bucki's appeals to expunge his record continued to June 1999, when the regional court dismissed his plea. In December 2004, his bid for annulment was again rejected. The buck stopped with that court, which found that while many partisan activities were aimed at supporting an independent Polish state, the actions attributed to Bucki—participating in the killing of fourteen people—"were a criminal abuse of the military nature of these organizations and their capabilities."

Neither was the court persuaded by Bucki's arguments that the partisans were motivated by reports that two Jews in the area had been stealing from local area residents. The court found that these executions "were carried out in two different places, on completely different people, families hiding from the Germans, who were shot without any reason." On top of that, the court ruled that once the partisans found the Jewish families in hiding, they executed them on the spot after making no attempt to find out who they were or whether they were guilty of any crime.

The appeals court in Kraków upheld that decision. But Bucki kept going.

In 2006, the man who for fifty-five years contended he was too ill to serve his sentence enjoyed enough health to press his case before the Supreme Court in Warsaw. But that final scheme was the end of the line. The high court ruled in December 2006 that it had found no new evidence on which to base an annulment of his record. The court was not persuaded by his assertions of torture or that other defendants had been coerced into falsifying information against him. It was just too late, the court ruled, saying, "This cannot be proven today," noting that by then, too many witnesses were dead. "Bucki does not deny his involvement in the killings, yet his intentions at those times remain unclear—in particular in Chruszczyna Wielka where a Jewish family has been executed," ruled the court.

By the time I was reading translations of these court records in 2017, that ruling from 2006 stood out as the voice of another judicial era in Poland. The PiS government was facing widespread criticism for taking a wrecking ball to the independent judiciary, which it has discredited as a collection of holdovers from the communist era.

In November 2017, a massive demonstration by hard-right nationalists played out on the streets of Warsaw. They shouted support for a "white Europe," "clean blood," and to "get the Jews out of power." One opinion piece on the protest was headlined, "Ninety Percent of Polish Jews Died in the Holocaust. So Why Are Poland's Nationalists Chanting 'Get the Jews Out of Power?'"[15]

Within months of that public outpouring, the Polish government enacted a law criminalizing any public speech that blames Poland or Poles for participating in the Holocaust. It came at a time of historical revisionism in neighboring Hungary, which actually allied with Germany during the war.

POLIN museum director Dariusz Stola linked the law to a Polish "obsession with innocence"—the nation's conviction that it is "morally blameless thanks to its resistance and widespread suffering, with millions killed in the war." Stola said Poland has nothing but its sense of innocence. "Poles lost the war. They lost a lot: family members, cities, libraries, churches, 20 percent of their territory and national independence. Little was left but their innocence," Stola said. "When you lose everything it's good to at least be innocent."[16]

While the law was under consideration, Polish authorities detained Princeton professor Jan Gross, the author of the *Neighbors* book about Jedwabne, during a visit to his native land on suspicion of slandering Poland. His high-profile detention was widely considered payback. Gross had rankled the Polish government with his hyperbole in 2016, stating in a German newspaper that "the Poles, for example, were indeed rightfully proud of their society's resistance against the Nazis, but in fact did kill more Jews than Germans during the war."[17] In response, the Polish government moved to strip Gross of the prestigious Order of Merit of the Republic of Poland that he'd been awarded in 1996 for opposing communism.

But Poland's 2018 law, rooted in its longstanding pique over newscasters and even President Barack Obama mistakenly referring to the Third Reich's killing factories in Poland as "Polish death camps," ignited a global diplomatic crisis. It drew widespread outcry from governments in the United States and Israel, and dismay from scholars around the world.

Michał Bilewicz, a Holocaust researcher at Warsaw University, said, "the new law aims to silence Polish historians, as it is obvious that this law would not be effective in sentencing anyone outside of the country."[18]

The uproar was so sustained that eventually the PiS government amended the law. It still penalizes public speech that deviates from the narrative of pure innocence, but violators no longer face up to three years in jail.

Stola said in 2016 that the policy was still a problem. "Poland was on the right side of this war, and Poland lost it to Hitler and then lost it to Stalin," Stola said. "We are not responsible for what happened seventy years ago, but we are responsible for what we do with this past today. And I think the right thing to do is to talk about it."[19]

Dominik Ogórek and wife, Kate. She sees the rationale for the mandated history law; he does not.

# 14

# No History Without Truth

Just months after the Holocaust memory law went into effect, Sammy and I landed in Poland to attend the wedding of our friends' son, who I'd known his whole life. We had roles to play: Sammy was playing guitar in the wedding band, and the groom's parents asked us to add something Jewish to the festivities.

On our way to the wedding by train from Wrocław, once again I thought of Hena. Had she settled somewhere on this bucolic landscape dotted with red tile roofs in former German territory? Maybe she was enjoying old age in obscurity.

The wedding venue itself spoke to a complicated history. It was set on a sprawling estate that German chancellor Otto von Bismarck gave as a reward in 1866 to Field Marshal Count Helmuth von Moltke for his role in winning the war against Austria that resulted in the creation of the modern German state.[1] Moltke famously devised modern methods of moving armies in the field, especially by train, leading to great military successes.

But the legacy of the family and the estate pivoted under his great-grandnephew, who used it as a place for plotting with confederates against Hitler. Their plans failed, and the Gestapo hanged Moltke in 1945 for treason. A son followed in his father's footsteps years later and renovated the property as the home of the Krzyżowa Foundation for Mutual Understanding in Europe, which invites groups of teens from Poland and Germany to learn together about democracy and human rights. Its purpose is to "inoculate" young people today against extremist ideology.

It was an inspired choice in 2018 for the union of bright young people eager to make the world better at a time when Poland was searching for its footing under a right-wing populist government. The Catholic ceremony was performed in a quaint church on the property. The bride had a Jewish grandfather, and the groom's parents suspected their family trees included Jews somewhere, and that may have motivated the request for us to add some Jewish flavor to the reception.

We chanted the blessing over the wine in Hebrew, wondering whether the well-traveled friends of the wedding couple would recognize the kiddush. Apparently not. Several young attendees came up to us afterward and said, "I like your song."

It would be almost impossible for Jewish culture or ritual to be familiar to these twentysomethings, having grown up in a homogeneous society generations removed from when Jews composed a significant minority. The Jews we saw depicted in Polish culture were Hasidim or nineteenth-century characters out of *Fiddler on the Roof.* Here we were, a blue-eyed couple wearing modern clothes, blending into the crowd, except for my husband. His shredding on electric guitar definitely stood out.

What did young people in Poland even know of Jews now? Politicians and media stories often depicted descendants of Polish Jews as greedy for seeking avenues to reclaim or get restitution for property seized under German occupation and kept by Poles. Negative cultural references abounded with few actual Jews around to test the stereotypes. The most obvious examples were the ubiquitous statuettes known to Poles as *żydki,* or little Jews. They filled tourist shops and kiosks, particularly the troll-like Orthodox rabbi figurines clutching a symbolic one-grosz coin or a bag of money. Poles had defended the *żydki* as portraying Jews as talismans for good fortune in money matters. But the appalling caricatures spoke to an enduring need to mock Jews even in absentia.

Before the wedding we had recovered from jet lag in Wrocław, and toured an exhibit at the only synagogue that survived the Holocaust, the historic White Stork, which had been rehabbed and reopened. We stayed at the Hotel Monopol, a landmark that had been exquisitely renovated, and now boasted a salt mine spa and gracious rooftop dining that I described in a travel piece for the *Boston Globe,* accompanied by Sammy's photographs. The hotel and the city itself hardly resembled the grim place Cousin Sam and I stayed in on the fateful trip in the 1990s when he gave up the Hena search.

The Wrocław we found in 2018 was a bustling college town. For the young people we met along the way, it was normal that everyone's grandparents or parents had been dislocated from somewhere else in 1945. Stalin had his way with the postwar map, booting the German population out of Breslau, and replacing them with Poles ejected from eastern territories.

Wrocław had a history of reviving itself in upstart ways. For decades, it had nurtured a vibrant underground music scene, from jazz to punk rock. We took it in, visiting a jazz club and then followed our ears to a hipster nightclub with a band-leader bringing up one talented soloist after another. It was a compelling scene that made us daydream about being regulars there.

Also intriguing was the city's history dating to the 1980s as home to a daring anti-communist underground movement. That rebellious spirit permeated the local arts scene in a way that was visible from the street level. Images of dwarfs symbolizing the Orange resistance to communism started as street graffiti. They evolved into pint-size metal sculptures that took on a whimsical air. The dwarfs multiplied until there were hundreds all over the city. Ferreting out these fine examples of political art had become a tourist's game, attracting visitors of all ages and origins.

The lively vibe fueled my hopes that Hena might have rebuilt a good life in this beautiful city on the Oder River. I had no fresh intel on Hena, and the mood trending out of Warsaw could not be more discouraging. Why would anyone pipe up now and share new revelations on wartime murders of Jews by Poles? At the time, the PiS government's idea of relenting in the face of international backlash to the new law was to remove the threat of jail time for violating it, leaving in place financial penalties for alleging Polish complicity in the Holocaust.

But we had other people to see, and after the wedding, we headed east by train to Kraków, which had turned into a vibrant tourist town. So much had changed. I could hardly believe it was the same place where a guy with a new-looking parka had stood out so starkly. Now visitors flocked there on promises of fairy-tale views of the towering Wawel Castle and people-watching in the Market Square, where we passed a lot of beery Brits engaged in the burgeoning pastime of stag pub crawls. Other vendors hawked handbills for welcome shots, strippers, and even VIP strip club access. We sidestepped those offers and stayed at a four-star hotel and dined on a spectacular Italian meal for half the price it would have cost in another major destination.

The next morning, we picked up a rental car and Gosia, our trusty translator, and headed into the countryside to visit Danuta and her son, Dominik.

Leaving the city in morning rush hour, Sammy's GPS issued instructions in English while Gosia's offered swishing Polish prompts. Sammy trusted hers, given its home court advantage. Before every turn he heard the directions in English and then asked Gosia if the Polish GPS agreed.

"You know it's just an algorithm," I piped up, laughing from the back seat.

On earlier trips, navigation guidance came from Sam following his nose. Sometimes his hunches and memories took him off the beaten path, leading to discoveries. A major one resulted in him finding the farm where Great-Aunt Frymet had been buried after her murder by a Polish policeman.

I later saw the place with Sam. I remember being taken aback by the squinty-eyed farmer. The fellow gestured toward the edge of his freshly planted field where a woman's body had been found in a shallow grave. Sam asked whether she was killed there or somewhere else. The man folded his arms across his chest and shrugged. He said he wasn't home at the time. A Polish policeman had long ago been convicted of her murder and died in jail. But the farmer seemed put out by our showing up to see the place where the body of a woman who happened to be a sister of Sam's father and my grandfather had been discarded in his field.

Gosia's GPS was saying *lewo* and *prawo*, reminding me of how Sam used to drive up to old guys in villages and voice those words in the form of a question. I smiled at the memory. I could feel his presence, and maybe at that moment, he was watching us, Wizard of Oz–style, via Google Earth.

We passed undulating fields of ripening rye and cabbage that looked ready for harvest. A wave of familiarity washed over me, and I thought of the generations of relatives who had lived here. My husband, whom I had not even met when I first started coming here, had bolstered my belief in the importance of returning, of showing up. He too was finding himself feeling somehow woven into this Polish tapestry regardless of how Jews had for so long been excluded from being considered part of the Polish diaspora.

"We were Poles for over a thousand years, but they still don't accept us," Sammy said. "In the years between the two wars, we were the leading songwriters, cinematographers, and poets. It's just such a loss for us and for the country."

Sammy's experience of getting shivers looking at road signs for places where his forebears had lived reminded me of my first trip with Cousin Sam when he said he got "electric shocks" at the sight of landmarks from childhood and the dark days that followed. He smiled in recognition again and again on those trips, recalling his footsteps from another era.

The identity Poland still conferred on him and our relatives as "Polish citizens of Jewish nationality," the legal reference that I had read over and over in the court documents, rankled me. Being Jewish was not a nationality. Our murdered relatives were not just visiting. After helping to build, nurture, and protect this country, why couldn't we belong here? Sam repeatedly said, "This does not matter." It was not up to anyone in Poland to decide whether he was Polish. "I've lived all over the world," he said on every trip. "But here I am at home."

Not only his home. For a very long time, Poland had been a garden for Jews, a center for Jewish culture, where religious tolerance and autonomy were legally protected. Jews were prolific, innovative, patriotic and resourceful. That was a Poland that Sam understandably missed.

But the "Jews in the garden" taunt that was hurled at Danuta in the schoolyard signaled another means for destroying the Jewish population besides the genocidal Germans.

I admired the stunning beauty of the harvest landscape we were passing, feeling wistful about a place where many generations of my family had lived until we were removed by the occupiers and some locals as well. In my mind, I heard the voices of Majdecki, Wacław, Luszczyńska, and Sodo detailing how hidden family after hidden family did not survive because they were murdered by Poles. The voices of these people who offered unflinching accounts were quieted by natural deaths. In their absence, a national law against defaming the Polish nation walled off any discussion or revisiting of these murders, cementing the deniability of the role of Poles.

The attack on the Sodo farm was the possible exception because the court records had garnered the attention of Holocaust scholars and the prosecutions were referenced in the Tadeusz Kozioł book. It had become perhaps one of the best documented cases of an elaborately staged execution of a Jewish family by Polish gunmen. Even though Kozioł and his interviewees tried to cast doubt on whether the killers were partisans, the voice of the court in 2004 in defendant Bucki's case clinched it when it found that his participating in the killing of fourteen hiding Jews (including the nine killed in Bełzów) was "a criminal abuse of the military nature of these organizations and their capabilities."[2]

We easily found the Sodo farm this time, especially with navigation help in two languages. In another first, Danuta knew we were coming. Even her dogs yipped a playful welcome, unlike the racket of alarm they made on unannounced arrivals.

I greeted Danuta with a bouquet of freshly cut flowers. She had set her table for tea, draping a starched white cutwork cloth specially for us. She asked after Cousin Sam. I told her he was still sharp at ninety-four, delivering food to poor people and playing poker most days with guys in his development.

Turning to the history that bonded us, I shared what I had not said in Cousin Sam's presence, when he was always running the show. I told her how much I appreciated all that I'd learned from his resilience and optimism. She smiled in admiration of him and nodded. She said that she too had been inspired by the example of elders, even those she had never met.

"I really admire my grandparents. What they did was so brave and good."

Until then, I had not realized she never knew the grandparents who tried in vain to rescue the Dulas. But she was quite well-acquainted with grief, having lost both parents by age eighteen, followed by the death of her brother, the last member of her immediate family.

Nevertheless, she expressed sympathy for the family that her family tried to save. "You know it was a pit in the ground. Even during the winter, they were in that pit," she said.

It was remarkable to think that I'd met Danuta when she was thirty-three and now she was close to sixty. She said many of those years were a blur of backbreaking farm work for little income.

It was my first time sitting with her after learning the extraordinary details from court records about the gunmen and their murderous military attack and their brutalizing of her grandfather for financial gain. The court records, which she said Dominik had shared with her, included testimony about her neighbor Edward Kozioł directing the attackers to the hiding place of the Jewish family on their property.

Our conversation was somber and quiet with me asking questions and Gosia translating. It was a sharp contrast to the last visit, when I had trouble keeping up even with Gosia there because of Cousin Sam's boisterous interruptions and side conversations. What emerged from this conversation with Danuta was how she was affected by the lingering resentment of villagers who had ostracized Danuta's grandparents, parents, and family. Rather than easing, the views of people living in this hilly enclave of close-set houses and prying eyes had only hardened against them over time.

The neighbors blamed the Dulas for getting killed, for "going outside at night when the war was almost over," as Danuta put it. "People noticed," she said, "but they kept that information for themselves. Farmers didn't even talk with each other about it." Somehow, she said, "that rumor found its way to these so-called partisans."

I was taken aback that she was still letting her neighbor Edward Kozioł off the hook even though he had been convicted and even locked up for diming out the Dulas. And I took her "so-called partisans" reference as sarcasm.

I asked her what she thought of how villagers regarded the men convicted of killing the people in hiding versus how her family had been treated.

She took her glasses off and laid them on the table as if considering the comparison for the first time.

"It's interesting that everybody knew who did this but nobody was saying anything bad to them. People were mean to my family but not to the killers."

For Danuta, the snubbing had continued to the present. When the author Kozioł described the attack on the Sodo farm, he relied on the account of the oldest man in the village, Tadeusz Nowak, the one who said he was sleeping in a briar patch when he heard gunshots. Nowak discouraged the author Kozioł from even talking to Danuta about the events that had occurred on her own property, even though she had learned details from her father and uncle.

Danuta said Nowak told the author, "No, don't go there. They don't know anything. Don't talk to them and don't mix in their lives."

And not long before our visit, she discovered that some villagers were still fuming about our visits. "I was talking with someone who was asking about your visit. I told him that you wanted to visit that place, and during the conversation, they said that because of what my grandparents did, the whole village was put in danger and could have died. People were still mad at my grandparents that they risked the lives of other people."

"You are kidding!" I said. "Even now?" I shook my head. "And you could not say, 'Poles killed them, not Germans'?"

Danuta shrugged. It was a stigma she had borne her entire life. To us, she and her uncle's wife had said the Dulas should not have been murdered. But in conversation with locals, the former population of Jews had been reduced to a threat, and those who eliminated Jews, according to this logic, had made their community safer. Jews were outsiders then and now. A taint attached to anyone who had contact with us.

Even before Poland outlawed blaming Poles for involvement in the Holocaust, it was already a taboo.

"Even after your visit with the movie cameras, people were saying a lot of stupid things. I don't even want to repeat those stories! That you came back to reclaim your old property, that you want to pay us or give us gold! So many stupid stories! Even my cousin once asked me, 'After they lived here, at your place, didn't you look for hidden gold?'"

As for the assailants who were accused of involvement with fourteen or more murders, Danuta said she knew now that the men who were also involved in other murders ultimately caught breaks. "The courts changed these punishments and finally amnesty freed those people."

But beyond the facts of the Dula murders themselves, the Sodo family's experience within their community undermines the Polish narrative. The PiS government insists that Poles engaged in widespread efforts to help Jews during the Nazi occupation, a narrative that dates back to the start of the communist era.[3] It has been pumped up and enforced in what is called *polityka historyczna* (historical politics) ever since the mid-2000s, starting with the Jedwabne debate.[4] I would learn about this from the work of Holocaust scholar Joanna B. Michlic, who has written extensively on the aftermath of Jedwabne on Poles, and from getting to know her when she was in residence at Brandeis. What is totally absent from this version of Polish history is the notion that these "righteous Poles" suffer from a stigma in their own communities.

Scholars like Michlic in her book *Poland's Threatening Other* have written about how Polish society never allowed Jews to rejoin it after World War II, and later the revelations about Jedwabne ignited vitriolic backlash "for putting an end to the self-image of Poland as a community of victims and heroes only."[5] They strummed old themes saying that Jews supported Bolshevism and welcomed the Soviet invasion. In other words, Jews were guilty of crimes against Poland and "Poles were the 'real victims' vis-à-vis Jews."[6]

The murders of the Dulas likewise had become embedded and entwined in a frustrated community mindset. No matter what any records or eyewitnesses said, the partisans simply could not be considered responsible. The fault had to lie elsewhere.

After all, it was now against the law to say otherwise in Poland. The law had sealed a contorted history, even what happened on this very property. Danuta said she was aware of how the push for the law got started.

"This new law that made a buzz around the world theoretically applied to talk about 'Polish death camps,'" she said, sounding like she found that impetus plausible. "But every thinking man knows these were German death camps."

We walked to the Dula graves, framed by a thick apron of lawn. We said Kaddish, although it seemed like an impotent gesture in the face of what I knew in detail about what befell this doomed family. Anger in me bubbled up with memories of court testimony and accounts of villagers Kozioł quoted blaming the Dulas for daring, after eighteen months of sitting beneath a barn, to take a nighttime sip of fresh air. As if they were to blame for the neighbors' betrayal and the executions that followed.

Only Danuta's grandfather acknowledged seeing anyone pull the trigger in the executions of the five adults he had long protected. And the only man he recognized or remembered was the one who held a gun to his own head.

We hiked to the upper fields, and Danuta announced some big news: Dominik was about to become a father. She smiled and giggled. She could not wait to become a spoiling grandmother. How nice to share her joy.

We stood together, taking in the panoramic view of the valley around Kazimierza and its captivating beauty. I felt an undeniable connection to this place despite the atrocities and inability of this community to face what had happened.

Afterward, she walked us to the car. I could feel neighbors stealing glimpses of Danuta's visitors from their windows overlooking her yard.

I said the busybodies would be gossiping again. She said, "They always do."

I apologized for my floral offering. "I'm sorry I don't have any gold for you."

She laughed hard. She does not wear gold anyway, she said. And we were always welcome to visit.

I put my arm around her. She stiffened. A flash of paranoia shot through me. Was I the first Jew she had ever touched? Then she giggled. We were on display for her surrounding neighbors.

I spun around and waved, smiling and pivoting in each direction until I'd waved to everyone in view of the Sodo farm.

———

Originally, we'd hoped Danuta's son, Dominik, could meet us at her house, but he could not get away from work, so we drove east for over two hours toward the Ukrainian border to see him.

I looked forward to seeing the boy I'd met more than twenty years before on the day the Shoah Foundation interviewer had told him to remember that his family had done something good. Now he was a twenty-nine-year-old engineer with a wife who was a month away from giving birth to his first son.

We pulled into the city of Stalowa Wola, squinting at the blinding September sun until Dominik's apartment block cast a long shadow. This industrial city built by the Soviets as a steel town had paved over most anything green.

Dominik welcomed us warmly and presented beautiful cakes his wife, Kate, had bought for our visit. After chatting about the baby and how the couple had met, we turned to the events that had brought us together. Each of us reflected on whether we would have had the guts of Dominik's great-grandparents to hide fugitive Jews. Dominik said he didn't think anyone today was up to the brave acts of his great-grandparents' generation. He had never known his great-grandfather, Kazimierz Sodo, and on the day I met Dominik, he was too young to understand what his great-uncle was talking about.

"My mom explained a little and I asked a lot of questions." Over time, he picked up more details overhearing his parents' conversations. But with such knowledge grew his conviction that the truth should be shared.

In his village, however, everyone wanted to forget about the situation. "Particularly the people who were there, they lied about this situation. It was difficult to live in this place, for sure." The second part—about who killed the hidden Jews— came later. "To be honest with you, maybe only when you sent me these documents."

But Dominik said that he made sure to tell everyone he knew about the story of what happened on his family farm.

I asked what they thought of the new law that sought to whitewash Poland's WWII history. His wife jumped in before Dominik could answer.

Kate said, "I don't want to sound rude, but for one hundred years, Poland was nonexistent. Now they are trying to make patriotism alive for a new generation," she said. She described the experience of her parents, who met in a German forced-labor camp, and how they suffered from the Russian invasion early in the war and then from the German occupation as well. She praised the PiS government because "they talk about the sacrifices people made. Every country tries to make their own heroes and teach their youth their own history."

Dominik and Kate were sitting side by side facing us. His eyes widened when she defended the law. He asked me, "What in the USA do people think about this situation? Almost everyone I told about this history tells me that they are surprised that Polish people were killers. Not German soldiers, but Polish people."

I told him, "Most Americans don't think about it at all. And Jews just think about—understandably—what happened to them." I said I was afraid that with the new law, change was even less likely. "And who knows what history will be repressed next?"

Dominik nodded and smiled. "OK, for me, history should be only true and it doesn't matter how it looks."

This statement was so simple and so pure. I could hardly keep from jumping up and down and cheering.

"Exactly," I said. "As soon as we start to shade the truth, mold the truth, we lose something. Once you face it, even if it's ugly, you can move on," I said. "How will Poland ever move on?"

Kate said, "It will always be like this."

I said, "But if we don't try as much as we can to face what really happened, we won't know what the truth is."

Kate said, "But you see you are very passionate about this, and you are very interested in this. It has touched you in a kind of personal way. It happens with all people. You can't just be objective about this. You must see both sides, and one will always be the one you identify with."

But Dominik wasn't having it. He declared with full conviction, "There is no history without truth. The truth is the truth. My son will know the truth."

We had been talking for hours and I was reluctant to leave them. We embraced warmly. I could hear Dominik saying those words over and over in my mind all the way back to Kraków and well beyond. After I got home, I listened to the recording over and over, his words washing over me like a balm: "My son will know the truth."

Kazimierza Wielka locals attending a ceremony honoring the nearly three hundred Jews slain at the site by Nazis in 1942. The victims had fled deportation and some filtered back to town while others lost their hiding places. The same monument that Sam and Judy found desecrated in 1991 and that Sam autographed in an act of defiance has been rehabbed and become the centerpiece of the ceremony that Judy and her husband attend as honored guests of the city representing their family in 2021.

# 15

# Honored Guests

The placard in the hands of a driver outside the Kraków airport read, "Mrs. and Mr. Rakowsky." I giggled. Aides to the mayor of Kazimierza had conferred on my husband my surname. We had flown in as invited guests to enjoy the "Great days of Jewish culture in Kazimierza," the city's first celebration of its kind.

The mayor's driver sped through Kraków's roundabouts that spun us like a giant lawn sprinkler into the countryside. In record time we found ourselves sitting in the mayor's office in Kazimierza, where I had not been welcomed since Knopek concocted a ruse for the pursuit of Hena. Now we were representing the family that had lived here for generations, namely Cousin Sam, the city's oldest Holocaust survivor. At age ninety seven with the COVID-19 pandemic raging, he begged making the trip.

Mayor Adam Bodzioch, an elfin man in perpetual motion, greeted us warmly, his eyes crinkling above his mask. He offered us cappuccinos and jelly-topped cookies like the ones my Polish grandmother used to make, and that I had always thought were a Jewish confection. Bodzioch honored us as dignitaries and bestowed a mother lode of city-branded swag— lapel pins, soccer bags, books, and plaques. We presented maple syrup from New England—which our hosts thought was only sourced in Canada—and Kentucky bourbon.

With the mayor's photographer chronicling our every move, I thanked the mayor for his hospitality. I asked the mayor why Kazimierza was putting on its celebration of Jewish culture now. The mayor said his own life experience offered motivation. He grew up hearing his parents describe Jewish friends and how they gave bread to Jews fleeing the Germans.

While sounding straight forward, I had learned from Sam that even giving bread to Jews during the war was fraught with politics. Sam visited former neighbors who acknowledged privately that my great-aunt Frymet had knocked on their door at night during the war and that they gave her bread. But when the topic came up in front of other people, they said they had sold her bread. It was astounding that decades after the war that they would be too guarded to admit to any wartime kindness to a Jew, even a next door neighbor who ultimately was murdered anyway.

Our visit came on the heels of events that had thrust Poland ɔ an unflattering international spotlight for major events in memory wars," causing tremendous uproar and division. It started with publication in 2018 of a major two-volume study, *Dalej jest noc. Losy Żydów w wybranych powiatach okupowanej Polski* (*Night without End: The Fate of Jews in Selected Counties of Occupied Poland*). The 1640-page study of nine Polish counties determined that Jews trying to elude Nazi persecution in small Polish towns were caught in death traps. Jews had a 1.5–2.0 percent chance of surviving the Holocaust in Poland due not only to actions by the Germans but also their own neighbors.[1]

The tome devoted a two-hundred-page section to a study of the county that includes Kazimierza. I was dying to know what it said.

Cousin Sam had ordered the book, published only in Polish. The day his copies arrived at his Florida home, he sat down and read the entire segment on the county of Miechów. He phoned me flush with excitement.

"They have in the book my father's name, and it has my uncle's name for running the food pantry and kitchen for Jews during the occupation," he said.

His reaction was focused on the proof of life, like when he saw his birth certificate in a Polish archive and when he saw his name and grades in books at his old school.

The study examined Jewish life and Polish-Jewish relations in the area before the war and under German occupation, including forced labor and mass deportations to the Bełżec death camp. It also chronicled episodes of the murder of Jewish men, women, and children by members of local underground organizations.

*Night without End* was proof on a grand scale. On a video call after a marathon reading session, Sam held up the shipping paper from the book and giggled. "It's an amazing book. This is one of the best books written about the history of Polish Jews. It's unbelievable," he said. "They don't hide anything."

I told him that the Polish government was upset with the book.

His response: "They cannot deny this. This is fact. It's all over the place Poles killing Jews. In every district, Poles were killing Jews. It's not political. They're robbing Jews, killing Jews, stealing, selling out Jews to Germans, Polish police."

He also felt vindicated and at the same time dismayed by the sheer volume and detail of the revelations in the entire study, which included more than thirty-five hundred footnotes. One reviewer called it "an unprecedented reconstruction of the daily reality of genocide, meticulously demonstrating the extent of local Polish participation in hunting down and murdering their Jewish neighbors. No amount of apologetic arguments will be able to dispel the well-documented findings of this volume or dispute the general conclusion that numerous victims might have survived but for the greed and callousness of the surrounding Polish society."[2]

In Sam's view, "this is the biggest book and the best one I've ever seen about what happened to the Jews. The biggest chapter is about my area. It's probably one of the worst ones. More Jews were killed there than maybe anywhere."

The segment on Miechów was authored by Dariusz

Libionka, with whom I had corresponded many years earlier at the start of his research on the district. It relied on some of the same IPN files Przemek had obtained, detailing the murders of the Ptasniks and Czosneks at the Pabis farm and the Dulas on the Sodo farm. But the most astonishing revelation of the book was how frequently partisans staged massacres of Jews in hiding in our home county. Libionka put together a table organized by date, responsible underground group, and the number of Jews killed. AK, the largest and most structured organization, holds the most, tallying seventy-two Jews killed in 1943 and 1944 in that county.[3]

A fifty-person AK unit staged an invasion of a farm hiding three Jewish families on May 5, 1944, following the Sodo attack of May 3 and the Pabis farm attack of May 4. They murdered a family of six, including four children. The AK also killed the wife and daughter of the rescuer, Konieczny. Four people escaped the melee, only one of whom survived the war. Some of the attacks, as the Dula court records demonstrated, involved members of multiple groups united in common purpose.

In fact, the killing of Jews in hiding by the underground in 1944 was so widespread that a Jewish partisan group sounded the alarm to the Polish government in exile, which, according to Libionka, attempted an intervention. But for all the revelations in the chapter, it did not mention the murders of the Rożeńeks in Zagórzyce.

I emailed Joanna Tokarska-Bakir, the Polish historian who

had authored *Jewish Fugitives in the Countryside, 1939–1945* and many other works that involved IPN research in the same geography as Libionka's chapter. In an email, she put words to my takeaway from *Night without End*, which left me bereft over the possibility of finding the trace of Hena.

Tokarska-Bakir said, "The problem with detecting any traces of their murders is quite significant when there are such numerous crimes in the area."[4]

After all these years of chasing one woman who survived a massacre, thinking it would stand out in people's minds and memories, her remark made clear that was unlikely. The sheer frequency of these massacres destroyed not only lives but memories. These partisan attacks on Jews just happened so often that they were not memorable.

The defenders of Polish honor in the face of such overwhelming evidence still found a way to mount an attack on *Night without End*.

A government-organized and -funded NGO sued the book's editors, Jan Grabowski and Barbara Engelking, for libel, claiming they had damaged the reputation of a long-dead mayor of a village in northeast Poland who was described in a Holocaust survivor's testimony as having robbed her during the war and betraying eighteen Jews hiding in a nearby forest to the Germans. The dead mayor's niece claimed—just like some of the Dulas' murder defendants—it was impossible because he had taken actions to save other Jews.

I felt I understood the thinking of those suing the editors

based on comments that Dominik's wife, Kate, had made about Poland's need for recognition of their own suffering.

But the judge in the Grabowski and Engelking case took Polish grievance to a new level. In a thirty-seven-page verdict, District Court Judge Ewa Jończyk ruled that the editors must submit a written apology to the niece of the dead mayor because they had published inaccurate but not untrue information about the man, violating his niece's right to a positive national identity.[5]

The judge wrote, "We can assume that ascribing to Poles the crimes of the Holocaust committed by the Third Reich can be construed as hurtful and striking at the feeling of identity and of national pride." She went on to say that such accusations risk striking "against the feeling of national belonging and provokes a feeling of harm."[6]

Anything that causes damage to this undefined sense of dignity, the judge put on a par with other legal protections. "To blame Poles for the Holocaust, for the killing of Jews in World War II, and for seizing their property touches upon the sphere of national legacy, and consequently is completely untrue and hurtful, and can impact one's feelings."[7]

In that same period, the government of Poland passed a law permanently slamming shut the door on heirs with hopes of seeking restitution for property taken by Germans and kept by Poles. The property law sparked a row with the United States and Israel, which recalled its highest diplomat in Poland.

Sam had strong feelings about the restitution law but no

skin in that game. Decades ago, Sam's father had pursued compensation, and the Rakowskis had received a check for $3,500 from the U.S. Treasury for the house.

The legal challenge to *Night without End* garnered plenty of international media attention, but the litigation had nothing to do with the study devoted to his home province. Sam spent hours poring over those two hundred pages, reveling in the details about local Jewish life before the war and how the community functioned under occupation and the destruction that followed. On our video chats, he gushed about the segment on his county.

He said, "I read this and I'm back in Kazimierza Wielka."

Now, I was back in Kazimierza—not as Sam's silent "secretary" but as an invited guest. For the first time, I actually stayed overnight in town, hosted by the city at a former palace built by the sugar factory society that overlooks the grounds of the former sugar refinery. The sprawling property was long owned by nobles in the Łubieński family, who became magnates in the 1800s. The Germans occupied the factory during World War II, until the summer of 1944. That's when several partisan units of the underground took over Kazimierza Wielka.[8]

The partisans who attacked the Sodo farm, according to the court records, had rearmed and reloaded between massacres with weapons stored at the sugar factory. I had no reason to believe that everyone in the underground around here was complicit in the executions and robberies of Jews in hiding. But how many knew and turned a blind eye?

I gazed out our hotel window at the crimson horizon. So many disturbing details that I'd learned since my last time here came flooding back.

What a wild ride. This decades-long attempt to crack one cold case had led to so many others. Grisly murders of whole families of Jews in hiding—my own relatives—had been concealed for so long. The cover-up was ongoing, and it ran deep and all the way to the highest levels of the government. The government had stacked the deck against the truth getting out or being believed, even in the face of so much evidence, by undermining independent thought in the courts and the media.

Weeks before we arrived, an appellate court overturned the libel judgment against editors of *Night without End*, finding that the lower court's decision threatened academic freedom. The appeals court absolved the Holocaust historians of the order to apologize to the niece of the late mayor. But the case laid bare the government's laser focus on codifying Poland's historical innocence. Pushback seemed limited or muted. After all, even Dominik's wife, Kate, who knew what happened on her husband's family farm, saw the need to elevate national pride over unflattering truth.

Kazimierza bucked the national trend by holding its first Jewish cultural celebration at a time when such festivals were on the decline in Poland. Poland was turning sharply inward under the nationalist conservative PiS government and had discouraged the practice of celebrating the ghost population of Jews. The widespread cultural shift that the PiS government cemented was far from subtle.

The government purged Dariusz Stola from the top position at the POLIN museum, despite the high praise and coveted international awards it garnered under his stewardship. Stola was punished for voicing opposition to the Holocaust memory law.[9] Sealing his fate was an exhibit the museum put on under his leadership detailing the communist government's campaign in 1968 of expelling Jews as anti-communists. It was an ironic twist of the traditional anti-Semitic narrative that vilified all Jews because some held high-level positions in the communist government after the war. It was also effective. By the end of the 1960s, about twenty thousand Polish citizens of Jewish descent left Poland. The anti-Jewish events of 1968 are well known and established. But the PiS government tarred Stola with "politicizing the museum."

The PiS government's story was that nearly every Pole selflessly aided Jews during World War II. If that were so, then why had neighbors and villagers given so much grief to generations of Mlekos and the Sodos? For the Kazimierza celebration, Cousin Sam urged the mayor to invite the Mleko family, who were his brave and generous harborers, as well as the Sikorskis, who hid the late Ray Fishler, and Danuta Sodo Ogórek and her family, who hid the Dulas.

I did not know whether it was widely known beyond their neighborhoods that the Mlekos and Sikorskis rescued Jews. But many were aware of the Dulas' stay on the Sodo farm and how that ended. I echoed Sam's request and learned that the mayor was already in the process of inviting all rescuers he knew of.

Emails were flying between us and the mayor's office, and with Tadeusz Kozioł, who was working on a new edition of his book. I also was in touch with a leader of cultural efforts in the nearby town of Busko-Zdrój, where such celebrations of Jewish life had anchored the community calendar for nineteen years. Thanks to Google Translate, I was able to communicate on Cousin Sam's behalf and to supply material from Sam to Kozioł for his new book. It included information Sam was so intent on conveying to future generations about the Jewish shopkeepers and artisans who once flourished in Kazimierza, as well as information and images memorializing Sam's family.

Mayor Adam Bodzioch tiptoed on a tricky path. Other area politicians who had spearheaded events commemorating Jewish history and restoration projects of Jewish cemeteries and synagogues had lost government grants and reelection bids. Bodzioch hoped to avoid that fate. Already he had finessed a politically conservative landscape in a province that was one of the dozens around the country that touted their intolerance by approving resolutions declaring themselves an "LGBT-free zone," in which LGBT people were not welcome, measures that the European Union found so bigoted that it threatened to cut off funding.

Bodzioch, a veterinarian turned politician, had built up a reservoir of goodwill over four terms in office before taking a break in 2014, a time of surging support around the country, particularly in rural areas, for the nationalist populism of PiS. He staged a comeback in 2018, beating his PiS incumbent by a wide margin.

He brought enthusiasm and a grounded sense of calm to the job with a style that mirrored Cousin Sam's in the form of a high-touch charm offensive. Bodzioch showed up everywhere. Appearing and chronicling events at schools, sports, and meetings on Facebook, he collected "likes" even better than votes.

Sam had never met the mayor despite his many trips. But they made up for it by connecting via video chat, phone, email and the mayor's inveterate updates on Facebook. Sam offered historical local tidbits, and the mayor honored his contributions and indispensable perspective. They bridged the distance of time and geography, building mutual support for future educational and cultural events.

Sam repeatedly stressed, "In life before the war, we had good relations between the Jewish community and everyone else." Every correspondence with the mayor Sam signed his name with, "son of Kazimierza Wielka."

The evening we arrived, the mayor and an aide treated us to dinner in the hotel. We ordered hearty meals of borscht, meat, and pierogi, while the mayor, who said he'd already dined, tucked into a massive ice cream sundae with a child's delight.

I asked the mayor why it had taken the city so long before hosting its first Jewish cultural festival.

The events were five years in the making, he acknowledged, and overdue. The city had learned a lot from the example of nearby Busko-Zdrój, a spa town that was already successful at drawing tourism. Beyond somber remembrances, Busko had developed a full slate of musical and theater performances, lectures, and ceremonies for its Jewish festival. Kazimierza was following Busko's example but was still at the starting gates in building local support. At any rate, Bodzioch figured the time was right. The generation that had lived through the war and had known Jews, like his own parents, who had Jewish friends, was dying out.

But what about the chilly reception to such festivals from the national government?

The mayor shrugged, offering an impish grin. "I don't care," he said.

He quoted a well-known survivor of Buchenwald, Jakub Goldberg, who became an influential Polish and Israeli historian: "There's no Polish history without Jews."[10]

I wished I'd had the presence of mind in that moment to respond with the rest of that well-known quote: "There's no Jewish history without Polish history."

I told him how important these events were for my family and for Sam, whom I was updating in regular calls.

Mayor Bodzioch nodded and turned serious. "It's important for us too."

The next day dawned misty and gorgeous, recalling the lush beauty of this land. The sweet, smoky fragrance of farmers burning leaves made me nostalgic for those early trips with Sam. Then it hit me: seventy-nine years ago to the day, Jews had awakened to loudspeakers blaring orders to report to the market square. And my great-grandmother Pearl, alone in her house, had opened her eyes on the last day of her life.

I shivered at the thought. We were in the right place on this anniversary. We got an early start, heading over to join the mayor and the events team in preparations for the day.

The mayor gave us a ride to Słonowice, and reviewed his own speech on the way. It felt surreal to be consecrating the monument that long ago Cousin Sam and I had found abandoned and covered with swastikas. I wondered what attendees of today's events had grown up hearing about the mass execution there. Was it widely known that many of the town's Jews had fled the roundup but their hiding places were not sustainable so they filtered back to town? Did they know that the Germans had locked them in the school? During that confinement, a brother of Sam's uncle Isaac jumped out an upper-floor window one night and got away. The rest were marched out of town in view of everyone, forced to strip before strangers, humiliated to the end. They stood naked before the pit awaiting their own executions, looking down on the bodies of relatives and neighbors who had been alive moments before.

Based on the sheer numbers of incidents Libionka chronicled in *Night without End*, I figured that someone who would be on hand today knew or was related to someone who betrayed or committed violence against Jews in hiding during the war. But the deep and pervasive pride in the Polish partisans had long suppressed and denied any reckoning with such offenses. Every Pole in the underground had earned full status as a military veteran—even those convicted of participating in multiple murders of Jews. Each was awarded full veterans' benefits, which at one point included a shiny new Fiat. The denial was complete.

At the monument site, I noticed the change. No longer was it surrounded by the spindly white birches that I recorded on video following Sam to the obelisk. In maturity, the trees spread a canopy of leaves that obscured the mass grave somewhere nearby.

I awakened from that memory and turned around. I saw a long line of dressed-up middle-aged people, women in heels and men in blazers, trudging up the hilly dirt road. Cynical thoughts melted at the sight of the purposeful looks on the faces of those who had chosen to take this path into these woods.

I swallowed hard, choking back sobs rising in my throat at the sight of solemn young scouts in red kerchiefs standing at attention by the obelisk. In 1942, the Germans ordered local scouts to dig the pit in advance. Now uniformed Polish soldiers stood as sentries by the spruced-up monument bedecked in colorful ribbons. I had met the survivor Ari Mellor, who settled in Canada after the war and later put up this monument. Finally it was drawing formal attention to this community's loss.

The mayor took the podium. "I feel emotional standing here today in a place where the gates of hell opened seventy-nine years ago. In the place where the Nazis, the torturers, murdered about three hundred people of Jewish origin—citizens

of Kazimierza Wielka and the surrounding area. The silence
of this place is apparent. Here, in Słonowice, as in Oświęcim
and many other places in Europe, you can hear the echo of the
excruciating screams and cries of men, women, and children
who cry out to us from the abyss of the anguish they have expe-
rienced. Could we not hear that scream? To suppress it is indifference and arrogance.

"Today, we bow our heads over the grave where our relatives and neighbors rest, a shoemaker who has been torn off
from the workshop, a shopkeeper who will never serve bread
again, an accountant who left unfinished bills, a child who will
never cry again. These people were one quarter of our population. They worked here, built houses that may still be standing. Ladies and gentlemen, this grief that squeezes the heart is
a prelude that begins a new stage in the history of Kazimierza
Wielka. Today we are all witnesses to history. We are committed to the memory."

After the many dignitaries were recognized and offered
their own words, it was my turn. I looked out at about one hundred people who had turned out here, roughly a third of the
number buried nearby. I addressed the crowd in English, with
Gosia standing beside me translating my words.

"'Here I am, *hineni*,' Abraham, Moses, and many prophets
said to God in the Old Testament. Showing up is very important in our long tradition, as the phrase appears many times in
four of the five books of Moses.

"Tonight is the Sabbath that falls between our New Year's

celebration of Rosh Hashanah and next week's most holy day of Yom Kippur. We call it Shabbat Shuvah, the Shabbat of Returning. We return here because of all that you are doing to make us welcome.

"It's a big deal," I said, pausing. "It may not be what everyone else in Poland is doing now, but you are here. *Hineni.*"

I talked about my first time visiting this place, when Sam and I were sad that it had been defaced. Sam had scratched his name on the back and declared, "Hitler missed one."

He was here. *Hineni.*

"Samuel Rakowski, who is now a sharp, optimistic ninety-seven-year-old living with his wife, Bilha, in Florida, introduced me to this place not just as one of tragedy but also as the town where the family of my great-grandmother Pearl Chilewicz came from and where my great-grandfather started a lumberyard, with materials that went into nearby barns, houses, and bridges, and where our relatives had stores up and down Sienkiewicz Street."

I thanked the mayor and everyone who made the event possible on behalf of Sam and our family, and then said the quiet part out loud. "We also thank the Mlekos for hiding our family, who survived, and the people like the Sodos, who hid our cousins the Dulas, and others who hid the Rożeńeks and my great aunt Frymet Rakowski, even though they were still murdere

"You stepped up and showed up and were very h *Hineni.*"

After my speech, my husband joined me at the mic

and we chanted Kaddish, the prayer for the dead, in Aramaic. This was not something that Gosia could translate. But in context, I hoped everyone got the meaning.

I waved to the Mlekos in the crowd. Could this community finally forgive their brethren, actually the grandchildren and great-grandchildren, for hiding Jews? I did not see Danuta and hoped she had not stayed away because of this stigma. It turned out, I learned later, that she had remained home to oversee workers digging on her property to install water pipes. She was afraid they would dig up the Dulas' bones, and she might be blamed for them. After over three-quarters of a century, it was astounding that she was the one worrying about trouble.

After the speeches, the mayor and other officials placed floral wreaths by the monument. In conversation with the mayor the previous evening, I had mentioned that Jews show respect for the deceased by placing small stones on Jewish graves. The mayor had taken it upon himself to bring stones from his own yard so that we could follow our tradition. The audience may have been puzzled by this practice, but it was so touching when the mayor handed me the stones that Sammy and I proceeded to place on the monument.

Next the group reassembled at the local library for the launch of Koziol's latest book, the one full of photos and descriptions of Sam's family history. It was followed by musical stage performances. Then I was invited to the stage to meet rise guest, Monika Anielska. I did not recognize the blond walking toward me in front of a standing-room-only crowd as the former teenager who once showed me her Beatles collection while her grandfather and Sam reminisced. I embraced the granddaughter of Guca awkwardly, embarrassed that I did not recognize her. Although Guca minimized any financial benefit he accrued from the Rakowski lumberyard, in the town's eyes, Monika and I symbolized the transfer of a signature Jewish business to a local Polish family.

After the program, two young schoolteachers came up to me saying they were new to town and wanted to educate their students about the former Jewish population. Could Cousin Sam come visit and teach their students about the Jews? I thanked them but said Sam had come here so many times but was no longer up to international travel at age ninety-seven. Maybe we could arrange a video chat.

The crowd had swelled for the big draw: a groaning buffet from a local Jewish-style restaurant. Roast goose, smoked fish, soups, and salads were so popular that even with the mayor's help, I could hardly squeeze into the buffet. The sharp-elbowed crowd delighted in this culinary vestige of Jews.

During a break in the festivities, we FaceTimed with Sam and Bilha, who had watched livestreams of the events on Facebook. They were beaming. What a proud day for Kazimierza, they raved. "Good job representing the family."

Tamar and David, Sam's children, who had shown up here with their father, were also moved. David watched the speeches online and emailed, "One only needs to sit back and reflect on what happened there, at the place not so long ago, to our family and relatives. It is very personal, and thank you for being there and sharing with the town officials and people how personal it was and is. You bring honor to the memory of those that are lost and for those that still remember."

That evening a sizable crowd turned out at an amphitheater in the park with *Fiddler on the Roof*–type skits and songs, leaving Jews somewhere in the 1800s. Sammy nudged me and rolled his eyes. In the gathering darkness of the park, Kozioł, the author whose first book had started with dismissive references to Jewish history and misdeeds of partisans, insisted on posing with me and his family for a group photo. I saw, to my surprise, that he was weeping. He said, with translation help from his daughter, that he felt very differently after writing his book. Now he had nothing but sadness about what happened to the Jews.

Standing nearby was Danuta. She was enjoying an acrobatics performance with a friend. "It's interesting who is here," she said, "and who is not here." She shot me a knowing look that I took to mean people like her suspicious neighbors.

Speaking of absences, the mayor said he had invited his predecessor, Tadeusz Knopek, the fellow who tried to help us smoke out Hena with a faux inheritance. But Knopek, now a member of the PiS party, declined attendance.

The next day, the mayor hosted us at a youth sporting event where we enjoyed his barbecued lunch, which, like everything else, he chronicled on Facebook. Leaving the school, my husband said, "They are so sincere and such true allies to us." I nodded. But Sammy continued, "It's just so awkward and sad because the Jews are gone, and they have no way to learn about this past and this lost population of Poles."

"I know," I said. "After two generations of denying memory, it's gone."

In our few free hours, we took advantage of the mayor's offer that his driver Janusz would take us wherever we wanted to go. Of course I asked him to drive us to Zagórzyce for one last round of stops seeking clues to the Hena mystery.

I stood again atop the hill where the house once stood, the place where Hena's parents and siblings were forced out the window into a hail of bullets. What had become of this sixteen-year-old whose search led us to this hidden history of her family and the Dulas? I don't know who she could trust with her life when partisans were running around killing Jews with impunity. I could not stop wondering: Where did she run and find safety? How did authorities later locate her and summon her for testimony?

We swung by the house of the granddaughter of the Radziszewskis, where her mother had spoken so freely to me in 2001. The worn woman who had once disparaged her own handwriting for resembling Hebrew seemed not to remember me. She said her mother had died and no one in her family knew anything about the Rożeneks. Even after she heard her mother describe to me the cruel details of the killings and the haunted cherry tree she, said no one talked about it.

Before we left town, we talked to Sam and Bilha again. "Did you find the cousin?" they asked.

"Not yet," I said, a little defensively.

The mayor came through with Hena's grade cards. In first grade her marks were mostly *dobry*, or good. She made friends, pleased her teachers, and showed willingness to learn. Over the next few grades, she continued doing well at learning Polish, but she was just so-so at math. By fourth grade, she was picking up *dobry* grades (equivalent to a B) in biology and history. She missed only two days of school the entire year. At the end of the school year in 1939, she completed fourth grade. Her teachers approved her advance to the fifth grade in the fall. But Hena never got the chance to attend. The German invasion ended her formal schooling at age eleven.

The grades made her more real than anything we'd found since my conversation with Mrs. Luszczyńska, who recounted that Hena sent her baby presents after the war. I could picture this popular young girl absorbing ordinary disappointments until she was forced to flee her home and, after hiding for eighteen months, witnessing the murders of her family by sadistic gunmen.

Following the festivals, we hopped a westbound train to Wrocław, a parallel journey to Hena's many years before. In Wrocław, I was looking forward to finally meeting the obliging police detective I had corresponded with occasionally since Bienkowski had connected me in 2006. This FBI Academy graduate, a pro at untangling financial crimes, had found what appeared to be a trace of Hena. He had dug into databases and had made another round of calls. His candor was refreshing.

His take on the Rożeńek murders was unflinching. He openly lamented to me that "the bastards who killed her family were Poles."

He thought he could see us before he went to an international conference. I did not know if there was any hope, but I figured this guy was the best one to scale hurdles no one else could. He said he could find our hotel, which was near the police station. I watched him loping toward us, a lean fellow carrying a backpack. Sammy said, "Do you think he's packing?"

He led us to the tram. I was trying to match his long strides, asking him how we would ride without tickets. He said, "You are with me, and I am a police officer, and if anyone asks, you are visiting cops from the States."

Five stops away, we got off on the city's edge and headed to his apartment building. In his comfortable flat, we met his thirteen-year-old daughter and very polite ten-year-old son, who could hardly wait for permission to dive into the éclairs specially purchased for our visit.

He apologized at great length for not hosting us overnight in his apartment, saying it was not large enough to accommodate two additional people, something I never remotely expected.

We dined with his wife on goulash he'd made for us in advance, along with ratatouille, kasha, hot beets, and sauerkraut. Their gracious efforts were touching.

Next, we headed off without his wife to the market square. Over pints and slices of brown bread spread with lard (clearly, we don't keep kosher), he grilled me on the Hena case. He thought it was worth another look at the possible lead to the woman who had lived in a nearby city until 2006 and who had some background details that matched Hena's.

"Did you ever have an address for her before she emigrated?" I asked.

"I would have gotten the address when I accessed the file illegally back then, when it was easier. Now it would not be possible." He took a slug of beer. Evidently, the wheels were turning. "Maybe I made a mistake by not accessing the address then." But then he added that if she had left the country or died, he would not have been able to see the address in the system.

Then he asked, "How do you know she survived?"

I laid out all the pieces from the partisan leader Augustyn Wacław, the one-legged former policeman, and the daughter of her would-be rescuer who got the baby presents after the war.

I told him Wacław said members of the farmers' partisan group were responsible for killing the Rożeńeks. Without missing a beat, he named a right-wing partisans' group known for killing Jews and collaborating with the Germans.

It made me realize that some in law enforcement knew a lot more than was popular to say.

"I phoned a colleague before we left the house who knows our computer system very well, and he confirmed that I would not have been able to see the address in 2006 if she was dead or left the country."

"Of course," I said, impressed by his effort.

Then he asked me why I had not arranged for anyone to track the woman he'd turned up who had emigrated to Israel in 2006.

"I can," I said. "But I'm doing everything here that is possible while I'm here, and I thought I'd be able to find the address she had around here."

He nodded.

Before we parted for the night, he ran down the checklist of his tasks and mine: he'd try once again for an address with some informal inquiries, and I'd work on the Israel end of the lead.

The next morning, I sat down with my laptop outside the hotel and drilled into the Israeli databases with the information on the woman our officer had found.

"Oh no," I said, frowning at my screen. I had been copying Hebrew lines from Yad Vashem documents into Google Translate. "It's not her. The first names of the parents are similar to Hena's but this person has a whole different story, coming from Tashkent by way of Lublin. Anyway, it's just all wrong."

I wrote to our policeman and told him to stand down. The lead was not worth following. Another dead end.

That left only one task for my remaining time in Poland: submit a formal application as a relative to the IPN for investigative records of the Rożeńek murders, something which Sam and I had tried under previous governments. I could take advantage of this officer's knowledge of how records might be kept and his recommendations in drafting the application.

I also had another new recruit to the cause, a PhD student with Jewish roots in Wrocław who was active in efforts to preserve Jewish graves. I'd met her by hopscotching contacts through a study-abroad program for U.S. colleges. With the policeman's advice and the student's familiarity with government procedures, we put together the request for all documents relating to the Rożeńeks' murders. Somewhere in the government's records, I fully believed, a dusty folder or digital file was waiting for me.

On our last day in Wrocław, this new friend left our hotel lobby clutching the envelope with the IPN application headed to the post office. I was afraid to hope too much but returned home feeling optimistic.

Soon our ally on the ground, who like many linked with these pursuits preferred not to be named due to the political climate in Poland, said the IPN rejected my application. I needed to back up every statement with notarized original documents, and I had to prove I had a blood connection to the person about whom I was seeking information.

This hurdle seemed insurmountable. Cousin Sam had told me pointedly over the years that Hena was his first cousin on his mother's side. "You are not related," he said over and over.

This was a job for Sammy. He was a pro at cross-referencing genealogy databases, combing through so many boxes on the computer screen that create family trees. Sammy took a deep dive into database hell. He spent countless hours sorting through Rakowskis, Banachs, and Rożeńeks, the latter a family name that was once quite common in our part of Poland. I was busy assembling documents for the application.

One day, I heard an exultant shout from my husband's home office. "I got it. Here it is. You are related. You are absolutely related to her!"

He discovered that in the village of Kazimierza Wielka with its one hundred Jewish families, of course there was a lot of mingling, with children numbering seven, eight, or nine—as in Sam's mother's family. "Of course," I said. "Who else were they going to marry?" It turned out that Hena's grandmother was a sister to my great-grandmother Pearl.

Was it close enough? I took the partial family tree and a pile of documents that I got notarized and then certified with an apostille stamp and ribbon from the Massachusetts secretary of state's office. I shipped the package off to Poland at great expense to make sure they got there.

In Wrocław, our friend hand-delivered the application to the IPN office. Then she told me to brace for another long wait.

I hoped I might get a file the size of the one Przemek got, or maybe just a brief investigative report that gave a date for Hena's appearance when she was asked to identify two suspects in her family's deaths, which might list an address for her at the time.

The next time I saw Wrocław friend's name in my inbox, my hopes swelled. This could be it. But I did not see any attachment or signs of a bulk file to download.

Instead the news brought another letdown.

The IPN purportedly had reviewed all the documents,

forms, and stamps. But it rejected my request. I read the email again and again. I had a hard time taking in this information. The institute had proof that a verified relative of Hena's had scaled every bureaucratic hurdle and followed every requirement in seeking these records.

This did not matter.

Why? According to the government, Hena was still alive. Therefore, she would need to approve the request.

Where? On what basis did officials reach this conclusion? Like the long cavalcade of people, officials, and archives that *had* to know about Hena, the government shrugged.

For its part, Poland said, "*Nie wiem.*"

# Epilogue

I had trouble giving up on Hena.

After we got back, Kozioł's daughter sent photos of us together. She included the one of him shedding tears over the sad fate of the local Jewish population.

I thanked him in an email, lamenting that after so much effort, Sam never found his last surviving cousin. "Sam cares so much about Kazimierza Wielka and everyone he knew there. He actually believed that his relationships with people from childhood who he still respected would mean that they would tell him the truth."

Kozioł said he would ask around.

Meanwhile, Guca's granddaughter Monika and I kept in touch. I sent her Hena's birth certificate and asked one more time whether her aunt remembered anything about her. I also sent a photo of the crystal bell she gave me when she was a teenager, which I have always cherished. She cheerfully wrote right back, sending news clips from the recent events. She also said, "I talked with my aunt. She doesn't remember Frania or Hena Rożeńka. She was five years old in 1939. Now she is eighty-seven years old. She looks good but doesn't remember everything. Regards to you and Sam from my family."

Kozioł got back to me a few weeks later. He had visited Monika's aunt, who he described as "the daughter of Guca, the one who took over the timber yard from Józef Rakowski." Kozioł knew Monika's aunt Maria in a different way. She was his former neighbor and had been his wife's longtime workmate.

"She remembers that after the war Hena went somewhere and then wrote a letter to a woman in Zagórzyce with whom she stayed after the tragedy," Kozioł said. "She said that she made a life for herself, got married, apparently concealed her Jewish origins, and that she is very well," he said, quoting Maria. "And she asked not to look for her."

After all the times Sam had asked her, now Maria was said to have corroborated the decades-old tip, but in a way that could not be followed up.

I thought of the city clerk who told me, "Even if she changed her religion, she had to change the place where she lived."

"As for the perpetrators of the Rożeńeks' murder," Kozioł said, "nobody knows today."

Nobody knows, I thought, or wants anyone to know.

I asked Kozioł why Maria, who just a few years ago sat next to Cousin Sam teasing him about memories from childhood, never responded to his pleas for information about Hena. As a girl, Hena's teachers found she made friends easily. She may once have counted Maria as one.

Why on that last visit did she pull a tablecloth trick on Sam about the one tidbit she had previously shared, that she used to play in the house of the Rożeńeks' rescuers with a girl who had giggled about a secret she could not tell? Why did she gaslight Sam while flirting with him?

She thought, Kozioł said, if she answered his questions, "It might upset him."

And turning a deaf ear to his pleas would make him feel better?

I thought of Hena crouched in the dark that night, smelling the gun smoke wafting over from the bodies of her parents and siblings. After the panic subsided, she must have made a move like Kozioł's information suggested. At a time of nightly attacks by squads of gunmen on Jews in hiding, somehow she found someone to take her in. I had no way of knowing whether she was alone then. But concealing one teenage girl might have seemed manageable. If she was still with a guy, hiding them both would have been more difficult. Either way, she would have been seventeen at war's end, and could have blended in among the many displaced Poles on the move, starting over.

It turns out an agency was formed that provided support for Poles forced to resettle from the eastern territories within the changing borders of the nation. An entity known as the State Repatriation Office (*Państwowy Urząd Repatriacyjny*, or

PUR) provided resources that could help her get an apartment and a job far away from her dangerous hometown and the killers of her family.

PUR could have paved the way for her journey when she "went west." Of course there is no record of Hena having taken advantage of those services under her accurate name. She may have chosen a new identity to remain incognito at a chaotic time when no one was tracing identities. Kozioł did confirm for me a fact that added credence to the information provided by Radziszewski's daughter: she married Slanisław Lushinski in 1946 and gave birth to her first child in 1947. That added up with Mrs. Luszczyńska's account of her father visiting Hena near Wrocław and bringing back baby gifts.

That's as close as I got to finding a happy ending for Hena.

She escaped Zagórzyce with her life. But what kind of postwar life was it? She could melt into the crowd of displaced people around Wrocław, where no one had a local past. Perhaps when her children grew up, she told them they were Jewish. If so, they might have been as confused as the young men I met at the rabbi's house in Warsaw after the Jedwabne exhumations.

I don't know who to thank for rescuing Hena a second time. Perhaps the descendants of this second rescuer do not even know that their family harbored this teenager after her family was murdered. Maybe the rescuer became the contact point for authorities seeking Hena as a witness against defendants in her family's slayings. Hena appeared but did not cooperate. No one was ever held responsible for five members of her family who died on a rainy May night after each was forced into a fusillade of gunfire.

I could hardly offer Kozioł a sufficient reason for the second rescuer to share more details or even their identity with me. The presence of relatives of the Rożeńeks' killers in the area and the way other righteous Poles were treated offered little motivation to go public about their brave actions in shielding Hena. The experience of generations of Sodos, who were publicly known to have hidden the Dulas, was hardly encouraging. Even though the Dulas were murdered and those convicted in the crimes received amnesty and full veterans' benefits, the Sodos bear the stigma for harboring them.

As *Night without End* established, the burden of saving many Jews in Poland fell to residents of tiny villages like Zagórzyce, requiring enormous sacrifices, even though research shows that the Germans very rarely punished Poles in that area for hiding Jews. In fact, scant support exists for the mandated historical narrative of the Polish government. In particular, the government insists that it was the norm during the war for Poles to rescue Jews. But if that were the case, if so many had been righteous gentiles saving Jews, why do the neighbors and communities persist in their anger and abuse of the grandchildren and great grandchildren of the brave rescuers we met?

Kozioł's reasoning that the truth about Sam's cousin Hena might upset him hits on a viable legal tenet in today's Poland. The judge in the libel case against Grabowski and Engelking decided that regardless of the truth of the evidence that the village mayor had betrayed Jews leading to their murder, they were still liable. Why?

"To blame Poles in any way for the Holocaust provokes a feeling of harm...and consequently is completely untrue and hurtful." The judge found that Poland as a nation and Polish people as individuals could not be considered responsible for the Holocaust in any way. "The unprecedented historical events which constitute the legacy of the community and of its individual members and which are considered factual beyond any discussion cannot be made relative."[1]

The judge's ruling slammed the door on inquiries or public discussion of attacks by Poles that we now knew were happening frequently in the spring of 1944. She held that paving over the past is essential to avoid the risk of hurting feelings of national pride.

The passage of time in stony silence, ignoring buried truths, together with official practices of sealing records and protecting feelings, wipes away historical memory. Then who can say for sure what happened?

This opinion in a government-backed libel case is disturbing. That it is being baked into laws, policies, and judgments in Poland is alarming. Protecting people from hurt feelings they might suffer from exposure to facts threatens not only how we remember the past, it also endangers how we resolve disputes, uphold treaties, and live under the rule of law.

Fortunately, an appeals court judge in Warsaw overturned this ruling and found, "There is no personal right in the form of national identity, attachment to the Polish nation, or national pride." The Appeals Court upheld "the importance of a free historical debate in a democratic society, including difficult and painful issues."[2]

Professor Jan Grabowski, who expects that Poland is not done attacking him or his work, is sounding the alarm for what Poland is doing in conflating the genocide of Jews with the suffering of non-Jewish Poles, something scholars call "Holocaust envy," mandating a false equivalency.

"When a society is steeped in the contemplation of its own suffering and brought up in a tradition of innocence and victimhood, there is little room for recognition or appreciation of the suffering of the other," Grabowski said in a talk on Poland's Holocaust distortion.[3]

While Poles cling to innocence, Sam has clung to family. The rare survivor to emerge with both parents, he started over in Israel without them, and even changed his surname. But after a while, the pull of family brought him to the U.S., where he went to work in his father's business. Having followed family himself, he just cannot believe that Hena, who had witnessed her parents' murder, would not seek surviving relatives.

Sam stood tall in a place where so many tried to kill him. Well into old age, he was still unearthing nuggets of information about lost people, connecting dots, and even as he learned ugly truths in his hometown, he still offered solace to people he wasn't so sure about. He darned many holes in the fabric of our family and our people. At the same time, he continually bears witness to the crimes against so many.

It seemed like his showing up again and again would jog memories. Surely it did. He disrupted the deliberate amnesia about the homegrown violence that together with the Germans' mass killings destroyed the lives of some six hundred people in the community.[4]

But the "prince of the city" could not loosen lips sealed by fear or some sense of solidarity with those involved in the murders. It was easier to abide by the local code and keep quiet. Denial proved more powerful than allegiance to a man they had known and perhaps even admired when he was a schoolmate, neighbor, and son of a leading businessman. That was before all Jews and their property became fair game.

The stonewalling took its toll. The consideration that Guca accorded young Sam during the occupation, walking with him when Sam was barred from the trains, did not carry over to those postwar visits. Even as an old man, Guca refused to help Sam track his surviving cousin or even confirm that she had survived. It couldn't be more personal.

Sam rationalized his disappointment, trying to convince himself, "This does not matter."

But it does.

For my part, I went from drilling down on how Sam survived to trying to find out whether and how Hena survived. The impenetrable walls raised by everyone from local townspeople to national institutions kept pulling me in deeper.

I was fortunate to have a front-row seat to Sam's amazing interactions with workers and neighbors across his native geography at a time when he could connect with people who remembered our relatives. I got to see him pull from his mental database names and places where people lived, worked, and tried to hide. He parlayed that knowledge again and again to find out the hidden fate of several murdered relatives.

As a young adult, I got to know Sam just when he was ready to focus on his wartime experiences. It coincided with the height of my own curiosity about my own identity. I saw in him my poppy's sunny pragmatism and my father's charismatic stubbornness—the Rakowski essence.

I hungered to learn this history from a living relative rather than from handed-down stories. With Sam, it all came back to life before my eyes. Through Sam, I saw that our family's long life in Poland was far more meaningful than the way it ended.

My investment in the quest for Hena ultimately outpaced Sam's. He gave it up, he said, in favor of returning to Poland on trips that offered him more success and satisfaction. On those trips when there was "no room in the car" for me, he underscored my outsider status. I hail from what he calls the Yankee family, with parents born in America.

But Hena's elusive trail led us to places and people who unsealed a dark history. Above all, I wanted Sam to meet her again. All along I believed Sam that she was not my relative. But when my application for access to government archives required that I prove I was related to her, Sammy found that her grandmother and my great-grandmother were sisters. I told Sam about the discovery, but I didn't know if it sunk in.

Soon afterward, we visited him in Florida in March 2022 when he was honored by the United States Holocaust Memorial Museum. Sam was surrounded by four generations of his family—his children, a grandchild, and a great-grandchild—a true triumph of survival.

Watching them pose for photos, my mind drifted back once again to the mystery of the lost cousin. To save her own life, she had to change her identity. I was lucky. In following her path, I found my own.

As always, Sam introduced me as the Yankee cousin, a descendant of the Rakowski who left. But whether or not he recognizes it, Poland, the magnet for Sam well into his nineties, had turned into a strong draw for me. I feel responsible for paying attention to our history there or watch it disappear.

Whether the family tree that Sammy filled in with my blood connections to Hena finally sunk in or on some level he considered all our "Polish business" over the years, something prompted Sam to turn to me during that visit and say, "You're family."

Sam not only survived and lived through it—*durkh leben*—he thrived and tended the memory of our family, including those still lying in gardens in Poland.

What the next generation will learn about that true history is strongly in doubt. The inspiring young schoolteachers we met in Kazimierza wanted Sam to help them teach current students about the local history of Jews. But the winds blowing out of Warsaw do not bode well for adding such elements to the curriculum.

A generation ago, young Dominik had tried to find more information on what happened to the Jews hiding on his family farm. His teachers accused him of telling a tall tale.

Now Dominik is a father himself. His optimism and quiet strength remind me of all the forthright and brave people in Poland who helped us try to find Hena and who face a formidable challenge dealing with Polish-Jewish history in these times. I've met many people who are educating, investigating, piecing together fragments of lives, restoring some dignity and a sense of reality to the millions who were denied humanity and life. They face such pressure, the weight of a society and a culture that is deeply invested in wiping the fingerprints of Poles from those events despite what Grabowski described as "ample, uncontested, and easily available historical evidence."[5] Several cited the reality of their government situation and asked not to be named or associated with their good works.

But Dominik has clear plans to pass the baton. "My son will know the truth."

# Acknowledgments

I am deeply grateful to Cousin Sam for introducing me to the land that shaped my family for generations and has had a profound impact on me. In our travels, I met generous, righteous Poles who risked everything trying to save our relatives. Building bonds with their children and grandchildren, especially Danuta Sodo Ogórek, Dominik Ogórek, and Wioleta Mleko-Włowowicz has been a rewarding gift.

From my first footsteps in 1990, dear friend Colleen Fitzpatrick, then reporting from Poland, introduced me to wonderful Warsovians who became mainstays on my journey and valued friends. Over nine trips in a thirty-year span, I got a time-release view of the country's evolution. That included institutions such as the Emanuel Ringelblum Jewish Historical Institute, which rose from the rubble of the Warsaw ghetto to its glassy modern structure that houses artifacts and protectors of important history. Its genealogy department takes scraps of information and partial names, and reconstructs lives and families. I am grateful to Anna Przybyszewska Drozd and her former colleague Yale Reisner.

# Acknowledgments

I am deeply grateful to Cousin Sam for introducing me to the land that shaped my family for generations and has had a profound impact on me. In our travels, I met generous, righteous Poles who risked everything trying to save our relatives. Building bonds with their children and grandchildren, especially Danuta Sodo Ogórek, Dominik Ogórek, and Wioleta Mleko-Włowowicz has been a rewarding gift.

From my first footsteps in 1990, dear friend Colleen Fitzpatrick, then reporting from Poland, introduced me to wonderful Warsovians who became mainstays on my journey and valued friends. Over nine trips in a thirty-year span, I got a time-release view of the country's evolution. That included institutions such as the Emanuel Ringelblum Jewish Historical Institute, which rose from the rubble of the Warsaw ghetto to its glassy modern structure that houses artifacts and protectors of important history. Its genealogy department takes scraps of information and partial names, and reconstructs lives and families. I am grateful to Anna Przybyszewska Drozd and her former colleague Yale Reisner.

My considerable needs for help with translating Polish, but some Yiddish, Hebrew, and Russian fell at first to Sam, but then I got invaluable on-the-ground aid from Daga Landau and Małgorzata Lewińska, who not only provided language help but read people and situations well. The extensive print translation needs fell to an evolving roster of translators, particularly Lucjan Zaborowski, Przemek Swadzka, Regina Swadzka, and Katka Reszke.

The mayor of Kazimierza Wielka, Adam Bodzioch, deserves special thanks for his commitment to opening a door to the Jewish history of Kazimierza and welcoming us in celebrating it. He has charted a path that I hope successors follow. Małgorzata Grabska, a teacher and community leader in nearby Busko Zdrój has provided insights to present day dynamics in putting on such Jewish cultural remembrance events, joining the expert former Chmielnik mayor Jarosław Zatorski.

Special thanks to Tadeusz Kozioł for his efforts to chronicle the local imprint of the late Ray Fischler and Sam (Rakowski) Ron, and his interest in remembering the history of the Jews in Kazimierza.

I appreciate the help I received over the years from law enforcement contacts developed on my day job. I'm grateful to the far-flung FBI alumni network, including Richard S. Swensen, Michael Pyszczymuka, John Bienkowski, and John Gamel.

There are many people I cannot thank by name at their request. Others I refer to for similar reasons only by their first names.

I name my husband, Sam Mendales, who only joined three Poland trips, but also lent his expertise in photography, videography, and genealogy to this project. He also shared many insights and indulged endless discussions about European history and the Holocaust, not to mention oodles of support and partnership.

I was able to turn this tale into a book thanks to help over the years from writing teachers and coaches, including Jami Bernard, the three-act structure wizard, and muscular verb champion Anne Bernays and her Nieman Foundation fiction writing course. I benefited from the feedback and camaraderie of Mark Kramer's Kitchen Table Workshop.

Thanks are due as well to Irena Grudzińska Gross for her critique, Cate Ferson for Polish contacts, Cheyenne Paris for citations help, and Maya Reisz for her organizational prowess.

I am indebted to Sara Rimer, whose writing I admired since my college days at the *Michigan Daily*, and who introduced me to Avery Rome, an amazing developmental editor who hones arcs of action and characters with a great sense of story and of humor.

Sara first introduced me to literary agent Susan Canavan of the Waxman Agency, who quickly grasped the story and its potential. With her wise shepherding, it landed at Sourcebooks. I am deeply grateful to Anna Michels, editorial director of Sourcebooks, for sage edits and stewardship, and to Findlay McCarthy, the talented assistant editor.

Author friends E. B. Moore, Michael Arkush, Larry Tye,

and Stephanie Schorow helped light the long path. Special thanks to Farah Stockman for spurring me to pick this story up again and keep my bearings. Thanks to writer friends Judy Fahys, Stacy Mattingly, Chris Woodside, and Karen Weintraub for timely encouragement.

And to Rabbi Liza Stern, thank you for the reminders that I am lucky I get to tell this story.

# Reading Group Guide

1. Before reading the book, what, if anything, did you know about Poland's role in World War II? What was the most surprising thing you learned while reading?

2. How would you characterize Stefan? He was the originator of the quest for Hena but proved slippery when Sam tried to follow up. Why do you think he mentioned Hena to Sam when they first reconnected? What caused his change of heart later?

3. The Rożcńek family (of which Hena was the only survivor) and the Dula family (their cousins) both successfully found hiding places. Why weren't those hiding places durable?

4. Sam is convinced that Hena would have reached out to find her family after the war if she survived—or at least that she *should* have done that. Do you agree with him that

her silence signals her demise? If not, why do you think she
has maintained her secrecy?

5.  How does Poland justify the legal gag orders that prevent
    anyone from acknowledging the mixed history of their
    partisans? Should a sense of patriotism or comfort be
    valued over truth? Can we be proud of our countries *and*
    acknowledge their unrevised histories?

6.  What reasons did partisans give for conducting their own
    pogroms outside of any Nazi influence? What benefits did
    they seek?

7.  In the latter half of the book, Sam has ostensibly given up
    the search for Hena, though he occasionally still discovers
    new information. Why do you think he started to withdraw
    from the investigation? Why can't he give it up entirely?

8.  What are some of the factors that make it so difficult to
    find information about Hena in Polish archival records?
    Would any of these obstacles be removed if Poland lifted
    their restrictions about WWII history?

9.  Although Poland is defensive of their reputation as saviors
    of Jews, individual families who sheltered Jews are heav-
    ily ostracized in their communities for generations. What
    causes this dissonance?

10. Despite the constant disappointments, Sam remains proud of his Polish heritage and fosters great affection for his hometown. How do you think you would view your childhood community if you were in Sam's position?

11. At the conclusion, Hena is still missing, though the search continues. Even in her absence, what is Hena's legacy?

# A Conversation
# with the Author

**How did you first approach Sam about his past experiences? Do you have advice for readers who would like to start similar conversations with their loved ones and learn more about family history?**

I showed interest in Sam's past. Before, he had not widely shared it, and he responded to that interest. Asking simple questions about a loved one's early life and showing you care enough to follow up can lead to surprising results.

**In moments like the one where you and Sam are told that you may look at his old table but not take it, how did you maintain your composure? Was there ever a time you wanted to leave an interview early or something even more drastic?**

My head was spinning when she said that, essentially accusing us of wanting to steal furniture. But it came in the oddest of social situations from someone Sam considered an old friend. In many of these encounters, delays in translation made it difficult to act in the moment. But if I had understood in real time the remark of the woman who said Jews should not complain because "so many of you survived" I would have had a strong retort. Sadly, I don't believe it would have changed her opinion.

**You have been searching for this truth for over thirty years now. What kept you invested through so many false leads and dead ends? Was there ever a point that you wanted to go along with Sam's dictate, "This does not matter"? In those moments, how did you rekindle your motivation?**

The wonderful people who helped us in Poland spurred me on at many turns—fresh eyes and ideas of new recruits to the quest fueled my curiosity and hope all over again. They also reminded me that you cannot judge a country by its government or its worst, small-minded people. By nature, I'm loathe to give up. I kept thinking I just needed to pull one more thread and all would be revealed.

**What do the other members of your extended family think of the many trips both you and Sam have devoted to this quest? Do they understand your obsession?**

Our extended family adores and respects Sam and his efforts to discover the fate of lost relatives. I'm not sure anyone quite understands why I have gone to Poland so many times, but my family knows how I am digging on a story, like a dog with a bone.

**In the process of looking for Hena, you and Sam discovered the fate of another branch of the family and many other**

details that you weren't specifically looking for. What would you say has been the biggest surprise of the search?

The biggest and saddest discovery was that the way they died was not rare and how unwelcome efforts to reveal what happened to them are in Poland today.

**Most of the information you uncover is devastating in one way or another. What strategies helped you weather the news of betrayals and murders?**

I don't have Sam's seasoned Teflon for managing loss, but the balm of connecting with good people in Poland, particularly those who tried to save our relatives, has meant so much.

**How have your trips to Poland changed your own life? What is Hena's legacy for you, even if you haven't yet found her?**

It may sound corny, but I found strength getting to know and accept parts of myself and who I am along the way. Hena was on her own and went through way too much at such an early age. She inspires me just as Sam does for how he found his own way in the world despite everything that happened to him.

**Many of the recent book bans in the United States target titles that deal with the history of slavery and race in this country. How would you compare those attempted bans to Poland's gag rules about the Holocaust? Based on your experiences in Poland, do you have recommendations for maintaining a record of true history and combating revisionist agendas?**

Book bans, hijacking curricula, and the legal notion that we have a right to pride in our country's history—in Poland and the U.S.—are a scourge that calls on all of us to be vigilant. I saw in Poland how librarians there, just as in the U.S., are on the front lines of these battles. At the core of all this suppression of history is a fear of learning unflattering facts, as if truth is the enemy. But how will we grow as people and societies if we do not face mistakes and figure out how to live together? We need unflinching support for academic freedom, cultural exchanges, and honest displays of history in museums and in public discourse.

# Bibliography

"Archive of Jewish War Graves." Zapomniane. Accessed July 24, 2022.
https://zapomniane.org/en/.

Armstrong, John Lowell. "The Polish Underground and the Jews:
A Reassessment of Home Army Commander Tadeusz Bór-
Komorowski's Order 116 against Banditry." *Slavonic and East
European Review* 72, no. 2 (1994): 259–76. http://www.jstor.org
/stable/4211476.

Associated Press. "New Polish Historical Policy Could Silence Holocaust
Debates." *VOA News*, March 22, 2016. https://www.voanews
.com/a/new-polish-historical-policy-could-silence-holocaust
-debates/3249438.html.

Associated Press. "Poles to Exhume Mass Grave of Jews Killed in
Massacre." *Los Angeles Times*, May 25, 2001. https://www.latimes
.com/archives/la-xpm-2001-may-25-mn-2305-story.html.

Bartov, Omer. *Erased: Vanishing Traces of Jewish Galicia in Present-Day
Ukraine*. Princeton, NJ: Princeton University Press, 2007.

Bauer, Yehuda. *Flight and Rescue: Brichah*. New York: Random House,
1970.

Bikont, Anna. *The Crime and the Silence: A Quest for the Truth of a
Wartime Massacre*. Translated by Alissa Valles. London: Windmill
Books, 2016.

"Chapter XXVI, Shawnee Township: 1885." Ohio Genealogy Express.
Accessed July 24, 2022. http://www.ohiogenealogyexpress.com

/allen/allenco_hist_1885/allenco_hist_1885_chpt_xxv_shawnee
.htm.

Crowe, David M. *Oskar Schindler: The Untold Account of His Life,
Wartime Activities, and the True Story Behind the List.* Cambridge,
MA: Westview Press, 2004.

Daum, Menachem, and Oren Rudavsky, dirs. *Hiding and Seeking: Faith
and Tolerance after the Holocaust.* ITVS International, 2005.

Day, Matthew. "Smolensk Air Disaster 'Was Caused by Mystery
Explosion.'" *Telegraph*, April 10, 2014. https://www.telegraph.co.uk
/news/worldnews/europe/poland/10758863/Smolensk-air-disaster
-was-caused-by-mystery-explosion.html.

de Pommereau, Isabelle. "Son of an Anti-Nazi Hero Uses Family Estate to
Nurture Democracy and Rule of Law." *Christian Science Monitor*, July
6, 2012. https://www.csmonitor.com/World/Making-a-difference
/2012/0706/Son-of-an-anti-Nazi-hero-uses-family-estate-to-nurture
-democracy-and-rule-of-law.

Dobrowolska, Joanna. "A Complicated Peace: Nationalism and
Antisemitism in Interwar Poland." Master's thesis, Utah State
University, 2018. https://digitalcommons.usu.edu/etd/7103/.

Elowitz, Jodi. "Heroism and Sacrifice as Represented in Nathan
Rapoport's Warsaw Ghetto Monument." Society Pages, April 22,
2018. https://thesocietypages.org/holocaust-genocide/heroism
-and-sacrifice-as-represented-in-nathan-rapoports-warsaw-ghetto
-monument/.

Elsby, Liz. "Rapoport's Memorial to the Warsaw Ghetto Uprising—a
Personal Interpretation." Yad Vashem. Accessed July 24, 2022.
https://www.yadvashem.org/articles/general/warsaw-memorial
-personal-interpretation.html.

"Encyclopedia of Camps and Ghettos, 1933–1945." United States
Holocaust Memorial Museum. Accessed June 30, 2022. https://www
.ushmm.org/research/publications/encyclopedia-camps-ghettos.

Engelking, Barbara. *Holocaust and Memory: The Experience of the
Holocaust and Its Consequences: An Investigation Based On Personal
Narratives.* Edited by Gunnar S. Paulsson. Translated by Emma

Harris. New York: Leicester University Press, European Jewish Publication Society, 2001.

Engelking, Barbara. *Such a Beautiful Sunny Day...: Jews Seeking Refuge in the Polish Countryside, 1942–1945*. Translated by Jerzy Michałowicz. Jerusalem: Yad Vashem Publications, 2016.

Engelking, Barbara, and Jan Grabowski, eds. *Dalej jest noc. Losy Żydów w wybranych powiatach okupowanej Polski* [Night without End: The fate of Jews in selected counties of Occupied Poland]. 2 vols. Warsaw: Centrum Badań nad Zagłada Żydów, 2018.

Fogelman, Eva. *Conscience and Courage: Rescuers of Jews during the Holocaust*. New York: Anchor Books, 1994.

Friedländer, Saul. *Memory, History, and the Extermination of the Jews of Europe*. Bloomington: Indiana University Press, 1993.

Friedländer, Saul. *The Years of Extermination: Nazi Germany and the Jews, 1939–1945*. New York: Harper Collins, 2007.

Gessen, Masha. "Historians under Attack for Exploring Poland's Role in the Holocaust." *New Yorker*, March 26, 2021. https://www .newyorker.com/news/our-columnists/the-historians-under-attack -for-exploring-polands-role-in-the-holocaust.

Gessen, Masha. "Poland's Ruling Party Puts an Extraordinary Museum of Polish-Jewish History into Limbo." *New Yorker*, September 23, 2019. https://www.newyorker.com/news/our-columnists/polands-ruling -party-puts-an-extraordinary-museum-of-polish-jewish-history-into -limbo.

Grabowski, Jan. "Hijacking Memory of the Holocaust: From Treblinka through Auschwitz to the Warsaw Ghetto." June 12, 2022. Video, 25:30. https://www.hkw.de/en/app/mediathek/video/91276.

Grabowski, Jan. *Hunt for the Jews: Betrayal and Murder in German-Occupied Poland*. Bloomington: Indiana University Press, 2013.

Grabowski, Jan. "Rewriting the History of Polish-Jewish Relations from a Nationalist Perspective: The Recent Publications of the Institute of National Remembrance." *Yad Vashem Studies* 36, no. 1 (January 2008): 253–70.

Grabowski, Jan, and Barbara Engelking, eds. *Night without End: The Fate of Jews in Selected Counties of Occupied Poland.* Bloomington: Indiana University Press, 2022.

Grabowski, Jan, and Dariusz Libionka. "Distorting and Rewriting the History of the Holocaust in Poland: The Case of the Ulma Family Museum of Poles Saving Jews during World War II in Markowa." *Yad Vashem Studies* 45, no. 1 (2017): 29–61.

Gross, Jan Tomasz. *Neighbors: The Destruction of the Jewish Community in Jedwabne, Poland.* Princeton, NJ: Princeton University Press, 2001.

Hackmann, Jorg. "Defending the 'Good Name' of the Polish Nation: Politics of History as a Battlefield in Poland, 2015–18." *Journal of Genocide Research* 20, no. 4 (2018): 587–606. https://doi.org/10.1080/14623528.2018.1528742.

Hilberg, Raul. *Perpetrators, Victims, Bystanders: The Jewish Catastrophe 1933–1945.* London: Harper Collins, 1992.

Holc, Janine P. "Working through Jan Gross's *Neighbors*." *Slavic Review* 61, no 3 (2002): 453–59. https://doi.org/10.2307/3090294.

Judt, Tony. "The Past Is Another Country: Myth and Memory in Postwar Europe." Daedalus 121, no. 4 (Fall 1992): 83–118. http://www.jstor.org/stable/20027138.

Kozioł, Tadeusz. *Dodatek do kwestii martyrologii i zagłady społeczności żydowskiej w Kazimierzy Wielkiej i okoliach* [Supplement to the Issue of Martyrology and the Holocaust of the Jewish Community]. Odonów, Poland: Cultural Society of Odonów, 2017.

Kozioł, Tadeusz. *Żydzi w historii Kazimierzy Wielkiej* [Jews in the History of Kazimierza Wielka]. Busko-Zdrój, Poland: Buskie Stowarzyszenie Kulturalne, 2021.

Kucia, Marek, Marta Duch-Dyngosz, and Mateusz Magierowski. "The Collective Memory of Auschwitz and World War II among Catholics in Poland: A Qualitative Study of Three Communities." *History and Memory* 25, no. 2 (2013): 132–73. https://doi.org/10.2979/histmemo.25.2.132.

Lanzmann, Claude, dir. *Shoah*. New Yorker Films, 1985.

Leslie, Roy F. *The History of Poland Since 1863.* Cambridge: Cambridge University Press, 1983.

Libionka, Dariusz. "Documents of the Polish Underground State concerning the extermination of the Jews." In *Guide to the Sources on the Holocaust in Occupied Poland*, edited by Alina Skibińska, translated by Jessica Taylor-Kucia, 251–58. Warsaw: European Holocaust Research Infrastructure, 2014.

Mendelsohn, Daniel. *The Lost: A Search for Six of Six Million*. New York: Harper Perennial, 2006.

Michlic, Joanna B. "'At the Crossroads': Jedwabne and Polish Historiography of the Holocaust." *Dapim: Studies on the Holocaust* 31, no. 3 (2017): 296–306. https://doi.org/10.1080/23256249.2017.1376793.

Michlic, Joanna B. "'I Will Never Forget What You Did for Me during the War': Rescuer-Rescuee Relationships in the Light of Postwar Correspondence in Poland, 1945–1949." *Yad Vashem Studies* 39, no. 2 (2011): 169–207. https://research-information.bris.ac.uk/ws/portalfiles/portal/10934473/MichlicYadVashemStudiesDec.2011.pdf.

Michlic, Joanna B. *Jewish Children in Nazi-Occupied Poland: Survival and Polish-Jewish Relations during the Holocaust as Reflected in Early Postwar Recollections*. Search and Research 14. Jerusalem: Yad Vashem, 2008.

Michlic, Joanna B. "Many Faces of the Memory of the Holocaust in Post-Communist Poland." In *Legends and Legacies 11: Expanding Perspectives on the Holocaust in a Changing World*, edited by Hilary Earl and Karl A. Schleunes, 144–179. Evanston, IL: Northwestern University Press, 2019.

Michlic, Joanna B. *Poland's Threatening Other: The Image of the Jew from 1880 to the Present*. Lincoln: University of Nebraska Press, 2006.

Michnik, Adam. "Poles and the Jews: How Deep the Guilt?" *New York Times*, March 17, 2001. https://www.nytimes.com/2001/03/17/arts/poles-and-the-jews-how-deep-the-guilt.html.

Michnik, Adam. "The Shock of Jedwabne." In *In Search of Lost Meaning: The New Eastern Europe*, edited by Irena Grudzinska Gross, translated by Roman S. Czarny, 204–12. Berkeley: University of California Press, 2011.

Mikics, David. "The Day We Burned Our Neighbors Alive." *Tablet*, October 20, 2015. https://www.tabletmag.com/sections/arts-letters /articles/anna-bikont-jedwabne.

"Obchody 75. rocznicy powstania Narodowych Sił Zbrojnych" [Celebration of the 75th anniversary of the establishment of the National Armed Forces]. Institute of National Remembrance, September 16, 2017. https://ipn.gov.pl/pl/aktualnosci /41742,Obchody-75-rocznicy-powstania-Narodowych-Sil-Zbrojnych -Warszawa-16-wrzesnia-2017.html.

Pileggi, Tamar. "Poland Moves to Strip Jewish Holocaust Scholar of Award." *Times of Israel*, February 14, 2016. https://www.timesofisrael .com/poland-moves-to-strip-jewish-holocaust-scholar-of-award/.

Polonsky, Antony, ed. *"My Brother's Keeper?": Recent Polish Debates on the Holocaust*. London: Routledge, 1990.

Polonsky, Antony, and Joanna B. Michlic. *The Neighbors Respond: The Controversy over the Jedwabne Massacre in Poland*. Princeton, NJ: Princeton University Press, 2004.

Popowycz, Jennifer. "Nazi Forced Labor Policy in Eastern Europe." National World War II Museum, March 14, 2022. https://www .nationalww2museum.org/war/articles/nazi-forced-labor-policy -eastern-europe.

"Populations and Migration." *YIVO Encyclopedia of Jews in Eastern Europe*. Accessed June 30, 2022. https://yivoencyclopedia.org /article.aspx/Population_and_Migration/Population_since_World _War_I#id0ezsbi.

Raack, R. C. "Stalin Fixes the Oder-Neisse Line." *Journal of Contemporary History* 25, no. 4 (October 1990): 467–88. https://www.jstor.org /stable/260758.

"Sachsenhausen." United States Holocaust Memorial Museum. Accessed July 24, 2022. https://encyclopedia.ushmm.org/content/en/article /sachsenhausen#prisoners-in-the-camp-.

"Schindler's Lists." United States Holocaust Memorial Museum. Accessed June 20, 2022. https://www.ushmm.org/online/hsv/source_view.php ?SourceId=20610.

Skibińska, Alina, and Jakub Petelewicz. "Udział Polaków w zbrodniach na Żydach na prowincji regionu świętokrzyskiego" [The participation of Poles in crimes against Jews in the Świętokrzyskie region]. *Zagłada Żydów* 1 (2005): 114–48. https://doi.org/10.32927/ZZSiM.151.

Sobieski, John. *The Life of King John Sobieski: John the Third of Poland, a Christian Knight, the Savior of Christendom.* Boston: Richard G. Badger, 1915.

Sommer, Anna. "Auschwitz Today: Personal Observations and Reflections about Visitors to the Auschwitz-Birkenau State Museum and Memorial." *Les Cahiers Irice* 7, no. 1 (2011): 87–94. https://doi .org/10.3917/lci.007.0087.

Stola, Dariusz. "The Polish Government in Exile and the Final Solution." In *Contested Memories: Poles and Jews during the Holocaust and Its Aftermath*, edited by Joshua D. Zimmerman, 85–96. Piscataway, NJ: Rutgers University Press, 2003.

Stutz, Eli. "Saved by Keeping Shabbat." *Israel National News*, April 14, 2010. https://web.archive.org/web/20211217071934/https://www .israelnationalnews.com/news/137018.

Teller, Adam. "Polish-Jewish Relations: Historical Research and Social Significance: On the Legacy of Jacob Goldberg." *Studia Judaica* 15, no. 1–2 (2012): 29–30.

Tokarska-Bakir, Joanna. "How to Exit the Conspiracy of Silence?: Social Sciences Facing the Polish-Jewish Relations." *East European Politics and Societies: and Cultures* 25, no. 1 (2011): 129–52. https://doi .org/10.1177/0888325410387640.

Tokarska-Bakir, Joanna. *Jewish Fugitives in the Polish Countryside, 1939– 1945: Beyond the German Holocaust Project.* Translated by Yecheskiel Anis, Ewa Gedroyc, Nicholas Hodge, Jerzy Jurus, Jessica Taylor-Kucia, and Benjamin Voelkel. Eastern European Culture, Politics and Societies 18. Warsaw: Peter Lang, 2022.

Tokarska-Bakir, Joanna. "The Ultimate Lost Object." Paper presented at the Second Annual Polish Jewish Studies Workshop, Princeton University, Princeton, NJ, April 17–19, 2015. https://doi.org /10.13140/RG.2.1.3613.0725.

Tokarska-Bakir, Joanna, and Avner Greenberg. "The Unrighteous
    Righteous and the Righteous Unrighteous." *Dapim: Studies on the
    Shoah* 24, no. 1 (2010): 11–63. https://doi.org/10.1080/23256249
    .2010.10744397.
Translation of ruling of Judge Joanna Wisniewska-Sadomska, Court of
    Appeal in Warsaw I Civil Division, I ACa 300/21, Judgment on
    Behalf of the Republic of Poland, August 16, 2021.
van Pelt, Robert Jan, Luis Ferreiro, and Miriam Greenbaum, eds.
    *Auschwitz: Not Long Ago. Not Far Away.* New York: Abbeville Press,
    2019.
Vinokour, Maya. "90% of Polish Jews Died in the Holocaust. So Why
    Are Poland's Nationalists Chanting 'Get the Jews Out of Power'?"
    *Haaretz,* November 13, 2017. https://www.haaretz.com/jewish
    /holocaust-remembrance-day/2017-11-13/ty-article/why-polish
    -nationalists-chant-get-the-jews-out-of-power/0000017f-e7fe-d97e
    -a37f-f7ffb30e0000.
"Warsaw Ghetto." Yad Vashem. Accessed July 24, 2022. https://yadvashem
    .org/holocaust/about/ghettos/warsaw.html.
Wauchope, Mary. "*The Counterfeiters*: Seeking Moral Lessons from a
    Holocaust Thriller." *Shofar* 28, no. 4 (2010): 57–71. http://www
    .jstor.org/stable/10.5703/shofar.28.4.57.
Wolentarska-Ochman, Ewa. "Collective Remembrance in Jedwabne:
    Unsettled Memory of World War II in Postcommunist Poland."
    *History & Memory* 18, no. 1 (2006): 152–78. https://muse.jhu.edu
    /article/196874.
Wróbel, Piotr. *Historical Dictionary of Poland, 1945–1996.* New York:
    Routledge, 1998.
Zimmerman, Joshua D. *The Polish Underground and the Jews, 1939–1945.*
    Cambridge: Cambridge University Press, 2015.
Zimmerman, Joshua D. "The Polish Underground Home Army (AK) and
    the Jews: What Postwar Jewish Testimonies and Wartime Documents
    Reveal." *East European Politics and Societies: and Cultures* 34, no. 1
    (2020): 194–220. https://doi.org/10.1177/0888325419844816.

# Notes

## PROLOGUE: HENA IN HIDING

1   Jennifer Popowycz, "Nazi Forced Labor Policy in Eastern Europe," National WWII Museum, March 14, 2022, https://www.nationalww2museum.org/war/articles/nazi-forced-labor-policy-eastern-europe.

## CHAPTER 1: LOST AND FOUND

1   David M. Crowe, *Oskar Schindler: The Untold Account of His Life, Wartime Activities, and the True Story Behind the List* (Cambridge, MA: Westview Press, 2004), 237.

2   Mary Wauchope, "The Counterfeiters: Seeking Moral Lessons from a Holocaust Thriller," *Shofar* 28, no. 4 (2010): 57–71, http://www.jstor.org/stable/10.5703/shofar.28.4.57.

3   "Sachsenhausen," United States Holocaust Memorial Museum, accessed July 24, 2022, https://encyclopedia.ushmm.org/content/en/article/sachsenhausen.

4   "Schindler's Lists," United States Holocaust Memorial Museum, accessed June 20, 2022, https://www.ushmm.org/online/hsv/source_view.php?SourceId=20610.

## CHAPTER 2: THE OLD COUNTRY

1   Mark Tolts, "Populations and Migration: Population since World War I," *YIVO Encyclopedia of Jews in Eastern Europe*, October 12, 2010, https://yivoencyclopedia.org/article.aspx/Population_and_Migration/Population_since_World_War_I.

2   John Sobieski, *The Life of King John Sobieski: John the Third of Poland, a Christian Knight, the Savior of Christendom* (Boston: Richard G. Badger, 1915), viii.

3   "Encyclopedia of Camps and Ghettos, 1933–1945," United States Holocaust Memorial Museum, accessed June 30, 2022, https://www.ushmm.org /research/publications/encyclopedia-camps-ghettos.

4   Joshua D. Zimmerman, *The Polish Underground and the Jews, 1939–1945* (Cambridge: Cambridge University Press, 2015), 13–35.

5   Joanna Dobrowolska, "A Complicated Peace: Nationalism and Antisemitism in Interwar Poland" (master's thesis, Utah State University, 2018), 25, https:// digitalcommons.usu.edu/etd/7103/.

6   Joanna B. Michlic, "Many Faces of the Memory of the Holocaust in Post-Communist Poland," in *Lessons and Legacies XI: Expanding Perspectives on the Holocaust in a Changing World,* ed. Hilary Earl and Karl A. Schleune (Evanston, IL: Northwestern University Press, 2019), 144–79.

7   Marek Kucia, Marta Duch-Dyngosz, and Mateusz Magierowski, "The Collective Memory of Auschwitz and World War II among Catholics in Poland: A Qualitative Study of Three Communities," *History and Memory* 25, no. 2 (2013): 132–73, https://doi.org/10.2979/histmemo.25.2.132.

8   R. C. Raack, "Stalin Fixes the Oder-Neisse Line," *Journal of Contemporary History* 25, no. 4 (October 1990): 467–88, https://www.jstor.org /stable/260758.

9   Raack, "Stalin Fixes the Oder-Neisse Line," 469–71.

10  Tadeusz Kozioł, *Dodatek do kwestii martyrologii i zagłady społeczności żydowskiej w Kazimierzy Wielkiej i okoliach [Supplement to the issue of martyrology and the Holocaust of the Jewish community]* (Odonów: Cultural Society of Odonów, 2017), 12–13; Tadeusz Kozioł, *Żydzi w historii Kazimierzy Wielkiej [Jews in the history of Kazimierza Wielka]* (Busko-Zdrój, Poland: Buskie Stowarzyszenie Kulturalne, 2021).

## CHAPTER 3: BARNYARDS

1   Zimmerman, *Polish Underground,* 371.

2   Roy F. Leslie, *The History of Poland Since 1863* (Cambridge: Cambridge University Press, 1983), 234.

3 Leslie, History of Poland, 235–36.

4 Dariusz Stola, "The Polish Government in Exile and the Final Solution," in *Contested Memories: Poles and Jews during the Holocaust and Its Aftermath*, ed. Joshua D. Zimmerman (Piscataway, NJ: Rutgers University Press, 2003), 85–96.

5 Leslie, *History of Poland*, 235–36.

6 "Obchody 75. rocznicy powstania Narodowych Sił Zbrojnych" [Celebration of the 75th anniversary of the establishment of the National Armed Forces], Institute of National Remembrance, September 16, 2017, https://ipn.gov.pl/pl/aktualnosci/41742,Obchody-75-rocznicy-powstania-Narodowych-Sil-Zbrojnych-Warszawa-16-wrzesnia-2017.html.

7 Szymon Rudnicki, "Mogą żyć, byle nie u nas... Propaganda NSZ wobec Żydów" [They can live, but not with us... Propaganda of the NSZ toward Jews], Wiez, September 20, 2017, https://wiez.pl/2017/09/20/moga-zyc-byle-nie-u-nas-propaganda-nsz-wobec-zydow/.

8 Stola, "Polish Government in Exile," 87.

9 Joshua D. Zimmerman, "The Polish Underground Home Army (AK) and the Jews: What Postwar Jewish Testimonies and Wartime Documents Reveal," *East European Politics and Societies: and Cultures* 34, no. 1 (February 2020): 194–220, https://doi.org/10.1177/0888325419844816.

## CHAPTER 4: ORIGINS

1 Dariusz Libionka, "Documents of the Polish Underground State concerning the Extermination of the Jews," in *Guide to the Sources on the Holocaust in Occupied Poland*, ed. Alina Skibińska, trans. Jessica Taylor-Kucia (Warsaw: European Holocaust Research Infrastructure, 2014), 251–58.

2 "Warsaw Ghetto," Yad Vashem, accessed July 24, 2022, https://yadvashem.org/holocaust/about/ghettos/warsaw.html.

3 David Engel, "Poland Since 1939," *YIVO Encyclopedia of Jews in Eastern Europe*, March 14, 2011, https://yivoencyclopedia.org/article.aspx/poland/poland_since_1939; Ruth Ellen Gruber, "East-Central Europe," *American Jewish Year Book* 102, (2002): 445–79, https://www.jstor.org/stable/23604553; Geneviève Zubrzycki, "The Politics of Jewish Absence in Contemporary Poland," *Journal of Contemporary History* 52, no. 2 (April

2017): 250–77, https://www.jstor.org/stable/44504015; "Murder of the Jews of Poland," Yad Vashem, accessed July 24, 2022, https://www.yadvashem.org /holocaust/about/fate-of-jews/poland.html.

## CHAPTER 6: BREAKTHROUGH

1   Joel Brinkley, "Walesa, in Israel, Regrets Poland's Anti-Semitism," *New York Times*, May 21, 1991, https://www.nytimes.com/1991/05/21/world/walesa -in-israel-regrets-poland-s-anti-semitism.html.

## CHAPTER 9: CHECKING BOXES

1   Jan Tomasz Gross, Neighbors: The Destruction of the Jewish Community in Jedwabne, Poland (Princeton, NJ: Princeton University Press, 2001), 48–49; David Mikics, "The Day We Burned Our Neighbors Alive," *Tablet*, October 20, 2015, https://www.tabletmag.com/sections/arts-letters/articles /anna-bikont-jedwabne.

2   Janine P. Holc, "Working through Jan Gross's Neighbors," *Slavic Review* 61, no. 3 (2002): 453–59, https://doi.org/10.2307/3090294.

3   Ian Fisher, "At Site of Massacre, Polish Leader Asks Jews for Forgiveness," *New York Times*, July 11, 2001, https://www.nytimes.com/2001/07/11/world/at -site-of-massacre-polish-leader-asks-jews-for-forgiveness.html.

4   Mikics, "Day We Burned."

5   Associated Press, "Poles to Exhume Mass Grave of Jews Killed in Massacre," *Los Angeles Times*, May 25, 2001, https://www.latimes.com/archives/la-xpm -2001-may-25-mn-2305-story.html.

## CHAPTER 11: STRAINED TRUTH

1   Masha Gessen, "The Historians under Attack for Exploring Poland's Role in the Holocaust," *New Yorker*, March 26, 2021, https://www.newyorker .com/news/our-columnists/the-historians-under-attack-for-exploring -polands-role-in-the-holocaust.

2   Matthew Day, "Smolensk Air Disaster 'Was Caused by Mystery Explosion,'" *Telegraph*, April 10, 2014, https://www.telegraph.co.uk/news/worldnews /europe/poland/10758863/Smolensk-air-disaster-was-caused-by-mystery -explosion.html.

3 Eli Stutz, "Saved by Keeping Shabbat," *Israel National News*, April 14, 2010, https://web.archive.org/web/20211217071934/https://www.israelnationa lnews.com/news/137018.

4 Piotr Wróbel, email to author, April 25, 2007.

5 Seth Abramovitch, "'Aftermath' Dares to Unearth Terrible Secrets of Poland's Lost Jews," *Hollywood Reporter*, October 28, 2013, https://www .hollywoodreporter.com/news/general-news/aftermath-dares-unearth-terrible -secrets-651230/.

6 Hanna Krall, *Shielding the Flame: An Intimate Conversation with Dr. Marek Edelman, the Last Surviving Leader of the Warsaw Ghetto Uprising*, trans. Joanna Stasinska Weschler and Lawrence Weschler (New York: Henry Holt, 1986), 95.

7 Liz Elsby, "Rapoport's Memorial to the Warsaw Ghetto Uprising—A Personal Interpretation," Yad Vashem, accessed July 24, 2022, https://www.yadvashem .org/articles/general/warsaw-memorial-personal-interpretation.html; Jodi Elowitz, "Heroism and Sacrifice as Represented in Nathan Rapoport's Warsaw Ghetto Monument," Society Pages, April 22, 2018, https://thesocietypages .org/holocaust-genocide/heroism-and-sacrifice-as-represented-in-nathan -rapoports-warsaw-ghetto-monument/.

8 Joanna Tokarska-Bakir, "How to Exit the Conspiracy of Silence?: Social Sciences Facing the Polish-Jewish Relations," *East European Politics and Societies: and Cultures* 25, no. 1 (February 2011): 129–52, https://doi.org /10.1177/0888325410387640.

9 Antoni Sułek, "Ordinary Poles Look at the Jews," *East European Politics and Societies: and Cultures* 26, no. 2 (August 2011): 425–44, https://doi.org /10.1177/0888325411415402.

## CHAPTER 12: FAKE PARTISANS

1 Kozioł, *Dodatek do kwestii martyrologii*.

2 Kozioł, *Dodatek do kwestii martyrologii*, 12–13 (all translations by Przemek Swadzka).

3 Kozioł, *Dodatek do kwestii martyrologii*, 3.

4 Kozioł, *Dodatek do kwestii martyrologii*, 4–5.

5 Kozioł, *Dodatek do kwestii martyrologii*, 14.

6    Kozioł, *Dodatek do kwestii martyrologii*, 40.

7    Kozioł, *Dodatek do kwestii martyrologii*, 35.

8    Kozioł, *Dodatek do kwestii martyrologii*, 43.

9    Kozioł, *Dodatek do kwestii martyrologii*, 44.

## CHAPTER 13: DOCUMENTED EVIDENCE

1    "Chapter XXVI, Shawnee Township: 1885," Ohio Genealogy Express, accessed July 24, 2022, http://www.ohiogenealogyexpress.com/allen/allenco_hist_1885/allenco_hist_1885_chpt_xxv_shawnee.htm.

2    Act on the Institute of National Remembrance—Commission for the Prosecution of Crimes against the Polish Nation, December 18, 1998, Journal of Laws of 1998, No. 155, item 1016, https://www.legal-tools.org/doc/fc69d7/pdf/.

3    "Archive of Jewish War Graves," Zapomniane, accessed July 24, 2022, https://zapomniane.org/en/.

4    Ewa Wolentarska-Ochman, "Collective Remembrance in Jedwabne: Unsettled Memory of World War II in Postcommunist Poland," *History & Memory* 18, no. 1 (Spring/Summer 2006): 152–78, https://doi.org/10.1353/ham.2006.0005.

5    Jan Grabowski, *Hunt for the Jews: Betrayal and Murder in German-Occupied Poland* (Bloomington: Indiana University Press, 2013), 241–46.

6    IPN Ki 128/37 III K 83/51, GK 306/32, 1950–1953, Files of criminal case against Edward Grudzień and 19 other persons accused of killing Polish citizens of Jewish nationality and members of Polish People's Army in 1944, Court of Appeal in Kielce, translated by Przemek Swadzka. This file involves the May 1944 killing in the village of Chruszczyna Wielka of the Dula family of five at the farm of Sodo. Two weeks later, the same group assassinated nine Jews who were also hiding in the village of Bełżów. All quotations of court proceedings following are from this file.

7    Alina Skibińska and Jakub Petelewicz, "Udział Polaków w zbrodniach na Żydach na prowincji regionu Świętokrzyskiego" [The participation of Poles in crimes against Jews in the Świętokrzyskie region], *Zagłada Żydów* 1 (2005): 114–48, https://doi.org/10.32927/ZZSiM.151.

8    Yehuda Bauer, Yad Vashem, email to author, January 23, 2006.

9    Barbara Engelking-Boni, email to author, April 19, 2006.

10   Dariusz Libionka, email to author, April 26, 2006.

11   Libionka, "Documents of the Polish Underground State," 251–58.

12   "Dekret o wymiarze kary dla faszystowsko-hitlerowskich zbrodniarzy winnych zabójstw i znęcania się nad ludnością cywilną i jeńcami oraz dla zdrajców Narodu Polskiego," (Decree on the penalty of fascist-Nazi criminals guilty of murder and mistreatment of civilians and prisoners, and traitors of the Polish Nation), *Dziennik Ustaw* 27, no. 4 (September 1944).

13   Joanna Tokarska-Bakir, *Jewish Fugitives in the Polish Countryside, 1939–1945: Beyond the German Holocaust Project*, trans. Yecheskiel Anis, Ewa Gedroyc, Nicholas Hodge, Jerzy Jurus, Jessica Taylor-Kucia, and Benjamin Voelkel, Eastern European Culture, Politics and Societies 18 (Warsaw: Peter Lang, 2022): 74.

14   Tokarska-Bakir, *Jewish Fugitives*, 81–82.

15   Maya Vinokour, "90% of Polish Jews Died in the Holocaust. So Why Are Poland's Nationalists Chanting 'Get the Jews Out of Power'?," Haaretz, November 13, 2017, https://www.haaretz.com/jewish/holocaust-remembrance-day/2017-11-13/ty-article/why-polish-nationalists-chant-get-the-jews-out-of-power/0000017f-e7fe-d97e-a37f-f7ffb30e0000.

16   Associated Press, "New Polish Historical Policy Could Silence Holocaust Debates," VOA News, March 22, 2016, https://www.voanews.com/a/new-polish-historical-policy-could-silence-holocaust-debates/3249438.html.

17   Tamar Pileggi, "Poland Moves to Strip Jewish Holocaust Scholar of Award," Times of Israel, February 14, 2016, https://www.timesofisrael.com/poland-moves-to-strip-jewish-holocaust-scholar-of-award/.

18   Associated Press, "New Polish Historical Policy."

19   Associated Press, "New Polish Historical Policy."

## CHAPTER 14: NO HISTORY WITHOUT TRUTH

1    Isabelle de Pommereau, "Son of an Anti-Nazi Hero Uses Family Estate to Nurture Democracy and Rule of Law," *Christian Science Monitor*, July 6, 2012, https://www.csmonitor.com/World/Making-a-difference/2012/0706/Son-of-an-anti-Nazi-hero-uses-family-estate-to-nurture-democracy-and-rule-of-law.

2    IPN Ki 128/37 III K 83/51, GK 306/32.

3    Joanna B. Michlic, "'I Will Never Forget What You Did for Me during the War': Rescuer-Rescuee Relationships in the Light of Postwar Correspondence in Poland, 1945–1949," *Yad Vashem Studies* 39, no. 2 (2011): 169–207, http://www.yadvashem.org/yv/en/about/institute/studies/issues/39–2/index.asp.

4    Michlic, "'I Will Never Forget,'" 172.

5    Joanna B. Michlic, *Poland's Threatening Other: The Image of the Jew from 1880 to the Present* (Lincoln: University of Nebraska Press, 2006), 274.

6    Michlic, *Poland's Threatening Other*, 276.

## CHAPTER 15: HONORED GUESTS

1    Jan Grabowski and Barbara Engelking, eds., *Night without End: The Fate of Jews in German-Occupied Poland* (Bloomington: Indiana University Press, 2022), vii.

2    Omer Bartov, review of *Night without End*, book cover.

3    Barbara Engelking and Jan Grabowski, eds., *Dalej jest noc. Losy Żydów w wybranych powiatach okupowanej Polski* [Night without end: The fate of Jews in selected counties of Occupied Poland], 2 vols. (Warsaw: Centrum Badan nad Zaglada Zydów, 2018), 192.

4    Joanna Tokarska-Bakir, email to author, October 5, 2021.

5    Translation of ruling of Judge Joanna Wisniewska-Sadomska, Court of Appeal in Warsaw I Civil Division, I ACa 300/21, Judgment on Behalf of the Republic of Poland, August 16, 2021.

6    Jan Grabowski reading from the translated ruling of Judge Ewa Jończyk during an address, "Hijacking Memory of the Holocaust: From Treblinka through Auschwitz to the Warsaw Ghetto," June 12, 2022, video, 25:30, https://www.hkw.de/en/app/mediathek/video/91276.

7    Grabowski, "Hijacking Memory."

8    John Lowell Armstrong, "The Polish Underground and the Jews: A Reassessment of Home Army Commander Tadeusz Bór-Komorowski's Order 116 against Banditry," *Slavonic and East European Review* 72, no. 2 (April 1994): 259–76, http://www.jstor.org/stable/4211476; Kazimierza Wielka municipal website http://www.kazimierzawielka.pl/asp/62-rocznica-powstania-kazimiersko-8211-proszowickiej-republiki-partyzanckiej,40,artykul,1,148.

9    Masha Gessen, "Poland's Ruling Party Puts an Extraordinary Museum of

Polish-Jewish History into Limbo," *New Yorker*, September 23, 2019, https://www.newyorker.com/news/our-columnists/polands-ruling-party-puts-an-extraordinary-museum-of-polish-jewish-history-into-limbo; Anna Sommer, "Auschwitz Today: Personal Observations and Reflections about Visitors to the Auschwitz-Birkenau State Museum and Memorial," *Les Cahiers Irice* 7, no. 1 (2011): 87–94, https://doi.org/10.3917/lci.007.0087.

10   Adam Teller, "Polish-Jewish Relations: Historical Research and Social Significance: On the Legacy of Jacob Goldberg," *Studia Judaica* 15, no. 1–2 (2012): 29–30.

## EPILOGUE

1   Grabowski, "Hijacking Memory."
2   Wisniewska-Sadomska, I ACa 300/21.
3   Grabowski, "Hijacking Memory."
4   Engelking and Grabowski, Dalej jest noc., 177, 192.
5   Grabowski, "Hijacking Memory."

# About the Author

© Sam Mendales

Judy Rakowsky spent a three-decade journalism career at five metropolitan dailies as an enterprising reporter and breaking news editor focused on crime and legal affairs. At the *Boston Globe*, the *Providence Journal,* and *People Magazine*, she broke stories on major issues of the day from organized crime to priest sex abuse, domestic violence, and online bullying. Along the way, she garnered awards for feature writing, sensitivity to crime victims, and enterprise reporting. She lives with her husband in Cambridge, Massachusetts.